Praise for *Thou Shalt Innovate*

Avi identifies the secret sauce behind Israel's innovative prowess by telling the story of how that tiny country leverages its technology to better the lives of billions of people around the world. . . . This insightful and uplifting book shines a bright light on the country's heart and soul.

> – YOSSI VARDI, serial entrepreneur and Israel's unofficial ambassador of technology

Hundreds of millions of people around the world lack the most basic human necessities and health services. Amazingly, tiny Israel has risen to the occasion to help. Avi Jorisch's *Thou Shalt Innovate* is not only uplifting but tells the story of Israel's meteoric rise from fledgling state to established light unto the nations.

> – SIVAN YA'ARI, Founder and CEO, Innovation: Africa

Realizing the enormous strides that Israel, a young country like my own, has made in such a short period of time will provide readers of Thou Shalt Innovate tremendous hope. We can all celebrate Israel's incredible technological contributions that improve the state of humanity.

> – HIS EXCELLENCY, ROBERT DUSSEY, Foreign Minister of Togo

Thou Shalt Innovate grasps the truth of this era. Innovation is a sacred task and technology a sacred means enabling us to repair this world. This inspiring book calls us to expand our moral imagination in exercising the unprecedented power with which our generation has been gifted.

> – RABBI IRWIN KULA, President, National Jewish Center for Learning and Leadership (CLAL)

Thou Shalt Innovate is a book the world needs to pay attention to. In a rich and exhilarating narrative, Avi Jorisch outlines the roadmap for how Israelis innovate while making the world a better place, and how other countries and people can follow suit.

> – YAAKOV KATZ, Editor in Chief, *Jerusalem Post*; co-author, *The Weapon Wizards*

Thou Shalt Innovate

THOU SHALT
INNOVATE

How Israeli Ingenuity Repairs the World

AVI JORISCH

gefen
publishing house בית חוצאת לאור
JERUSALEM ◆ NEW YORK   Est. 1981

Scripture quotations based on *The Holy Scriptures According to the
Masoretic Text*, published by the Jewish Publication Society in 1917.

Chapter 8, ReWalk exoskeleton image by Mikhnenko773; chapter 17,
ancient Judean coin image by Zegomo, both available under CC BY-SA 4.0
license, https://creativecommons.org/licenses/by-sa/4.0/deed.en.

Cover Design: Mendelow Design/Sensical Design & Communication
Typesetting: Raphaël Freeman, Renana Typesetting

ISBN: 978-965-229-934-5

1 3 5 7 9 8 6 4 2

Gefen Publishing House Ltd.
6 Hatzvi Street
Jerusalem 94386, Israel
+972-2-538-0247

Gefen Books
140 Fieldcrest Ave.
Edison NJ, 08837
516-593-1234

orders@gefenpublishing.com
www.gefenpublishing.com

Printed in Israel

*   *   *

Library of Congress Cataloging-in-Publication Data

Names: Jorisch, Avi, 1975- author.
Title: Thou shalt innovate : how Israeli ingenuity repairs the world / by Avi
 Jorisch.
Description: Jerusalem, Israel : Gefen Publishing House Ltd., 2018.
Identifiers: LCCN 2017045170 | ISBN 9789652299345
Subjects: LCSH: Inventions--Israel. | Inventors--Israel. | Technological
 innovations--Israel. | Medical innovations--Israel. | Agricultural
 innovations--Israel.
Classification: LCC T27.I8 J67 2018 | DDC 609.5694--dc23 LC
record available at https://lccn.loc.gov/2017045170

For Eiden, Oren, and Yaniv – the next chapter is yours.

CONTENTS

Let There Be Light

I will also give you for a light unto the nations, that My salvation may be unto the end of the earth.

~ Isaiah 49:6

As my car rumbled over the road outside Jerusalem, I heard the code red blast over the radio. I looked back at my toddler sleeping in his car seat and felt fear spread out over my limbs. It was July 8, 2014, and I had just passed a security checkpoint. For weeks, all people could talk about was the impending war with Hamas. Israel had just begun a military operation in Gaza targeting Islamic militants. For years, Hamas — whose charter calls for "obliterating" Israel and replacing it with an Islamic theocracy — had used underground tunnels to smuggle arms and materials from Egypt. Around six thirty in the evening, I pulled up to my home on a quiet, leafy street and put my son Oren to bed. Then I waited. Sure enough, the air raid siren wailed. Hamas had started blasting rockets across the border. During that first night, the militant group shot a round of M75 missiles toward Tel Aviv and Jerusalem, two large cities many once thought were beyond its reach. As I carried my son four flights downstairs to a bomb shelter, I could see he was terrified. I could only imagine how scared other children in Israel and Gaza felt. A few minutes later we heard two loud thuds and knew it was safe to go back upstairs. Israel's Iron Dome missile defense system had successfully intercepted Hamas's rockets.

For the next seven weeks, the sirens blared as this scene repeated itself. The fear never went away, but my family, like the rest of Israel, found comfort in the Iron Dome. I marveled at this invention. It kept Israel from descending into the chaos and carnage that was engulfing the Middle East: the Islamic State was taking over large swaths of territory in Iraq and Syria, raping and murdering "nonbelievers" on a massive scale; the Assad regime was slaughtering its own people with barrel bombs and chemical weapons, while millions of refugees were flooding over the border into Turkey, Jordan, and Lebanon; and in Egypt, Islamic militants were waging a bloody insurgency in the Sinai Peninsula.

It was depressing. I grew up thinking my generation would see peace in the Middle East. As a graduate student, I studied Islamic history and Arabic, moved to Cairo, and traveled around the region hoping to witness a lasting change. But the people of the region have been plagued with a seemingly never-ending violence.

Yet something else happened in the summer of 2014. I came to learn that the Iron Dome was not the only Israeli innovation saving lives. Almost by chance, I began to notice the other innovations around me that were making a real difference in fostering a kinder, gentler world. After every crisis — whether it was a rocket that came crashing down, a traffic accident, or a random heart attack — almost immediately appeared an emergency responder riding on a kind of half ambulance half motorcycle (known as an ambucycle), dispatched using an Uber-like application on a smartphone. My Jerusalem gardener pointed out that he used a special dripper that I soon learned was being used by farmers all over the world to conserve one of our most important resources — water — and feed our growing world population. One of my colleagues was diagnosed with Parkinson's and began undergoing deep brain stimulation to help with his symptoms. I learned that the device that was used had been designed by Imad and Reem Younis, an Arab couple from Nazareth. Their innovation has revolutionized brain surgery through a GPS system that allows surgeons to insert an electrode device into the exact affected part of the brain to treat all kinds of movement and psychiatric disorders.

These stories were like small rays of hope cutting through the darkness I felt was overtaking the region. I wanted to connect with this inspirational side of Israel. I began to deliberately seek out social innovators who were working on challenges – small and large – that were making life better for millions if not billions of people around the world.

Like many others, I was aware of Israel's incredible record of innovation, and had read *Start-Up Nation,* Dan Senor and Saul Singer's great account of how Israel achieved economic success. But what I hadn't realized was the extent to which Israel's innovative spirit was having an impact far beyond Israel, addressing some of the world's most pressing social problems. It quickly became clear to me that Israel was much more than the "start-up nation." It was playing a disproportionate role in helping solve some of the world's biggest challenges. I didn't expect to be moved. But I was. I started to feel in my *kishkes* (meaning "gut" in Yiddish) that a different future was possible.

Eventually I met Yossi Vardi, one of the godfathers of the country's high-tech revolution. The following June, he invited me to attend his annual Kinnernet retreat, a gathering of tech entrepreneurs known for bringing together Israel's Jews, Christians, and Muslims, as well as Palestinians from the West Bank, among others. On a whim, I said yes.

Walking into Nazareth's Saint Gabriel Hotel felt like entering the *Star Wars* cantina. There were people playing Hacky Sack, flying drones, and jumping out windows onto large air cushions to test their velocity. I half expected to see Jabba the Hutt. Over the next few days, I met some of Israel's – and the world's – leading minds and was exposed to many of the other innovations that were coming out of Israel. I felt compelled to find out more and get to the heart of why there was so much social innovation taking place.

I began traveling across the country. I met entrepreneurs in their offices, on park benches, and sometimes even in their homes. I sat in Michel Revel's living room as he told me about the novel way he created Rebif – one of the leading multiple sclerosis drugs – by experimenting on foreskin. And I munched a pizza with Bernard Bar-Natan, the man who developed the Emergency Bandage, a unique life-saving product that instantly controls massive bleeding and prevents infections in trauma situations. I traveled to the northern part of Israel to meet Amit Goffer, the man who created the exoskeleton that allows paraplegics to walk. And Shlomo Navarro took me – and his large dog – to his basement office to explain to me exactly how he conceived of the Grain Cocoon, a magical bag that is playing a major role in the fight against world hunger by storing grains and killing bugs without having to resort to harmful pesticides.

The more people I met, the more I realized that these innovators were living a life beyond the horrors of war, one that involved hope and optimism. Rather than being consumed by bombs and bullets, they were inventing devices that they hoped would make the world a better place.

I also took the opportunity to cross the Green Line – the border created after the 1949 armistice between Israel and its Arab neighbors. There, I learned about the start-up scene in the Palestinian territories. Israelis and Palestinians are grappling with land disputes, water rights, refugees, and a host of painful issues; few have any illusions about peace. But many of the entrepreneurs I spoke to believe innovation can serve as a powerful bridge between two groups that have been fighting for generations.

If you only casually followed the news, you might think daily life in Israel is nothing but violence – war, suicide bombings, stabbings, car-ramming attacks. The country does suffer its share of turmoil. However, there is another Israel. If you take a look at the top ten problems facing the world, there is bound to be someone from Israel looking to solve them.

In the early twentieth century, the British writer G.K. Chesterton wrote that America is "a nation with the soul of a church."[1] Americanism, he seemed to be saying, is its own religion. The United States is a country with its own creed, its own set of beliefs and sacred scriptures – the Constitution and the Declaration of Independence and the enduring belief in the American dream. Israel, I've come to believe, is a nation with the soul of a synagogue, a country where Jewish prophetic tradition – whether consciously or unconsciously – has created a remarkable culture of innovation that is being marshaled in large part to solve the world's most formidable problems.

Jewish mystical tradition says that when God created the universe, He drew in his breath to make room for the wonders of the world. And when God said, "Let there be light," he sent ten radiant vessels to fill the darkness of his creation. Had the vessels remained intact, the world would have been perfect. But God's divine force was too powerful. It shattered the vessels and scattered their sparks. The majority of them fell to the ground in the land of Israel. Our purpose as human beings, Judaism argues, is to gather as many sparks as possible, to restore God's broken vessels and make the world a better place.

But how do we do this? For many Jews around the world, it means doing good deeds, charitable giving, and saving the environment. But for many in Israel, it increasingly means repairing the world through technology and innovation. If one paralyzed person can walk again, then perhaps no one has to be bound to a wheelchair. If one hungry person can eat, then perhaps we can solve world hunger.

This book will demonstrate what Israel is presently doing to make the world a better place and the impact the country is having globally. It will also hint at what Israel is capable of doing in the future. If it can contribute this much to the world while dealing with the current situation, imagine what the country would look like if it were not mired in war and constantly needing to defend itself and its borders.

There is no single narrative that fully describes the State of Israel. But there is also no denying that the country has extraordinary innovators who are bound together not by religion, money, or stature, but rather by their desire to save lives and make the world a better place. Those who stand for liberty, peace, and social justice should stand with these individuals – and the many others who are not featured in this book – in an effort to repair the world. Miracles took place in the Bible. But this book demonstrates how they continue to happen today whenever someone helps a hopeless person change his or her life. The pursuit of modern-day miracles is a universal yearning – with no one tradition holding exclusive rights over this impulse – but also one that has deeply taken root in this country the size of New Jersey on the Mediterranean Sea.

In recent years, there have been a number of awe-inspiring books about Israeli technology. *Start-Up Nation* rebranded the country and exposed readers to the story of the country's economic miracle. The country has few natural resources, a small population, and enemies galore. But Israel has still managed to produce more start-ups than Canada, India, Japan, Korea, and the United Kingdom combined. Outside of North America, the country has the largest number of companies on the NASDAQ. And as a share of gross domestic product, it has the highest level of venture capital in the Organization for Economic Cooperation and Development (OECD). *Let There Be Water* by Seth Siegel provided a gripping account of how Israel became a water superpower despite the fact that well over half the country is a desert. And *Weapons Wizards* by Yaakov Katz and Amir Bohbot gave an insider's look into the James Bond–like weapons systems Israel has created in the past seventy years. Each of these books focused on one particular aspect of Israeli technology.

And while *Thou Shalt Innovate* features ventures focused on agriculture, medicine, water, and defense, the heart and soul of this book revolves around the global impact of world-changing innovations and the people behind them. This is the collective story of how Israeli innovation is making life better for billions of people around the world and how Israeli ingenuity is helping to feed the hungry, cure the sick, and provide shelter for the homeless. And as policy officials, lawmakers, engineers, doctors, lawyers, bankers, aid workers, and other professionals of all kinds look to solve challenges – small and large – they should look to Israel to either find existing answers or innovate new solutions.

And as importantly, as countries around the world try to elucidate Israel's innovative "secret sauce" for their own populations and economies, they should look to the essence of Israeli culture for guiding principles.

Thou Shalt Innovate is a tale about Israelis who have chosen hope and healing over death and destruction. In a part of the world that has more than its share of darkness, these stories are rays of light.

PART I

The Country with a Spiritual Soul

CHAPTER 1

Israel's DNA

If I am not for myself, then who will be for me? But when I am for myself, then what am I? And if not now, when?

~ Ethics of the Fathers 1:14

[Israel] has been granted a great, historic privilege, which is also a duty...to solve the gravest problems of the 20th century.

~ David Ben-Gurion, "Israel's Security and Her International Position," *Israel Government Yearbook* 5720 (1959–60)

USING CHUTZPAH TO CHEAT DEATH

Israelis have a reputation for unconventional thinking, and the man who epitomizes this is Avi Yaron, my roommate at Yossi Vardi's Kinnernet retreat. I enjoyed chatting with him at the conference in northern Israel, and on the last day, I offered him a ride back to Tel Aviv; I wanted to get to know him better.

In the car, he told me his story, and I was so shocked I was worried I'd get into an accident. In 1993, Yaron's motorcycle crashed, and he was rushed to the hospital. There, the doctors gave him both good and bad news: the crash hadn't done much physical damage, but they had discovered a brain tumor. "I was in a complete state of shock," he recalls. "But I was not sure the doctors were completely honest and open with me."[1]

Under the best of circumstances, the doctors told him, he would likely become paralyzed on one side of his body and suffer significant mental impairment. Yaron was saddened, but knew he needed to find a way out of his predicament. "I decided to fight for my life," he says. "I went to the medical library and started learning – anatomy, biology...every time I thought I understood and took one

3

step forward, I took two steps backward. The worst part was that everyone around me thought I was going insane."[2]

Yaron improved his diet, consumed less coffee, and started sleeping only four hours a night because "it [sleep] was a complete waste of my time."[3] His tumor kept growing, and there was nothing his doctors could do. The problem was that the tools brain surgeons use to operate were too big. Yaron was told that maybe someone would create the technology in the next five years. Thinking he might not that have that long, he came up with a solution. He started a company called Visionsense and spent almost a decade developing a new type of operating scope modeled after the structure of an insect's eyes. "The technology works and saves thousands of lives globally now," says Yaron.[4]

As we drove through the Judean Hills, it struck me that Yaron had used chutzpah to cheat death. And in doing so, he had created a remarkable innovation that was now being used to help people around the world do the same.

What drove him, I felt, wasn't a singular expression of his character, but something larger, something definitively Israeli. It made me wonder: How did such a small country become a nation that felt a deep need to dispel darkness and bring more light to the world?

A LIGHT UNTO THE NATIONS

Israel's innovative success stems from a number of factors, including creating a culture that encourages its citizens to challenge authority, ask the next question, and defy the obvious. Various factors such as chutzpah, obligatory military service, renowned universities, smart big government, a dearth of natural resources, and diversity come together as national characteristics to explain how tiny Israel became a technological powerhouse. But rather than simply enriching people or making our lives more convenient, many Israeli tech companies also wind up making the world a far better place.

I started asking a variety of innovators why, and I got a variety of answers. Often, people cited a member of the family who inspired them – mothers, fathers, or spouses. But as I dug deeper, many ascribed their motivation to Israeli or Jewish culture. Eli Beer, the man behind the ambucycle and the founder of the United Hatzalah emergency medical response team, explained how his father always underscored the importance of "being a mensch and doing good." One of his earliest memories was traveling to the United States with his father to raise money to help Soviet Jewry emigrate to Israel, a population that for the better part of the 1970s and 1980s was not allowed to leave the USSR.

Shlomo Navarro, the creator of the Grain Cocoon, believes "it is inherent in our blood to do a revolution, to do something for the benefit of others." He remembers learning about the importance of these values at the Jewish school he attended in his native Turkey and as a member of a Zionist youth movement.

Bernard Bar-Natan, the creator of the Emergency Bandage, learned about doing good from his parents, both of whom were Holocaust survivors.

What happened in Israel, I realized, was part of a larger, unconscious process that's evolved and spread across the country. Reem Younis, the cofounder of Alpha Omega, Israel's largest Arab high-tech company, perhaps articulated this idea best. "It came from my father, the school I went to, and networking with Israelis," she says. "Israel's culture has spread through osmosis."[5]

LIKE THE PROTESTANT WORK ETHIC ... FOR JEWS

Since the Middle Ages, and possibly before, Jews have recited a prayer called Aleinu three times a day. The prayer instructs us, among other things, to repair the world. We believe we are partners with God, that we share a responsibility in spreading morality and justice around the world. The Mishnah, the classic body of rabbinic teachings codified around the second century CE, references *tikkun olam* ten times, mandating extra protection to those potentially disadvantaged for the sake of repairing the world.[6] And for his part, the prophet Isaiah called on the Jewish people to act as a "light unto the nations" (42:6).

The Jewish message of helping others is also strong in *Pirkei Avot* (Ethics of the Fathers), a compilation of ethical teachings put together by rabbis around the second and third centuries CE. Two of the most famous maxims include Rabbi Tarfon's statement "It is not incumbent on you to complete the task, but nor are you free to desist from it," and Rabbi Hillel's series of questions "If I am not for myself, then who will be for me? But when I am for myself, then what am I? And if not now, when?"

And perhaps the center of all Jewish teachings is to elevate the mundane and transform it into something holy. Before eating a single morsel of food, when one goes to the bathroom, at every single joyous occasion – and mournful ones as well – the pious recite specific blessings praising God and His various creations. Immediately following the Sabbath, candles are lit and the Sovereign of the Universe is extolled for distinguishing between sacred and secular and between light and darkness.

In Jewish tradition, this idea is known as being a "light unto the nations," an injunction first commanded by the prophet Isaiah. It has also come to mean taking responsibility for repairing the world, or engaging in *tikkun olam*. "There is no question that *tikkun olam* is at the very heart and soul of Zionist ideology," says Jerusalem-based Rabbi David Rosen, the former chief rabbi of Ireland and the American Jewish Committee's director for international inter-religious understanding.[7]

One of the most important Jewish philosophers, Rabbi Moses ben Maimon (commonly known as Maimonides or Rambam) famously wrote that there are eight levels of committing charity – one of the highest is to give charity anonymously, while the lowest is do so unwillingly. Similarly, the motivations driving the various Israeli innovators featured in this book cover a wide spec-

trum – some set out to make money, others to primarily do good.
But each one of them has in effect given charity and has significantly
impacted the lives of an untold number of people. While Israel is
certainly "not a country of all saints or do-gooders," as Yossi Vardi
gently explained to me as we sat staring at the Atlantic Ocean off the
coast of the Hamptons, Jewish culture has bred "a nation of people
who do seek higher meaning."[8]

Israel's founding fathers were inspired by these religious teachings. Chief among them was David Ben-Gurion, the country's first
prime minister and Israel's version of George Washington. "We
extend our hand to all neighboring states and their peoples in an
offer of peace and good neighborliness, and appeal to them to
establish bonds of cooperation and mutual help with the sovereign
Jewish people settled in its own land," said Ben-Gurion when he
declared statehood in 1948. "The State of Israel is prepared to do its
share in a common effort for the advancement of the entire Middle
East."[9] Even the national emblem of Israel, a menorah – the biblical
seven-branched lampstand – symbolizes Israel's desire to act as a
source of light.

The Old Man's words may sound ironic or cynical today, especially knowing what would ensue during the war (and the violence
that continues today in Israel, the West Bank, and Gaza). But Ben-
Gurion was sincere, and his words are part of a long tradition of
Jewish aspiration.

Five decades earlier, in 1896, Herzl, the founder of modern Zionism, touched on that idea when he laid out his vision for a modern
Jewish state. A central pillar of his treatise *Der Judenstaat* (*The Jewish State*) involves Zionists striving for social change: "Whatever
we attempt [in the state of the Jews] for our own benefit," he wrote,
"will redound mightily and beneficially to the good of all mankind."[10]
Several years later, in *Altneuland*, a utopian novel that became something of a founding document of modern political Zionism, Herzl
echoed that sentiment: "Once I have witnessed the redemption of

the Jews, my people, I wish also to assist in the redemption of the Africans."[11]

In the seventy years since the country's founding, Israel has faced enormous challenges: it has fought a war every decade, it has faced diplomatic and economic isolation, and its population has grown immensely as the nation has taken in millions from around the world. Along the way, Israel has come under heavy criticism, particularly in regard to its treatment of Palestinian Arabs. But for all its flaws, the young nation continues to exercise political, economic, and moral leadership that radiates well beyond its narrow borders.

For many in the Jewish community, repairing the world has meant doing good, saving the environment, and engaging in social activism. Just as the Protestant work ethic that took root among the early settlers in the United States is now ingrained in American culture, the words and vision of Israel's founding fathers – and their historical forebears – have deeply affected the country's multiethnic society.[12] For the Israelis featured in this book – who include doctors, scientists, agronomists, botanists, and engineers of a variety of faiths including Judaism, Christianity, and Islam – repairing the world has become a defining purpose. Israel's betterment of the world is a mosaic of one person at a time with one innovation at a time.

CHAPTER 2

Jews Cannot Remain Indifferent

Whoever saves a life, it is considered as if he saved an entire world.

~ Mishnah, *Sanhedrin* 4:9

THE COUNTRY WITH A BIG HEART

The men in the armored car hear the gunfire from miles away. It's a pitch-black night in December 2015, and ten heavily armed Israeli commandos are driving toward the Syrian border, where a civil war has been raging for four years. The driver speaks quietly into his handheld radio and shuts down the engine. The soldiers jump out into the freezing cold. Five of them creep over to the border fence.

On the other side is a wounded young man, hemorrhaging blood and wrapped in a stained duvet. One of the officers unlocks the barrier and drags the man back to the Israeli side of the border.[1] The man is around twenty years old, and somewhere on his journey over the Golan Heights, he was shot in the stomach and liver. An Israeli medic sticks an IV in the man's arm, and the commandos hoist him onto a stretcher. They quickly head back across the border to an Israeli field hospital.

The man the soldiers rescued isn't Israeli. He isn't Jewish. He's a Syrian militant, likely a member of the country's opposition. He could even be a member of Jabhat al-Nusra, Al-Qaeda's Syrian affiliate that has kidnapped UN peacekeepers and massacred Christians. And yet they saved him and gave him medical care.

This same scene repeats itself often, as jihadis and civilians alike seek refuge with their sworn enemy, Israel. Women, children, the elderly, and jihadis alike all get unconditional medical care when they cross the border. Since 2013, Israel has treated more than twenty-five hundred Syrians seeking medical care, which has cost the Israeli taxpayer tens of millions of dollars.[2] But it's not just Syrians whom Israel has helped. The country has sent aid delegations around the world, to Armenia, Argentina, Kyrgyzstan, Mexico, Rwanda, and Turkey, among others. "Israelis are among the first on the scene to aid in saving lives after disasters," says Eugene Kandel, the former chairman of Israel's National Economic Council. "The country is strong, and it has a big heart."[3]

The reasons for these aid missions vary; some have been pragmatic, others idealistic. But all are informed by the mission to be a light unto the nations, a desire to repair the world, and the darkness that prevails when this type of assistance is absent; many of Israel's founders experienced the horrors of the Holocaust and the pogroms. As Member of Knesset Isaac Herzog once put it, having felt the "world's silence…Jews cannot remain indifferent."[4]

WINNING FRIENDS AND INFLUENCING PEOPLE

The first decade following Israel's independence was particularly challenging for the fledgling state. Hundreds of thousands of immigrants arrived in a country that was surrounded by enemies, lacked natural resources, and was facing a food shortage. And yet it was during this time that Israel created a government agency to help others around the world. This decision may seem at best naïve, or at worst harmful for people at home. Yet a close reading of the speeches and memoirs of Ben-Gurion, Israel's first prime minister, and Golda Meir, its fourth, indicate that the country's decision to do so stemmed from a combination of self-enlightened interest and idealism.[5]

Critics often point to the beleaguered country's need for good PR and international support. Which is true. But it's also true, as Meir said, that Israel's foreign aid program "typifies the drive towards social justice, reconstruction and rehabilitation that is at the very heart of Labor-Zionism – and Judaism. It is a continuation of our own most valued traditions and an expression of our own deepest historical instincts."[6]

In the mid-1950s, both leaders were distraught over two events that eventually convinced the country's political leadership to get involved with international aid. From the prime minister's office in Jerusalem, Ben-Gurion would pace around and fire off instructions to his ambassadors around the world. In 1955, Israel was not invited to the Bandung Conference in Indonesia, whose participants included twenty-nine African and Asian countries. The goal was to promote economic cooperation and oppose colonialism. The attendees pledged their support to the Palestinian cause, making no mention of Israel's plight, which humiliated Jerusalem's diplomats. Israel was "excluded from that 'club' as well," recalls Meir. "We were being treated like unwanted stepchildren, and I must admit that it hurt."[7]

The second event occurred in 1956, after Israel, along with France and Great Britain, attacked Egypt to remove Gamal Abdel Nasser from power and control the Suez Canal. The assault succeeded, but after heavy pressure from the US and USSR, the three powers withdrew. Many countries around the world subsequently offered tremendous support for the Arab world's embargo of the Jewish state and anti-Israel resolutions at the United Nations. "We have to break the boycott on us by the hostile Arab states and build bridges to the nations being liberated on the black continent," Ben-Gurion said to his ambassador in Ghana, Ehud Avriel. "We have a lot more to offer the Africans than diplomatic gestures. We are prepared to assist them with social and material development."[8] Israeli policymakers concluded it was in their interest to expend more energy on third-world countries.

As the Zionist leadership looked around the world for allies, Africa seemed like a natural partner. Many countries there had recently achieved independence and faced similar challenges. And given the large number of countries on the continent, each of which had a United Nations vote and collectively made up a quarter of the important international body, Israel's Ministry of Foreign Affairs began to try to bolster its relationships in Africa.

Throughout the 1950s and '60s, Israeli experts – doctors, engineers, agricultural and water experts, among others – provided assistance across the African continent and earned a reputation for being capable and practical. Part of this decision had to do with garnering international support, which Israel partially achieved. "Yes, of course that was one of our motives," says Meir, who for much of that period served as foreign minister. "But it was far from being the most important motive.... We had something we wanted to pass on to nations that were even younger and less experienced than ourselves."[9]

In 1958, Israeli diplomats started to successfully make the case to high-ranking government ministers to create a governmental body to coordinate foreign assistance. That same year, Israel launched what eventually was called the Center for International Cooperation (or MASHAV in Hebrew). This office focused on providing technical training and courses, rather than just financial aid.

Within a year of opening this office, Israel sent out hundreds of technical experts around the developing world. It also trained more than a thousand people annually in centers around Israel, teaching courses that included agriculture, public administration, medicine, trade union management, women's empowerment, entrepreneurship, and community development.[10] What began as a modest assistance program eventually grew into a massive initiative that sent Israeli experts to developing countries around the world to train those in need. Over the course of the next fifteen years, thousands of Israeli experts, political leaders, and civil servants regularly traveled to Africa to offer humanitarian aid. About two-thirds of Israel's aid budget was dedicated to the continent during that period.[11] But Israel also spearheaded similar programs with India, Pakistan, Somalia, Mauritania, and Indonesia.[12]

During that same time, fifteen thousand people from ninety

countries around the world regularly came to Israel for training. According to historian Moshe Decter, Israel had developed one of the most extensive technical programs in the world.[13] A major reason: the Haifa-based Mount Carmel Training Center, which Meir founded in 1961 along with Swedish diplomat Inga Thorsson and Israel's Mina Ben-Zvi, who later became the center's founding director. The center became part of MASHAV but focused for many years on empowering women from the developing world through training programs, including teaching techniques, nutrition, entrepreneurship, and other forms of social welfare. "If I had gone to study in the United States, I might have learned the history of development," said one Kenyan student to Meir in the early 1960s. "But here in Israel I have seen development as it takes place."[14]

The training programs and assistance helped Israel's image in Africa, something Meir was surprised to discover on one of her trips to the continent. In 1964, she was slated to fly from Kenya to Nigeria, but before her plane took off, Israel's ambassador to Lagos warned her she would be greeted by massive anti-Israel demonstrations, orchestrated by the wives of Arab ambassadors. Meir considered whether it was wise to cancel her trip, but ultimately decided to go. As she landed in Lagos and got off the plane, there were in fact hundreds and hundreds of Africans. "This is going to be unpleasant," she thought.[15] But instead of finding angry demonstrators, she was greeted by a crowd of people who had either trained in Israel or had been trained by Israelis in Nigeria. As she descended the plane, she was greeted by throngs of people singing "Hevenu Shalom Aleichem," a Jewish folk song that translates to "We bring peace unto you." The next morning, Meir met President Nnamdi Azikiwe, who said, "We respect and greet you as an ambassador of true goodwill."[16]

Many Africans were amazed to learn the extent to which Meir stood up for their civil rights. During the same year as her trip to Kenya and Nigeria, she also attended the Independence Day ceremonies for Zambia, which included a trip to the Victoria Falls. At the time, part of the area was in Zambia and the other half in Southern Rhodesia. Meir and several other Israelis, along with their African colleagues, took buses to this wonder of the world. But when they got to the border, the Southern Rhodesian police had the "effrontery to refuse to let the blacks on my bus get out," recalls Meir. "Whites only," the policemen insisted. The police tried their best to get Meir to leave the bus, but she refused. "I have no intention of being separated from my friends," she said. When the bus returned to Lusaka, the capital of Zambia, President Kenneth Kaunda personally received Meir and thanked her for taking a stand.[17]

This sign of solidarity is at least partly why African leaders were not concerned that Israel would, as the colonial powers had, attempt to exploit their countries for natural resources. "Israel is a small country... but it can offer a lot to a country like mine," said Julius Nyere, the president of Tanzania in the 1960s. "We can learn a great deal... building the nation and changing the face of the land, physically and economically."[18] Israel was providing practical assistance with agriculture and putting in place policies meant to relieve poverty. "Like them, we had shaken off foreign rule," Meir recalls. "Like them we had to learn for ourselves how to reclaim the land, how to increase the yields of our crops, how to irrigate, how to raise poultry, how to live together and how to defend ourselves."[19] Even the United Nations recognized Israel's contribution. "The study of Israel's unique efforts and achievements in the field of economic development... provides the curious visitor with more useful hints for the solution of problems in under-developed economies than any other country known to me," said an official in 1964.[20]

OUT OF AFRICA

Yet the goodwill between Israel and many African countries would not last. Following the Yom Kippur War in 1973, thanks to pressure from the Soviet Union, and the Arab world, all but four of the thirty-two sub-Saharan African countries broke their diplomatic relationships with Israel, including the technical assistance programs on the continent.[21] OPEC barred countries from doing business with Israel. Ivory Coast president Félix Houphouët-Boigny told Meir at the time he had to choose "between his Arab 'brothers' and his Israeli 'friends.'"[22]

The diplomatic rupture had major implications for Israel's aid program. As a first step, Israel stopped funding for any African country that cut ties.[23] The country then moved its aid programs to Latin America and Asia. MASHAV, however, didn't stop providing training courses within Israel to Africans from countries that cut off diplomatic relations, or sending doctors and technical experts into the field. These doctors brought equipment normally unavailable in the host country, trained local staff, and often donated their medical equipment when they departed.[24]

Since this shift in 1973, Israel has dispatched some of the world's largest medical teams – often arriving first – to numerous natural disasters. As was the case with Israel's aid missions to Africa, these efforts helped improve the country's image around the world. But they were also driven by a very real desire to make the world a better place. In 1983, Israel created a specialized national search and rescue unit to provide aid, both at home and abroad. The country's rescue teams include medical doctors, engineers, logistics specialists, and rescue dog handlers.[25] "As I see it, [the aid missions are] part of the Jewish identity that obliges each and every one of us to aid people in time of need, anywhere in the world," the commander of the Israeli Air Force squadron responsible for flying aid missions around the world (who declined to provide his full name) said in an interview about the military's humanitarian efforts. "I have no doubt that whenever and wherever help will be needed, we will arrive. As an Israeli citizen and an IDF soldier, I see myself obligated to every person in need – whether he's Israeli or not. Our commitment to people in need is not a national one, but a universal one."[26]

Dov Maisel, United Hatzalah's director of international operations, who has partaken in numerous Israeli international disaster relief missions, agrees. "By going to disaster zones, we show that we are not only concerned about ourselves, but about doing the right thing." He continues: "When we go, we often get asked, 'What are you doing here? You don't owe us anything.' They realize we are there because we are your friend and we are coming to help you."[27]

In more recent decades, Israel has participated in numerous humanitarian relief missions, including in places such as Kosovo and Rwanda, where genocide was taking place.[28] "We cannot sit here and let children die . . . when we know there are treatments available," says Professor Dan Engelhard, formerly the head of the pediatric department at Hadassah University Hospital and a member of Israel's first medical team to provide foreign aid to Cambodia in 1978. "As doctors, we cannot allow ourselves to care if a person is Jewish or Muslim. All children have a right to live. When you treat a child, you don't care about politics."[29]

One of Israel's most impressive humanitarian missions occurred in Haiti. Colonel Ariel Bar, the IDF's chief medical officer, remembers it well. On January 13, 2010, the IDF was preparing for a massive biological and chemical attack. Bar was in charge of the logistics. Surrounded by soldiers, he was monitoring a variety of electronic devices when his personal cellphone rang. "Doc, a severe earthquake has occurred in Haiti. We are sending a rescue team and you have an hour and a half to be at the airport," said a colonel on the other end of the line.[30] Bar rushed home and packed a small bag. On his way out the door, he called his six-year-old daughter and mumbled something about going halfway around the world to save lives. He arrived at Ben-Gurion Airport in time to make the flight.

Bar's plane took off without receiving permission to land in Port-au-Prince or knowing what to expect when they arrived. The medical crew didn't know if they would have room to set up their sprawling twenty-six-tent hospital, or how they would unload the eighty tons of equipment they were carrying. Israel's medical team was the first to arrive on location, before any other country. Within twelve hours, they constructed what many doctors and policymakers have hailed as one of the best field hospitals ever built.[31] In the ensuing weeks, Israeli surgeons performed hundreds of operations, saved countless vital organs, delivered babies, and provided care to newborns. In one harrowing moment, an Israeli officer donated his blood to save the life of a three-day-old infant. And alongside their canine team, after eight days of searching, rescue officials erupted in joy when they found a man alive, buried deep in the rubble. As former US president Bill Clinton put it, "I don't know what we would have done without the Israeli hospital in Haiti."[32]

In 2013, the World Health Organization under the auspices of the United Nations put together a classification system to grade medical teams around the world that are able to react to disasters. Israel is the only country in the world to have received the top mark.[33] "Only a handful in the world could even think of" reaching that benchmark, said Dr. Ian Norton, the senior author of the "Classification and Minimum Standards for Foreign Medical Teams in Sudden Onset Disasters."[34]

Since its founding, MASHAV – which coordinates Israel's humanitarian aid programs – has trained close to 270,000 people in more than 140 countries.[35] Israeli rescue workers are often asked why they are motivated to travel halfway around the world to help people they have never met or to whom they have no prior connection. "It may sound [like] a simple cliché, maybe even cynical…[but] the IDF does everything it can to save lives and to help each and every human being," says Bar, the Israeli colonel. "When we save [the life] of one person, we feel that we save the world. So we save[d] the world several times in this mission."[36]

PART II

Local Challenges Make
for Global Solutions

CHAPTER 3

The Uber of Ambulances

Deliver me in Your righteousness, and rescue me; incline Your ear unto me, and save me.

~ Psalms 71:2

Eli Beer pictured with Hatzalah ambucycle (courtesy of United Hatzalah)

RADICALLY CHANGING EMERGENCY CARE

On June 2, 1978, Eli Beer was walking back from kindergarten with his eleven-year-old brother when a bus suddenly exploded next to them.[1] The blast was so powerful it shook a nearby building and blew out several windows around the neighborhood. A Palestinian terrorist group had planted a bomb to disrupt the eleventh anniversary of Jerusalem's reunification.[2] Six people died in the explosion, and nineteen were injured. Beer and his brother were so terrified, they ran away.[3] But the trauma of that day affected him deeply.[4] "I knew I would become an EMT," he says. "I decided that, someday, I would make it my business – my dream – to help the people I wasn't prepared to help on that day."[5]

21

A decade later, when he was fifteen, Beer took his first EMT course and became a volunteer for Jerusalem's Magen David Adom (Red Star of David), the Israeli branch of the International Committee of the Red Cross.[6] The experience was rewarding. But he often felt that he and his colleagues arrived too late.

One day, for instance, he heard from his dispatcher that a seven-year-old child was choking on a hot dog and needed immediate assistance. Beer's ambulance navigated as quickly as possible through Jerusalem's ancient streets. They arrived on the scene twenty minutes later only to find the boy blue in the face and unconscious. Beer and his team performed CPR. A local doctor heard the ambulance siren and came running over. He took the child's pulse and found nothing. The boy was dead. If the same doctor, Beer realized, had known about the incident a few minutes earlier, he could have saved a life. "This child died for nothing," Beer recalls thinking. "There had to be a better way."[7]

In Israel, a place known for devastating terror attacks, ambulances arrive at the scene of an emergency in about twenty minutes. After the choking incident, Beer wanted to find a way to speed up the process, to make it more efficient. Many people who could otherwise be saved, he says, were dying unnecessarily.[8] Shaving off a few minutes is critical. Responders often have just six minutes to save someone's life after a heart attack, for instance.[9]

His solution was to band together fifteen EMTs and form a local neighborhood first-aid group, to help get to emergencies more quickly. They all purchased beepers so they could keep in touch with one another, and Beer contacted the ambulance company that serviced his neighborhood; he wanted the company's ambulance manager to contact his group if there was an emergency in his neighborhood. The manager laughed. "Kid, go to school or go open a falafel stand," he said. "We are not interested in your help."[10] The manager threw Beer out of his office, but that didn't stop the

Jerusalem native. "[I had] an amazing Israeli innovation," says Beer. "Chutzpah."[11]

The next day the group of EMTs went out and bought two police scanners to allow them to listen to calls for help. "The hell with you," Beer thought, recalling the manager's words. "I'll save lives without your help."[12] That same day, as Beer listened to the scanners, he heard a distress call for a seventy-year-old man who had been hit by a car. He was a block away and ran to the scene.[13] When he arrived, Beer saw an old man lying on the ground with blood gushing from his neck. A relative told him the old man was on Coumadin, a blood thinner. Beer didn't have any medical equipment, but he knew the man would die if he didn't quickly stop the bleeding. So he took off his *kippah*, a Jewish religious head covering, and used it to apply heavy pressure to the wound. The bleeding stopped, and twenty-five minutes later, when the ambulance arrived, the old man was unconscious but breathing.[14] As the ambulance personnel put the man on a gurney, Beer noticed a tattoo on the inside part of his forearm – a series of blue numbers – the mark of an Auschwitz survivor.

Two days later, Beer received a phone call from the old man's son. "I was sure he was going to tell me that there was going to be a funeral," Beer recalls.[15] But the old man was alive. He wanted to thank Beer and requested he visit the hospital. When he arrived, the old man hugged him and thanked him for saving his life. At that moment, Beer knew his life's mission was to form an organization that would radically change emergency care.

Yet fulfilling that mission was going to be a lot harder than he ever imagined.

A LIFESAVING FLASH MOB

In order to expand his volunteer group, Beer had to solve two problems. First, he needed to construct a highly trained network of people all over the country. Second, he had to create a system that would ensure medics would be able to treat victims almost immediately.

With the help of Dr. Avi Rivkind, who heads up the Shock and Trauma Unit at the Hadassah Medical Center of Jerusalem,[16] Beer decided that all of his Hatzalah (meaning "rescue" in Hebrew) medics had to undergo a six-month, two-hundred-hour first-aid training course.[17] Candidates had to be over twenty-one and have a driver's license and a clean police record. "Medics, paramedics, and ambulance drivers play a crucial role in emergency medical care," says Rivkind, who serves as the unofficial chief medical advisor for Beer's organization. "Their professionalism determines the patients' chances of survival, the pace and extent of their recovery."[18] As more medics received training, however, Beer became increasingly frustrated with their inability to help those in need. Many drove cars and were delayed by parking and traffic jams.

He found an innovative solution. It was late 2001, and he was stuck in traffic. He pulled out his phone and started chatting. Before he knew it, a traffic cop on a motorcycle pulled up next to him and knocked on the window and gave him a ticket. Beer was mightily annoyed, but the incident sparked a unique idea: volunteers should ride motorcycles so they could weave through traffic and park anywhere. Beer went home and told his wife about his concept. "We should call it the ambucycle," she said. Part ambulance, part motorcycle.

Soon, Beer began to refit motorcycles as mini-ambulances. Each one contains a trauma kit, an oxygen canister, a blood sugar monitor, and a defibrillator. These vehicles aren't sexy, but like their innovator, they get the job done with chutzpah.[19] The ambucycles (and Beer's organization) aren't meant to replace traditional ambulances and paramedics, which are critical to helping those in need. But they are able to shorten the time it takes EMTs to provide first-aid and life-saving support. As Beer puts it, "We [are] . . . a lifesaving flash mob."[20]

Using police scanners to learn of emergencies, Beer's group

quickly expanded, first in Jerusalem, then Bnei Brak, followed by Haifa, Tel Aviv, and a number of smaller cities. Religious Jewish communities were the first to get involved. Beer attributes this to their lifestyle, which for men, centers around learning. Yeshiva students have the flexibility to take a break at any time – as opposed to attorneys, accountants, or others who tend to have a fixed schedule.

The summer of 2006 marked a critical moment for Beer, his cohorts, and other similar organizations that started all over the country. Many volunteer medics traveled to northern Israel as a war unfolded with Hezbollah. When Beer realized that some organizations were better equipped than others, he decided to unite the various groups. That way, he felt, they could reduce expenses and save more lives. At the height of the war, in the basement of a synagogue in Hadera, a city north of Tel Aviv, he met with the leadership of the various groups. After hours of bitter squabbling, he convinced most of them to join forces. Together, he believed, they could tend to anyone who is injured or sick within a minute and thirty seconds of being called. "If you get to someone within the first two minutes of a cardiac event," Beer says, "you have a 90 percent chance of saving them."[21]

The name of the new organization? United Hatzalah. As the meeting came to a close, people in the room "felt like they were on the verge of a revolution," recalls Dov Maisel, the organization's director of international operations. "This was going to change everything."[22]

"Eli figured out a way to overcome the bureaucratic antipathy by just doing good," says Peter Bloom, chairman of DonorsChoose.org and retired managing director at the private equity firm General Atlantic. "I think it is the force of Eli just going, 'If I do the right thing long enough, eventually people will come to see why I'm doing it.'"[23]

The next step was figuring out exactly how to make the group more efficient. Before the war, Maisel felt the group needed a specialized app that would dispatch medics using GPS technology. "In retrospect, if we were thinking about making money and not saving lives," Maisel says, "we would have been Uber."[24] But Hatzalah put the idea on hold due to the large development costs, which stood at more than $1 million. After the 2006 war, as the various neighborhood groups came together, Beer and Maisel decided they had to scrounge up the money. Thanks to a private donor, by the summer of 2007, United Hatzalah had a beta version for flip phones. But just as their technology was released, the first iPhone came out, and Maisel understood everything had changed.

In 2008, all EMTs started downloading a standardized GPS app to their smartphones. The system draws a perimeter around an incident and alerts the five closest volunteers through a series of loud beeps on their phones.[25] Anyone who identifies an emergency can call a toll-free central number in Israel (1221) that routes to the United Hatzalah nerve center, which blasts out the alert. All of the group's EMTs, Beer says, are guided by the same principle: "Think about every single patient...like he's your own mother or father. Run to him like he's your own son."[26]

ARABS SAVING JEWS AND JEWS SAVING ARABS

One thing, however, does stop ambulances and first responders: violence. Magen David Adom (MDA), Israel's primary ambulance organization, will not go into many Arab neighborhoods, unless accompanied by a security escort. There have been too many instances of rock throwing, Molotov cocktails, and gunshots. Palestinian militants have even burned MDA ambulances.[27] "MDA has a problem," says Muhammad Asli, an Arab medic and Jerusalem native. "The ambulances don't enter [Arab neighborhoods] unaccompanied, so the time that a family or a sick person waits for medical treatment is very long. This waiting time can jeopardize a person's life, and to our sorrow, there are many incidents like this in the east of the city."[28]

In 2006, Asli's father collapsed at home from a heart attack. It took more than an hour for the ambulance to arrive to his East Jerusalem home because the driver did not want to go to that part of the city without a military escort.[29] Asli's father died waiting; there was nothing his son could do about it. Like Beer, he decided to form a neighborhood association of first responders to try to save lives.[30]

Shortly after his father's tragic death, as he continued to mull over the idea, he randomly met Beer at the Hadassah University Medical Center, where Asli works as an X-ray technician. The two wound up chatting about United Hatzalah and the importance of saving lives regardless of a person's religion or nationality. Asli was intrigued by the conversation. In 2007, he and a friend, Murad Alyan, a registered nurse, called their new Jewish acquaintance to gauge his interest in starting a new chapter in East Jerusalem.[31] They decided to meet at United Hatzalah's main office and dispatch center at 78 Yirmiyahu Street, near the entrance to Jerusalem.[32]

As Asli walked into the building, he was immediately stopped by a United Hatzalah volunteer.

"What are you doing here?"

Asli looked at him. Before he had a chance to respond, the volunteer said, "Do you not remember me?"

"No," Asli said.

"Well, I am going to invite you to my daughter's wedding. Do you really not remember me? You are the one who helped my daughter when she was admitted to the emergency room a few months ago."

As the volunteer ushered him into the room where he was going to meet Beer, it was Asli's turn to engage in déjà vu.[33] Beer did not remember him. When Asli reintroduced himself, however, the two quickly picked up where they left off. "I felt part of the family," Asli recalls. "And I would be more than happy to continue with this [type of work]."[34]

All four men had a shared interest in emergency medicine. But as Beer listened to Asli, he realized the issue was personal. "Please start this [in Arab East Jerusalem]," Beer recalls him saying. "[There is] so much tragedy, so much hate. It's not about saving Jews. It's not about saving Muslims. It's not about saving Christians. It's about saving people."[35]

Shortly after the meeting, Beer, Asli, and Alyan started recruiting United Hatzalah volunteers among the city's Arab residents. Today there are more than forty volunteers in East Jerusalem.[36] Each decided that their families would be safer if they studied first aid.[37] "United Hatzalah helped me a lot," says Asli. "They gave me equipment and whatever I needed."[38]

In addition to East Jerusalem, there are United Hatzalah chapters in Tira, Kafr Kana, and Kafr Qasim, three predominantly Arab cities within Israel.[39] There are also about three hundred Arab and Bedouin volunteers of various faiths – including Druze, Christian, and Muslim – throughout the country.[40] Volunteers wear identification vests with Arabic and English-language United Hatzalah logos.[41] Today, the group's Jewish and Arab volunteers are going to places in Jerusalem, Arab cities within the Green Line, and even locations in the West Bank that are normally dangerous for each respective community. "We started hand in hand," says Beer. "Arabs were saving Jews. Jews were saving Arabs. Something special happened...it's an unbelievable situation...all of a sudden they had a common interest."[42]

United Hatzalah has helped break down preconceived notions and stereotypes among the volunteers. People who normally never interact with one another – including ultra-Orthodox and secular Jews, Christians, Muslims, Bedouin and Druze – now work together.[43] When Asli's uncle fell ill, it was a Jew from the disputed territories with a *kippah* who took care of him. Beer had a similar experience. A few years ago, when his father collapsed from a heart attack, one of the first volunteers to arrive on the scene was Muslim. "He saved my father," Beer says. "Could you imagine?"[44]

"Saving lives," he adds, "is important to all religions."[45]

A CRAZY IDEA

When Beer first started United Hatzalah, many called him meshuga (crazy). No one thinks that anymore. Beer's EMTs have been wildly successful. "United Hatzalah's innovation has helped save thirty-five thousand-plus lives a year, which – *dayenu!* – would be enough," says Mark Gerson, the founder of the Gerson Lehrman Group. "But in doing so, the group has also brought people together – Jews, Christians, Muslims, and Druze. In focusing on a common goal, saving lives, they have become brothers and sisters in solidarity."[46] In 2014, Hatzalah volunteers treated 245,000 Israelis, including 27,000 children. A quarter of the calls United Hatzalah fields are considered life-threatening. And since the organization's inception, EMTs have treated well over a million people.[47] "United Hatzalah is the essence of saving human lives before anything else," says Professor Alan Dershowitz. "It grows out of the heart and souls of people who just want to do good. There is no reward more important than the knowledge that you made the difference between life and death."[48]

Beer has accomplished all of this on a budget of about $5 million a year, the vast majority of which is raised via private donations in Israel and the United States.[49] No one in the organization – with the exception of a few paid staffers – is compensated, nor are EMT-related expenses reimbursed.[50] He has formed a robust volunteer corps of EMTs numbering more than three thousand Jewish, Muslim, Christian, Druze, and Bedouin volunteers in Israel. There are several chapters in various stages of development around the world.[51]

Not everyone, however, is supportive of Beer's work. When several donors learned that United Hatzalah embraced Arab volunteers, they pulled their funding. Fortunately, other donors found this appalling and stepped up their donations to compensate for it. "Some people thought I was doing this for political reasons," says Beer. "But real Zionism is treating everyone who lives in Israel in the best manner."[52]

In the next fifteen years, Beer envisions that every neighborhood in Israel will have an EMT volunteer. And he wants to see the group grow in other parts of the world as well. "I see lots of people who would run ... to save other people, no matter who they are, no matter what religion, no matter who, where they come from," he says. "We just need a good idea, motivation, and lots of chutzpah."[53]

CHAPTER 4

One Drop at a Time

No shrub of the field was yet in the earth, and no herb of the field had yet sprung up; for the Lord God had not caused it to rain upon the earth, and there was not a man to till the ground; but there went up a mist from the earth, and watered the whole face of the ground.

~ Genesis 2:5-6

Drip irrigation (courtesy of Netafim)

IRRIGATING ON POINT

On a crisp afternoon in the spring of 2015, Rafi Mehoudar paced backstage, waiting to make his entrance. It was the sixty-seventh anniversary of Israeli independence, and several thousand people had gathered at Israel's Mount Herzl National Cemetery in Jerusalem. The mood was festive, as ten of the country's luminaries came on stage to light a torch in honor of their achievements. Notable figures included Danny Gold, the innovator behind Iron Dome; Gavriel Iddan, the inventor of the PillCam; and Ehud Shabtai, one of the cofounders of Waze.

Then it was Mehoudar's turn. He walked up to the lectern in a dark suit, smiling as he looked out at the crowd of people waving blue-and-white Israeli flags. Mehoudar had helped develop modern drip irrigation, a system that waters crops one drop at a time, more efficiently and effectively than earlier methods. But before he left the stage, he sifted through his notes as if he was looking back in time. Then he praised his forgotten predecessor, a man who had not received the money or fame that came from his remarkable invention. "In honor of Simcha Blass," he said, "who against all odds advanced the use of drip irrigation fifty-five years ago."

Mehoudar lit the torch, and the crowd erupted in applause. The only problem: Blass was not alive to hear it. Some thirty-three years earlier, he had died a bitter man.

It was August 12, 1965. The taxi carrying Simcha Blass, an Israeli water expert, came to a screeching halt in front of a ramshackle building in Kibbutz Hatzerim, a socialist commune in the middle of the Negev Desert.[1] Israel had existed for less than twenty years, and it had already experienced three wars. Now the kibbutz was waging a battle to conserve one the world's most vital and finite resources: water.

Because of its remote and barren setting, the kibbutz had long struggled to get by, so Hatzerim's leadership decided to try something new. They wanted to start a business that would help earn extra money for the kibbutz's roughly one hundred inhabitants, and they'd been in negotiations with Blass for a project they felt could accomplish just that.[2] As Blass stepped out of the car, he steadied himself with his cane and slipped on long white gloves that extended to his elbows.[3] Peering out in the distance, all he could see was miles of sand.

The area was parched, and there was little the kibbutz could do. Israel's farmers had long used flood irrigation to water their fields. This method has been used for centuries in the Middle East in places like Egypt and Iraq, where people used the Nile, Euphrates, and Tigris rivers to support their crops. Farmers built canals and trenches for irrigation, but these systems took a massive amount of time, effort, and money. Even worse, agronomists estimate that more than 50 percent of water evaporates or drains into the soil before a plant's roots can absorb it.[4] Being a poor country, Israel couldn't afford to waste a single drop, yet it was wasting a whole lot more.

Blass had created an irrigation system he believed could save an enormous amount of water and fertilizer. Using pipes, small holes, and narrow plastic tubes, he believed he could build a device that delivered water directly to the base of the plant. The kibbutz hoped he was right. Most of Israel's academics, farmers, and government officials, however, were skeptical. How could dripping a small amount of water allow plants to grow and yield significant crops? But Hatzerim was willing to take a chance.

Blass signed away the rights to his invention to the kibbutz. In return, he received a small royalty on future sales and 20 percent of the shares in the company the kibbutz was building around his invention.

He left the kibbutz, satisfied with the terms. But his satisfaction was short-lived.

THE TREE OF KNOWLEDGE

A descendent of the Vilna Gaon, one of the world's most famous rabbis, Blass was born into a Hasidic family in Poland in 1897. Growing up, he enjoyed tinkering with clocks and was involved in the local Zionist youth group. When World War I broke out, he was drafted into the Polish army and served for two years. During his service, he created a meteorological instrument for measuring wind speed and direction. After the war, he enrolled in a Polish engineering institute, where he began thinking about how to use alternative sources of energy for internal combustion engines. Among his inventions was an engine that used alcohol derived from barley instead of gasoline.[5]

His passion for engineering was matched by his interest in a Jewish state. When he realized that Israel did not have enough barley for cattle, let alone engines, he decided to create a machine capable of planting large quantities of wheat, which he completed and tried to sell.[6] It never took off, but in 1930, he left Europe for Palestine, excited to return to the Jewish homeland.

Shortly after arriving with his wife, Yehudit, he began working on water projects for the Yishuv, the Jewish community in pre-state Israel. One day in the early 1930s, a friend invited Blass to his home in Karkur, a town near Haifa. As the two ate outside, Blass noticed something odd. In the field before him, he saw what looked like a fence of trees. One of them was much bigger than the others, but they were all the same species and likely planted at the same time. His friend told him the big tree grew supposedly without water. Intrigued, Blass started looking around.

What he found surprised him: the topsoil was completely dry, but a dripping faucet in the area had soaked the root system underneath the tall tree. He started digging and found an onion-shaped wet zone that kept the ground moist, with almost no surface evaporation.[7] "Water droplets raising a giant tree hit me like a mosquito in the mind of the evil Titus," Blass would later say.[8]

Over the course of the next twenty years, Blass often thought about that tree. By dripping water slowly to the base of a plant, he believed he could revolutionize the way farmers irrigate their crops. Yet his idea would have to wait, as Blass was slated to play a key role in the birth of the State of Israel. "I became busy with other plans," he recalled. "But the drop of water that grew a gigantic tree refused to leave me. It stayed trapped and sleeping in my heart."[9]

THE PERFECT DRIP

From the 1930s through 1950s, Blass became one of Israel's leading water experts. When he moved to Palestine, there wasn't much infrastructure. People would dig for water, pump it to the surface, and then carry it short distances or send it through pipes. And with millions of Jews making their way back to their ancestral homeland, it was clear to Israel's founding fathers that the country would need to provide these immigrants with a number of services.

It was only after he left government service in 1956 that Blass was able to dedicate himself to drip irrigation. In the late 1950s, he started playing with several different prototypes. He started working with metal pipes, mimicking what he had seen with the row of trees in the 1930s.[10] Yet during World War II, there was a worldwide rubber shortage, and that gave rise to a new substance: plastic. For several years, Blass experimented with various widths and discovered plastic tubing was a cheap and flexible way to deliver water.[11]

In 1960, Blass carried out his first successful experiment in an orchard of seventy trees in the city of Rehovot. He used a third less water to irrigate the plants.[12] Later trials showed drip irrigation was far more effective than flood irrigation and sprinkler systems, regardless of the plant it was watering or its location. Not only did it use less water, but the crop yield was significantly higher, too.

Decades after Blass had come up with his idea, drip irrigation was poised to change farming practices not only in Israel, but also around the world.

Blass was not the first person to try drip irrigation. The Chinese experimented with drip methods in the first century BCE. In 1860, researchers in Germany tried using underground clay pipe irrigation. The first recorded use of plastic occurred in Australia in the 1920s. But Blass utilized a different system that involved a dripper with a long, spiral micro-tubing water passageway that slowed the velocity of the water. A few years later, he improved his design by creating a two-piece dripper.[13]

For the better part of the early 1960s, Blass talked about his invention to anyone who would listen. Along the way, he met Dan Goldberg, a Hebrew University professor in the Department of Soil and Water Sciences. The two conducted a number of experiments together. But most people did not take his ideas seriously. Perhaps it was his gruff temperament, or maybe, as with other inventions, changing the status quo met stiff resistance.

Blass decided to leverage his old contacts at the Ministry of Agriculture, and the government began conducting a number of experiments in an almond orchard. The first resulted in complete failure when the ministry placed the plastic tubes incorrectly in the soil (the tree roots grew into the drippers and blocked the outflow of water). Luckily for Blass, one of the ministry officers succeeded in convincing his colleagues to carry out the experiment again. This time, officials placed the drippers at the base of the trees, and as predicted, the plants flourished, grew with less water, and produced a higher yield.[14] But even with the seal of approval from the ministry, his invention did not catch on.

By 1964, however, word started to get around that a "pensioner" (the Israeli term for a retiree) had some kind of system to save water.[15] The head of the Kibbutz Industrial Association, Aryeh Bahir, told Kibbutz Hatzerim's treasurer, Uri Werber, about Blass's idea.[16] Bahir knew that Kibbutz Hatzerim was looking to start a new business, and that it could not survive on agriculture alone. Luckily for Blass, the Hatzerim leadership wanted an industry with a strong connection to the land, recalls Werber. They also wanted women and the elderly to be able to play a role.[17]

Originally created to help farmers working in desert-like conditions, Blass's rudimentary device was a micro-tube wound around a sixteen-millimeter pipe. Because of the water's friction at the entry point, the dripper produced a flow rate of three to five drops per hour. The kibbutz members loved the idea of saving water and getting a larger yield. They didn't care that it wasn't in vogue.

Blass was skeptical. He believed in his invention, but doubted the kibbutz could manufacture his dripper and monetize the idea.[18] Werber, the community's treasurer, was persistent. "I was lucky enough, and maybe a little clever enough to go with my feelings and instincts," he says.[19]

Within a few months, Blass signed his contract with the kibbutz. In January 1966, the company began manufacturing drippers. Its name: Netafim, or drops of water.

DROWNING THE COMPETITION

After the first growing season, the kibbutz discovered that Blass was right; the results were exactly as he predicted. Some members even wanted to keep this innovation a secret in order to ensure Hatzerim closed as much business as possible.[20] In August 1966, the company completed its first sale to grape growers in the settlement of Bnei Atarot. The world's first commercial dripper had arrived.[21]

That same year, a Ministry of Agriculture official convinced four Arava Valley settlements to conduct an experiment, pitting their existing sprinkler system against Blass's technology. Within one month, the sprinkler-irrigated vegetables failed to grow, while the drip-irrigated vegetables – tomatoes and sweet peppers – yielded a phenomenal crop. This experiment and those that followed helped the Arava settlements become one of Europe's leading suppliers of winter fruits and vegetables.[22]

As Blass's invention received more recognition in the Arava, the area's settlements used Netafim's product to grow melons and watermelons, date palms and flowers, in both fields and greenhouses.[23] Later Netafim was the first company to sell micro-drippers to irrigate cotton and sugar cane.[24] "When we first introduced drip irrigation, everyone in Israeli academia explained to us why it can't work, and why the method would just kill the plants," says former Netafim CEO Oded Winkler. "It took us over five years [after the company was founded] to prove that such a position was just theory, not reality."[25]

Once the company became commercially successful, Blass filed for a patent in 1966 to protect his intellectual property.[26] In the early 1970s, he sold 100 percent of his rights to Netafim,[27] receiving a large sum of money, and lived the rest of his life in comfort.[28]

A few years later, however, he seemed upset about his decision. The inventor got together with Uri Werber, the kibbutz treasurer, and told him, "Here sits the man who robbed me. I didn't think right, and he took advantage of that."

Taken by surprise, Werber responded, "The only thing that I did was...believe in your invention and idea more than you did."[29]

He wasn't the only one. There was also a young upstart engineer who revolutionized the company, turning it from a small, kibbutz-run business into a worldwide water empire.

THE GROUNDBREAKER

Growing up, Rafi Mehoudar was anything but extraordinary. He was just another scrawny, dark-haired kid whose family had been living in Jerusalem for twelve generations.[30] His teachers felt he had limited intelligence. "Your son doesn't understand chemistry," they told his mother. "Maybe he will turn out to be great plumber."[31]

What helped Mehoudar, however, was his father, a failed businessman, who knew how to draw out his son's creative side. He had magic trick sets with items that included exploding cigarettes and cups that would spill their contents on anyone who drank from them. He would entertain the young Mehoudar with his magic and make him laugh. When young Rafi turned thirteen, his father bought him a tool kit that allowed him to build a solar energy collector and a small desalinization water station.[32]

After high school, like all Israelis, Mehoudar was drafted into the military, entering a special program that allowed its members to pursue academic studies along with military service. He enrolled in Israel's prestigious Technion, where he became intrigued by the ways humans can conserve water. Not only did he invent his own sprinkler irrigation system, he also worked on a toilet that he hoped would reduce the amount of water people flush.[33]

When he left the military, the Ministry of Defense's science office asked him to come back part-time to develop water-saving tools.

During his time there, he created a number of pressure regulators for sprinklers,[34] and the industry took notice.

In 1972, Netafim's then CEO, Oded Winkler, approached Mehoudar. He asked the young engineer to join the company's research and development department. But Mehoudar initially demurred; he thought many kibbutz members weren't open to new ideas. "I was quite suspicious starting to work with Hatzerim," he recalls. "Then I found that [they were] another animal. The people in Hatzerim that I met were very open to external ideas."[35] Mehoudar finally agreed to work with Netafim, but only as a consultant who was compensated with royalties for his innovations.

Shortly after Hatzerim and Mehoudar struck a deal, Winkler gave the young inventor a list of ten drippers that he wanted him to develop. Some were sensitive to temperature changes, while others worked only with the push of a button. It took Mehoudar six months to find solutions to nine out of the ten requests. He then presented Netafim with blueprints and products for these products. The company carried out his plans, and many of the drippers are still sold today.

As Ran Maidan, the company's current chief executive, puts it: "Simcha [Blass] invented the dripper, but Rafi really developed [it]."[36]

OUR NUMBER ONE ENEMY IS IGNORANCE

By 2050, the world's population will balloon to roughly nine billion people.[37] In fifteen years, experts say half of the world's inhabitants could be living in areas where there isn't enough safe water to drink.[38] The result will likely be a surge in demand for food.[39] This means that the world will need to grow more food with less water. To meet this need, humanity will have to find innovative ways to use existing land and water resources, which are already under heavy stress. "Water isn't just water," says Seth M. Siegel, author of *Let There Be Water*. "In the case of Israel, it's also an inspiring example of how vision and leadership can change a nation and transform the world."[40]

Less than 1 percent of the world's fresh water is potable. The vast majority of this precious resource is used for agricultural irrigation – over half of which is wasted due to inefficiency.[41] One way to conserve is to change the way we irrigate our crops, and the most efficient method is drip irrigation. "Water is one of the biggest challenges humanity is facing," says Oded Distel, director of the Israel NewTech program at the Ministry of Economy and Industry. "Israel's holistic approach can serve as a model to overcome the global water crisis."[42]

Today, Netafim is playing a key role in feeding the chronically undernourished and cultivating more crops. The company helps farmers, cooperatives, and governments conserve more water for the greater benefit of all. Netafim has grown into a global powerhouse with more than 30 percent of the global drip irrigation market, and it sells its products in more than 110 countries. "Our number one competition is ignorance," says Naty Barak, the company's chief sustainability officer.[43]

When Mehoudar stepped off the stage that night at Mount Herzl, he shook his head in disbelief. What he and Simcha Blass had launched helps feed nearly a billion people. "And this is just the beginning," says Mehoudar.[44] Blass may have died a bitter man, but what he and Mehoudar created has improved the lives of many – one drop at a time.

CHAPTER 5

Real Iron Men

As birds hovering, so will the Lord of hosts protect Jerusalem; He will deliver it as He protects it, He will rescue it as He passes over.

~ Isaiah 31:5

Iron Dome battery deployed near Ashkelon (courtesy of Israel Defense Forces)

MISSILES WERE MAKING LIFE UNBEARABLE

The warning sirens blared in Sderot, and residents of this Israeli town, about a half mile from Gaza, quickly took cover in the nearest bomb shelter. An eerie silence fell, and then everyone could hear the low-pitched whine of a rocket approaching, followed by a deafening boom. Windows shattered. Car alarms blared. It was July 2014, and a rocket had crashed into the exact spot where I had been standing three hours earlier. As the scene unfolded live on TV, I felt lucky to be home in Jerusalem. Since 2001, these rockets attacks have been almost a daily occurrence in southern Israel, as Hamas has fired missiles at Sderot and other Israeli cities in an attempt to kill people and disrupt daily life. To the north, near the Lebanese border, it was far quieter, but there, too, Israeli officials worried Hezbollah could create chaos. Over the past two decades, the group had amassed tens of thousands of rockets, and by 2004, many already felt war was inevitable.

The military needed a solution to these rocket attacks, but its experts were stumped. Life in Israel, they worried, was becoming unbearable. Later that year, the task fell on Danny Gold, the IDF official responsible for developing new weapons systems. In August, he put out a request for defense companies to submit ideas. Few took notice. So, the general with a dual PhD in electrical engineering and business started studying the matter on his own. His hope: to develop a system that could intercept missiles in mid-flight.[1]

At the time, the idea sounded like science fiction. In the 1980s, US president Ronald Reagan proposed an ambitious space-based anti-missile system, called the Strategic Defense Initiative, which critics lampooned as "Star Wars." The technology was extraordinarily complex, and subsequent presidents canceled its funding. Which is perhaps why almost no one in Israel's military leadership thought a similar system could work. Gold's colleagues and superiors called him "completely delusional."[2] Many Palestinian and Hezbollah rockets are only a few feet long and a few feet wide. They often fly erratically and can hit Israeli cities within seconds. How could any missile defense system thwart such unpredictable weapons?[3]

Gold was steadfast. "I saw what was going on," he says, "and I said to myself, with all the technology that exists in Israel, we must use it to protect human life."[4]

COULD IT BE DONE?

The sounds of rockets exploding outside his home shook Chanoch Levine to the core. It was the summer of 2006, and Levine and his wife were living in the Jezreel Valley in northern Israel. Their country was embroiled in a vicious war with Hezbollah. The group was firing missiles at a rate of about a hundred per day, and Levine's home was near some of the worst violence.[5]

That summer, he had returned to Israel after two years in Washington, DC, working with the US Department of Defense. As a senior engineer for Rafael Advanced Defense Systems, an Israeli defense technology company, he had worked on finding ways to reduce the damage inflicted by improvised explosive devices (IEDs). As missiles rained down not far from Rafael's offices in northern Israel, Oron Oriol called Levine into his office. Oriol headed the company's air-to-air missile program and tasked Levine with his new assignment: figuring out how to cheaply and effectively defeat the short-range missile threat. Levine's first task was to put together a team and prepare a proposal for Gold so Rafael could win a contract.

"Why are you giving me the position?" Levine asked.

"I have five people who are better than you. And every one of them knows air-to-air missiles better than you," said Oriol. "The problem is that the Minister of Defense is insisting we do this in three years. Every one of the others will do it in fifteen years. The minister is insisting we do it at $50,000. Everyone else is going to do it at a price of $1 million. I need someone who is coming from outside and will look at things differently."[6]

As he walked out of the meeting, Levine called his wife and told her he didn't think he would see her for the next five years. "I felt terrible," he said. "I wasn't certain it [the project] could be done."[7]

With the war ongoing, military officials became even more insistent that someone find a way to stop the rockets. Levine's boss put him to work and gave him an assistant and an empty office. "At first, I didn't know what to do with myself," says Levine. "I looked at the wall and asked myself, 'How do I even start?'"[8]

Israel's war in Lebanon lasted thirty-four days. But the death and destruction were devastating. During the fighting, 1200 Lebanese and 165 Israelis died. Most were civilians.[9] The conflict also forced roughly one million Lebanese[10] and three to five hundred thousand Israelis to flee their homes.

About three months later, in November 2006, Levine and his team presented their idea to Gold at the Ministry of Defense's office in Tel Aviv.[11] Levine began by providing an assessment of the necessary capabilities, the cost, the range, and the salvo requirements. The Israeli military has long recognized Rafael for its specialty in missile technology, and Gold's team was impressed with Levine's idea. Rafael proposed that it partner with the Israel Aerospace Industries to build a radar system, and a little-known company at the time, mPrest, to create the controls and provide data analysis.[12]

After about a month of internal deliberation, Gold chose Levine's team and gave them a paltry sum of 20 million shekels (about $5 million) to get started. Rafael's chairman, Ilan Biran, matched this sum, but only after Gold promised to secure more funding within a year or two from elsewhere.[13]

Even after the 2006 war, very few thought it was possible to stop Hezbollah's and Hamas's rockets. Initially, Prime Minister Ehud Olmert refused to fund the project after most of his military advisors slammed the idea. So Rafael was forced to start building a complex missile system with about $10 million dollars committed to the project – a fraction of what it would cost. As Levin puts it: "I was overjoyed that we got the money. But I was scared we wouldn't succeed."[14]

THE TOYS R US KIDS

In order to build an effective, low-cost missile system, Levine had to assemble a highly motivated workforce and scour the globe for cheap, durable parts. Levine's original team was extremely small. "We picked the best in the entire country," says Gold. "We had seventy-year-old missile experts working alongside…engineers fresh out of college…without any hierarchy. The one who is right is the one who decides."[15] The people on the team worked in shifts twenty-four hours a day. "Comptrollers and critics, like the pair of old guys in the Muppet Show, sat on the sidelines and criticized," says Gold. "It never really bothered us."[16]

It was an extremely challenging period for everyone who worked on the program. "We worked like crazy during the week, and the weekends during the development stage, which took several years," says Levine. "There was not a day I would get home before eleven at night. I forgot what my family looked like when they were awake. I never took a day off during three long years. But I am not sorry for even a second."[17]

Both Gold and Levine understood that the interceptor missiles would have to cost about a tenth of the average missile, which costs about half a million dollars.[18] If they didn't, the number of interceptor rockets that Israel needed would bankrupt the country. So Levine found ways to cut costs in the most unusual of places. Among them: a toy store. "One day, I brought to work one of my son's [remote-controlled] cars," he says. "We passed it around and we saw it had components that really worked for us."

Levine's son's car had been in the garage for about fifteen years and still worked perfectly. The engineer immediately went to the store and bought more of the components for 80 cents apiece.[19] "Our system," he says, "is the only missile in the world that has parts from Toys R Us."[20]

THREE, TWO, ONE ... NOTHING

Naming the system took a while, too. One of the project leaders, known only as Colonel Chico,[21] went home for a short weekend break. He and his wife started to brainstorm.

"Let's call the rocket Tamir, for *til meyaret*," a Hebrew acronym for "interceptor missile." And for the system itself, the colonel liked the sound of "Golden Dome." The following Sunday the team approved the name Tamir, but didn't like the name Golden Dome, because it sounded too ostentatious. So they changed it to "Iron Dome," and the name stuck.[22]

Aesthetics also played a role in the design of the system. According to one of the original team engineers, "I wanted the battery system to look super-modern and threatening, because it was obvious that within an hour of its use, it would be featured on the likes of CNN and Al-Jazeera."[23]

But as the project progressed, getting funding proved to be the biggest challenge. Levine and company were running low on funds and had little to show for their effort. Fortunately, in early 2007, Defense Minister Amir Perez committed $10 million.[24] And in the final months of 2007, following heated arguments with the Ministry of Defense and the entire defense establishment, Olmert lent his support to the project, and the IDF finally allocated $200 million.[25] This was enough for Rafael to build two full batteries and a large number of missiles.

The signing ceremony took place at the Ministry of Defense offices in Tel Aviv. It was a joyous occasion, but not everyone was exuberant. Defense Minister Amir Peretz came over to Levine looking nervous. He took the Rafael engineer aside and looked him straight in the eye.

"Can you do it?" Peretz muttered.

"Of course we can do it."

"I didn't believe a single word that came out of my mouth at that moment," Levine recalls. "But when the Minister of Defense asks you if you can do something, the answer is always yes."[26]

By March 2009, the Rafael team had put together what it believed was a missile that met the Defense Ministry's specifications.[27] To test it, Rafael set up a demonstration in the Ramon Crater in the Negev Desert. Almost spontaneously, Rafael's researchers began taking bets. They jokingly divided themselves into three self-labeled camps. The Anti-Semites thought the Iron Dome would miss the Qassam rocket by at least half a mile. The Boycott, Divestment, and Sanctions (BDS) team wagered it would miss by at least a hundred yards. And the Zionists were convinced the Tamir would come within ten yards of the enemy rocket.[28]

On the day of the test, the weather was typical for the desert, hot and dry. Rafael launched the enemy rocket. And then the countdown for the Iron Dome began. "In those moments," Levine jokes, "I experienced two heart attacks."[29] Five, four, three, two, one. Nothing. The Tamir rocket didn't rise. Levine asked his team to press the button again. Still nothing. A few minutes later, the Qassam fell into the crater completely intact.

Levine decided to try again. The engineers loaded another Tamir missile into the canister. Then they fired another Qassam, waited, and launched another Tamir. "My guy presses the button, and nothing [again]," says Levine. "And at that moment, I thought to myself, how do I get to the cliff and 'accidentally' just take an extra step?"[30] The Israelis left the crater feeling dejected.

Within twenty-four hours, Levine's engineers figured out the problem: a faulty wire. Someone had placed it incorrectly. A week later, the military brass and Rafael employees once again made their way to the Negev. The three teams once again took their bets. This time the countdown started at ten. The Qassam came flying out. "I look over at a guy from the anti-Semitic team and he is totally white," recalls Levine. "I lost a few more years of my life at that point." Levine held his breath. Suddenly both missiles appeared together on the video screen and hit one another. The Iron Dome missile had knocked the Qassam out of the sky. The group erupted in joy.

What began as an impossible mission had become a viable way to protect the country.

DESTROYING DEATH FROM ABOVE

There, were, however, a few problems. When it became clear that the Israeli government spent hundreds of millions of dollars on Iron Dome, Rafael's rivals lobbied the government to audit the project.

In 2009, State Comptroller Micha Lindenstrauss issued a report blaming Gold for launching a multi-billion-dollar effort without going through the necessary channels.[31]

While the report didn't suggest criminal or administrative charges against Gold, it led to a lot of bad press.[32] There were hundreds of engineers, developers, soldiers, and security officials involved in the project. But Gold received most of the blowback. And while the system was in theory ready to deploy, Israel did not have a sufficient number of batteries to fire the missiles, or a significant number of Tamir rockets, which cost about $75,000 apiece.[33] Both would be necessary for the project to save lives. And that meant more money.

To help, Israel approached its longtime ally and benefactor, the United States. In May 2010, President Barak Obama announced he would seek $205 million from Congress to deploy Iron Dome batteries around Israel. That same month, the US House of Representatives approved the funding almost unanimously.[34] The Obama administration, with support from Congress, had come to Israel's rescue, says Aviv Ezra, director for congressional affairs at Israel's Ministry of Foreign Affairs. "The challenge was not only to save lives, but also to prevent war and give a wider diplomatic window for decision makers."[35]

By March 2011, the Iron Dome system was fully ready for battle, and its capabilities were impressive. It could successfully target rockets, artillery, and mortars. It could strike down aircraft, helicopters, and drones. It could detect and intercept missiles of all kinds within a forty-three-mile range. And it could operate in a variety of weather conditions, including rain, fog, and dust storms.[36]

The system calculates with a high degree of precision where incoming missiles are projected to hit and whether or not the area is strategic or heavily populated. Iron Dome then fires a Tamir and sets out to hit the target. Often, Israel fires two missiles in case the first one misses.

In early April, the IDF placed two Iron Dome batteries around Gaza, one in Ashkelon and the other in Beer Sheva, and the military command gave permission to fire at any Hamas rocket headed toward Israel. On April 7, the IDF spotted its first opportunity. Hamas launched a rocket toward the coastal city of Ashkelon. Seconds later, Iron Dome fired.[37] Plumes of white smoke pocketed the sky. The Tamir missiles hit their targets. Five years after Levine began his research, the so-called impossible project was a resounding success. "In rocket science, we call this a miracle," says Yair Ramati, the former head of Israel's Missile Defense Organization.[38]

The system came just in time. When war broke out in 2012 between Israel and Hamas, the population took note of Iron Dome's capabilities. There was a video that went viral during the war of an Israeli wedding that took place in a city not far from Gaza.[39] As the warning siren blares, guests walk around, some toward the bomb shelter, others watching the sky. The video shows Hamas firing more than a dozen Qassams as Maroon 5's "Sunday Morning" plays in the background. And in a vivid display of fireworks, Iron Dome intercepts them all. The guests erupt in celebration.

By July 2014, Iron Dome had protected major Israeli cities from Hamas's rockets. Its success rate was 90 percent. Finally, Israelis felt safe enough to go about their lives. And as a result, many on both sides of the Atlantic Ocean believe the system has the potential to play an important role in bringing together Arabs and Jews to the negotiation table as well as to save lives on both sides of the border. "Iron Dome is an investment in diplomacy – helping to create the conditions conducive to peace," says Michael Oren, former Israeli ambassador the United States.[40] Washington policymakers tend to agree. "The Iron Dome is Israel's military response to all those who thought they could bring the country to its knees," says Ambassador Dennis Ross. "It has given the IDF protection, and in most cases, allowed it to avoid deploying ground forces into places like Gaza, which saves an untold number of Israeli and Palestinian lives."[41]

ISRAEL'S SHELTERING SKY

Today, despite the 2014 war, military experts believe there are tens of thousands of rockets in Gaza. They also believe there are still hundreds of thousands of missiles in Lebanon. Gold, however, isn't afraid. He believes Iron Dome can deal with this threat effectively – and with an even higher success rate. "The question is how many missile batteries you buy and deploy," he says. "Iron Dome is prepared for the future."[42]

Across the political aisle in Israel, Gold is considered a hero and has been vindicated. In 2012, Israel awarded him, Levine, and seven of Rafael's engineers with the prestigious Defense Prize for their role in creating Iron Dome.[43] By the end of the 2014 war, Israel had nine batteries in place, with more scheduled to come on line in the next few years. Since the system was officially activated, it has successfully hit more than a thousand incoming rockets. "That makes me feel very good," says Gold.[44]

Israelis feel good about the system, too. All across the country, vendors hustle Iron Dome–related clothing, paraphernalia, and bumper stickers. But none of this would have been possible without the determination and ingenuity of people like Gold and Levine. As Gold puts it, "Sometimes it's worth being Don Quixote."[45]

CHAPTER 6

Modern-Day Joseph

The most traditional prayer is for a successful harvest – that God provide sustenance – bread, the staff of life. The Grain Cocoon technology is an answer to the ancient yearning that all people be fed. Shlomo Navarro, the innovator, the creator of the Grain Cocoon, is a messenger of God. His story is contemporary Scripture.

~ Rabbi Irwin Kula, personal correspondence

Shlomo Navarro (*second from right*) demonstrates a Grain Cocoon in Kigali, Rwanda, 2002 (courtesy of Shlomo Navarro)

A BETTER WAY TO PROTECT CROPS

The sound was almost grating. In November 1994, Shlomo Navarro, an Israeli food storage expert, and several of his colleagues had traveled to a small warehouse in a village outside Asmara, the capital of Eritrea.[1] The country had just exited a thirty-year bloody civil war, but the villagers told Navarro they were losing a battle with a far more common enemy: bugs. In recent weeks, insects had infested their grain stores, and a famine was imminent. Almost immediately, Navarro knew they weren't exaggerating. As he walked through the warehouse, examining the bags of maize piled up to the ceiling, the sound of the insects buzzing inside the sacks grew louder and louder.[2]

The villagers relied on local agriculture to survive, and for years had tried various ways to prevent bugs from destroying their grain stores. Many used toxic insecticides, which a local store sold in unmarked plastic bags. Farmers spread the white powder on their post-harvest crops. They often did so by hand, without wearing gloves, unaware that the residue can remain on the skin even after washing. This can lead to extreme sickness and even death. Scientists say the use of some pesticides and chemicals has also worn away at the ozone layer, and over time, insects can develop a resistance to these chemicals, rendering them ineffective.[3]

Navarro felt he had a better way to protect the village's crops. It's called the Grain Cocoon, and it's a large, hermetically sealed bag for rice, grain, spices, and legumes. The bag can hold anywhere from five tons to three hundred tons of grain. It's composed of a strong material called polyvinyl chloride (PVC), so it doesn't tear easily.[4] When farmers seal it off, the bag traps bugs and their eggs inside and deprives them of oxygen, suffocating them to death. On average, Navarro says, the cocoon can save more than 99 percent of a farmer's crops. It can be used any time after harvest collection, and once grain is placed inside it, the insects generally die within about ten days. Farmers can then easily remove the dead bugs by using a sieve, among other techniques.[5]

The villagers were skeptical, but they were willing to give his idea a shot. Navarro and his team had traveled to Eritrea at the behest of the Lutheran World Federation, a relief organization the villagers trusted. After having a cup of coffee with the locals, the Israeli scientist showed them his device. In storage, it took up roughly as much space as a small file cabinet. But once he unfolded it, he explained that it could hold up to ten tons of grain. The villagers began filling the cocoon, finding as many strong men as they could to quickly finish the job. Then they sealed it up and waited. Two days later, they opened the bag and sifted through the grain. Trapped inside were hundreds of dead bugs. True to his word, Navarro had helped save the village from starvation and famine.[6]

THE HUNGER GAMES

Across the globe, 805 million people are chronically undernourished.[7] Like the villagers, many farmers in the developing world still use burlap sacks to store their goods. Insects can easily infiltrate these bags, often destroying more than half of a farmer's harvest. Reducing these losses, experts say, will play a critical role in the fight against world hunger. In fact, inefficient storage techniques result in the loss of roughly 1.3 billion tons of food annually. That's one-third of all food produced for human consumption, an amount sufficient to feed every starving person in the world.[8]

Already Navarro's invention is helping on that front. Not only does his Grain Cocoon protect the harvest from bugs and farmers from pesticides, it also helps the rural poor deal with the unpredictable forces of the free market. By storing grains immediately after a harvest, farmers can wait to sell them until prices rise. In cases of extreme poverty, Navarro encourages villages to invest in a communal cocoon so they can store excess grain collectively and use it as needed. Unless small farmers are able to make these types of choices, they and their families are often doomed to an endless cycle of poverty.[9]

Since Navarro's for-profit company,[10] GrainPro, officially introduced the cocoon in the early 1990s, a hundred countries around the world have adopted it and saved their harvests from insects, rodents, and other pests.[11] The company has sold millions of cocoons along with other, small-sized hermetically sealed bags across the developing world, including countries in the Arab world (many of which have no diplomatic relations with Israel), Africa, Latin America, and Asia. The cocoons have become especially attractive to farmers and development agencies because they can reuse the bags multiple times over the course of several years.[12] As Martin Gummert, a senior scientist at the International Rice Research Institute (IRRI), puts it: "The science and technology have been proven and the benefits are great. The challenge now is...making people aware."[13]

SHRAPNEL'S SILVER LINING

Today, Navarro, in his mid-seventies, is widely recognized as a modern-day Joseph – the biblical figure who saved Egypt from famine by convincing Pharaoh to store grain underground. And like Joseph's, Navarro's journey to become a much-heralded leader of grain storage was improbable. A native of Izmir, Turkey, Navarro decided to immigrate to Israel in 1963. He didn't have a passport or enough money for the trip. But at twenty-three, Navarro was idealistic and eager to help build a Jewish homeland. So after four of his friends bought tickets on a boat traveling from Istanbul to Haifa, Navarro asked them to smuggle him aboard. They agreed, and he left without saying goodbye, knowing his family would have tried to convince him to stay.[14]

For four days, as the boat crossed the Mediterranean, Navarro remained in hiding in his friends' cabins, intermittently popping out to eat and stretch his legs. Terrified of getting caught and sent back to Turkey, Navarro wasn't sure how he would get off the boat and into Israel without a visa. His friends suggested they smuggle him out in a laundry basket, but he ultimately decided to come clean. When the Israeli customs officer boarded the ship in Haifa to stamp passports, Navarro told him the truth. The officer stepped away and deliberated with his superiors, and the Turkish stowaway waited anxiously with his fellow immigrants. Soon, the officer returned. Navarro, he said, could leave the ship. His friends erupted in celebration.[15]

At the time, Israel had a tightknit Turkish community, and Navarro had distant ties to two prominent families, the Mizrahis and the Castros. Once he was in Israel, they provided him with food and shelter, and even helped him find a job.[16]

Navarro didn't know what he wanted to do with his life. But he had a strong Jewish education and had always been fascinated by the story of Joseph. Before immigrating to Israel, he had earned a college degree in agricultural engineering from Ege University, a prominent Turkish institution. It was there he learned about insecticides, how they could protect crops from bugs, but often with terrible consequences. Eventually, he found a job in Israel working with the Israel Plant Protection Service (IPPS).[17]

In the early years after his arrival, Navarro went back and forth between government work at the IPPS, graduate studies, and reserve duty in the Israeli army. In 1965, he married his high school sweetheart, who also made the trip from Turkey. The couple had three children, but a bloody conflict interrupted parenthood and work.[18]

Navarro fought in the 1967 war and emerged unscathed. Two years later, he joined an Armored Corps unit in the Jordan Valley, where they battled Palestinian militants who wanted to reclaim the territory that Jordan lost years prior. The militants ambushed Navarro and his team at a remote outpost. As the battle raged, a mortar exploded and riddled Navarro's legs with shrapnel. The blast shot him fifteen feet in the air. In a daze, he looked over and saw that one of his fellow soldiers was dead. With mortars exploding and bullets whizzing by, Navarro's comrades carried him to safety. The IDF evacuated Navarro to Jerusalem by helicopter, where he underwent surgery to remove the shrapnel from his legs. He received a medal of honor for his service.[19]

Navarro spent the next eight months in a lower body cast, recovering in the hospital. The injury left him with a slight limp – his friends and colleagues affectionately call him "slow-mo" for the way he walks.[20] But it gave him time to study two subjects he found fascinating: temperature manipulation and hermetic storage. Both became the basis for his doctorate in agricultural entomology, which he received from the Hebrew University of Jerusalem in 1974.[21]

A few years after he was released from the hospital, Navarro went on to work at the Israel Agricultural Research Organization's Volcani Center, a world-renowned institute that fosters research and development for agriculture, water irrigation, crop cultivation, and pest control. It was there that the Turkish-born scientist created the prototype for what eventually became the Grain Cocoon.

Navarro began his experiments with a simple question: Is it possible to store large amounts of grain for long periods of time, with almost no losses? Like many countries at the time, Israel was storing goods to withstand market swings, natural disasters, and war. Navarro set out to prove that it was possible to hermetically seal fifteen thousand tons of grain in silos. And just like Joseph, he started by digging a deep trench.[22]

The work began in 1979. The harvest was very good that year, but if history was any indicator, the country would lose more than 2 percent of it. Israeli authorities stored the bulk of the grain outside, and they needed a better method. Navarro, who was already well-known in his field, briefed the heads of the Ministry of Commerce. "I have a solution," he said, "but it has never been tested before outside the lab."[23]

He presented plans for what later became known as bunker storage. The plan began in haste at Kibbutz Magen, located in southern Israel. Organizers quickly built a trench that was 360 feet long, 165 feet wide, and 30 feet high. Over the next month, they lined the trench with polyvinyl chloride, poured in the grain, and covered it with another layer of lining, before welders used heat to hermetically seal the trench.[24]

Navarro was confident his plan would work. But he also felt a tremendous sense of responsibility. He was overseeing a project worth millions of dollars, and the grain served as a large part of the country's reserves. Over the next fifteen months, Navarro says he had many sleepless nights. Whenever a big storm arrived, he woke up and drove two hours from his home to check the site. There were never any problems, but that didn't stop him from doing the same thing over and over.[25]

After the trial ended, Navarro and his cohorts discovered the grain was as fresh as the day they put it in the ground. The loss ratio fell tenfold to 0.2 percent. And the next year, Israel built three more trenches.[26]

After years of searching for a safe and reliable way to indefinitely store grain and prevent it from being attacked by insects, Navarro had finally found it.

THE SRI LANKA EXPERIMENT

After his initial success, Navarro wrote a number of articles about his invention. In the mid-1980s, one caught the attention of Dr. Laurence Simon, an international development expert and the head of the American Jewish World Service, a New York–based nonprofit. In 1985, Simon traveled to the Volcani Center to meet Navarro, the organization's deputy director. He didn't have an appointment, but he was determined to meet the man whose invention he felt was so promising. He knocked on Navarro's door, walked into his office, and told him he wanted to try to recreate Navarro's experiment with smaller bags to help the developing world. The Israeli scientist wasn't enthused. "I don't have time for this project," he said. But Simon didn't give up. The next day he returned, again uninvited, and argued that the Jewish people should make this important contribution to the rest of the world. This time, Navarro agreed.[27]

Less than a week later, Navarro began to give the project serious thought. One night, he went to bed and had a dream about the device. Midway through the dream, he woke up, bolted upright, and hurried downstairs to his home office. "I sketched out the entire thing," he says, from the zippers to the straps. Soon, Navarro contacted Simon and let him know it would take a few months to build his invention. Simon was elated. He knew just the place to test it: Sri Lanka.[28]

A multiethnic nation that's home to twenty million Buddhists, Hindus, Christians, and Muslims, Sri Lanka is a tiny island nation located just south of India. For years, Simon had worked with Sri Lanka's largest NGO, Sarvodaya. So he knew the country was poor and suffering from massive post-harvest losses. The team brought its prototype, and the first test trial was set to begin in three villages where the NGO had good relationships with farmers. The villagers worried they would lose all of their grain, or enough to cause a famine. So Navarro and his colleagues promised to compensate them for any losses beyond what they normally expected. After extensive training and instruction, Sarvodaya sent cocoons out into the field. Three months later, they returned to find that the experiment was a success. The bugs had suffocated, and the grain was fresh and ready to be turned into food.[29]

Since then, Simon and Navarro have gone on to market the product throughout the developing world. They even managed to convince major relief organizations such as the United Nations World Food Programme and the Office of the United Nations High Commissioner for Refugees to adopt the technology.

In 1992, as more and more villages and development agencies began using their technology, Navarro, Simon, and other Israeli grain experts decided to start GrainPro. Simon and Navarro didn't want to rely on charitable donations or fickle development organizations. A for-profit company, they decided, was the best way to create enough Grain Cocoons to help the developing world. "We take our social mission very seriously," says GrainPro president Phil Villers. "But to be successful we have to be profitable, and we are."[30]

BATTLING BIG PESTICIDE

Despite all the benefits of the Grain Cocoon, pesticides still reign supreme in both the developing and developed world. A major reason: cost. Each cocoon, which stores upwards of five tons of grain, sells for more than $1,000, a hefty price tag for most poor farmers. GrainPro has developed hermetic storage bags for smaller quantifies, which cost much less, as little as $2 to $3.[31] But even that's expensive for many subsistence farmers, who have to rely on governments and NGOs to buy the product.

On the surface, using pesticides may seem cheaper to farmers. But Professor Maria Otília Carvalho of the University of Lisbon, an expert on entomology, ecology, and food storage, argues that in the long run, pesticides are in fact more expensive. "Given the health ramifications, potential loss of life and grain, to say nothing of the environment," she says, "using hermetic storage comes out ahead... it is the technology of the future."[32]

But when it comes to the developing world, Simon says cost isn't the only reason the cocoons aren't more widespread. Despite their harmful effects, pesticides remain popular because leading grain providers don't have real incentives to change their ways. From their point of view, they have storage and fumigation "down to a science," says Simon. They deliver a quality product that kills bugs at a reasonable cost. Simon says he and other grain storage experts have tried to convince industry leaders such as Archer Daniels Midland and Continental Grain to adopt Navarro's technology or other safe methods of hermetic storage – to no avail. As Simon puts it: "It is hard to introduce new technologies when some people don't see a problem."[33]

Yet pesticide-related problems persist, and it may only be a matter of time before large grain companies are forced to change their ways. As consumers develop greater awareness of food safety, a growing number of them have begun to demand organic products. In the United States, over the next few years, the organic market is expected to continue to grow at an annual rate of 14 percent.[34] As demand for organic food grows, Simon and Navarro hope the industry will have no other choice but to adopt their technology. In other words, they want the cocoon to kill more than just bugs.

RWANDA'S GOT A BRAND-NEW BAG

In 1999, just five years after the end of Rwanda's civil war, Dr. Tesfai Ghirmazion, the country's minister of agriculture, traveled to Israel to meet with officials at the Volcani Center. Among other things, he wanted to learn more about the Grain Cocoon. What he saw impressed him. "This is the technology I want for Rwanda," Navarro recalls him saying.[35]

Three years later in the summer of 2002, Navarro was in Lubirizi, a village about an hour outside Rwanda's capital, Kigali. There, Navarro taught more than two dozen people how to use his hermetic storage technology. At the end of the training course, Navarro again met with the minister. He wanted permission to perform an experiment. What would happen, he wondered, if they stored one of his bags for more than a decade? The minister agreed, and they sealed a maize-filled cocoon.[36]

Twelve years later, Rwandan officials working at the site opened the bag. What they found surprised them. The maize was as good as the day it was stored. Together with Navarro, the Rwandan government had proved that Grain Cocoons can work long-term.[37]

Gadi Loebenstein, former head of the ARO-Volcani Center and chief scientist of the Israeli Ministry of Agriculture, puts it like this: "The Grain Cocoon has lifted millions of people out of poverty. Using relatively inexpensive technology, farmers now have the ability to store their food over long periods of time and feed their families."[38]

CHAPTER 7

The Fourth Day

And God made the two great lights: the greater light to rule the day,
and the lesser light to rule the night; and the stars. And God set
them in the firmament of the heaven to give light upon the earth,
and to rule over the day and over the night, and to divide the light
from the darkness; and God saw that it was good.

~ Genesis 1:16–18

Physicist Shmuel Sambursky (*left*) and David Ben-
Gurion (*center*) with Harry Zvi Tabor (*right*) and his
Tabor Selective Surface solar panel (courtesy of
Tabor family)

HARNESSING THE SUN

Everyone was sweating profusely. It was the summer of 1955, and
the sun was blazing in the field behind Jerusalem's iconic Generali
Building. Harry Zvi Tabor, a physicist and engineer, had arrived
there to meet with some of Israel's founding fathers. There was Prime
Minister David Ben-Gurion, Finance Minister Levi Eshkol, and
Teddy Kollek, then director-general of the Prime Minister's Office.

This was not a celebratory affair. A few years earlier, the country had defeated six Arab armies to win its War of Independence. But the nation now faced a new challenge: hundreds of thousands of Jewish immigrants were arriving from all over the world. The economy was in crisis, fuel was scarce, and brownouts were common. The situation was so dire that the government had forbidden heating water between ten at night and six in the morning.[1] And the more the population grew, the greater the likelihood that Israel could go bankrupt.

Tabor knew the fledgling state would need a cheap and reliable energy source to serve its citizens. But where to find it? Other Middle Eastern nations had discovered an abundant supply of oil. Israel had none. It didn't even have coal, let alone a stable supply of water. What it did have, however, was sunlight. And plenty of it. But harnessing the sun to heat water and produce electricity was difficult. For years, scientists had tried and failed to create a device efficient enough for mass consumption. Tabor, however, believed he had a solution. Using his advanced knowledge of physics and applied engineering, he created a contraption he called the solar collector. The only problem: the device had never worked outside of the lab.

Now as Ben-Gurion and the others watched, Tabor placed his device in the middle of the yard and turned it on. The contraption began pumping water into pipes, and as the liquid moved, the panels attracted sunlight and heated the water.

Ben-Gurion was ecstatic. He immediately knew the solar collector would change the course of the country's future, and perhaps even the world.[2] The prime minister was so excited, he sent the British-born scientist to the United States to attend the world's first solar energy conference in Arizona. And he insisted Tabor ship his solar water collector to the meeting (the physicist thought it would be sufficient to bring a poster).[3] The collector became the hit of the conference, and suddenly Israel, a tiny, newly formed country, was well on its way to becoming one of the world's solar energy pioneers.

AN ACTIVITY OF CRANKS

Tabor was born in 1917 to Jewish immigrant parents who had fled the Russian pogroms and wound up in the United Kingdom.[4] As a child, he was a member of the Habonim Zionist youth movement, an organization that promoted Jewish, socialist, and Zionist values.

As he grew up, he developed an interest in physics, which he began studying at the University of London in the mid-1940s. There, he met Shmuel Sambursky, a physics professor at the Hebrew University and a disciple of Ben-Gurion. At the time, Sambursky served as the British Mandate's secretary of the Board of Scientific and Industrial Research, an organization that tried to utilize the scientific knowledge of world Jewry to benefit the soon-to-be established Jewish state.[5] He often traveled to London, and on one visit, he met the young British Jew through Tabor's girlfriend (and later wife).

The two scientists had a shared interest not only in physics but in Zionism. Their initial conversation, which took place at the British Colonial Office – a grand building that was designed to impress foreign visitors – was long and spirited. Tabor explained to Sambursky that Palestine had three systems of measurement: the metric, the British, and the Ottoman. "They measure things in okers or whatever it is, and that's not for a modern country," Tabor explained. "You have to have one system."[6] Both agreed that Palestine needed the equivalent of the British National Physical Laboratory to address this problem, among others.

When Sambursky returned to Palestine, he conveyed his impressions of the young Tabor to Ben-Gurion, who said, "Oh, we've got a physicist."[7] And a patriotic one, too. In 1947, Tabor was recruited by the Haganah – the Jewish paramilitary organization in Palestine – to go to France and use his engineering knowledge to help convert freight ships to vessels that could be used to carry illegal immigrants to Israel. As Jews languished in Europe after the Holocaust, Tabor did what he could to help survivors make their way to the Holy Land.

Two years later, Tabor decided it was time for him to make the journey himself. With no job or prospects in the newly formed Jewish state, he gathered his possessions and prepared to leave London. "My parents were flabbergasted that I was going without a job," he says. "They thought I was nuts. And looking back maybe I was."[8] But ten days before his departure, Ben-Gurion sent him a cable, inviting him to take a position at the physics and engineering desk at a scientific office that reported directly to the prime minister.[9] "That," Tabor says, "made life very easy."[10]

One of the first projects Tabor worked on was the one he and Sambursky had spoken about in London: unifying Israel's systems of weights and measurements. "You'd see grocers measuring things by putting stones on scales," he recalls.[11] But Ben-Gurion and Sambursky had bigger plans for him. In 1950, they launched the National Physics Laboratory of Israel, and Tabor became its first director.

With the physics laboratory in place, he started thinking about research and development possibilities. Solar energy, he decided, was a good place to start.[12] "In a country with no raw materials and no fuel, the sun was an obvious thing," says Tabor. "But it wasn't obvious to anybody else. At that time, harnessing solar energy generally was considered an activity of cranks."[13]

SIMPLE PHYSICS

The Romans were the first people who used solar energy. And they did it – about twenty-five hundred years ago – for a simple but important reason: to heat their baths. These baths faced the sun in the afternoon and had large windows made of clear glass, which allowed sunlight to filter in and trap the heat inside. Buildings with glass became so popular that Romans passed laws that made it a crime to block a neighbor's access to sunlight.[14]

Solar technology made almost no progress until about the mid-nineteenth century, when people – primarily in the United States – began using metal tanks to heat water. By the afternoon, these tanks had enough hot water to allow people to take a warm shower.[15] In 1891, Clarence Kept, an inventor in Baltimore, developed the first commercially viable "Climax" solar water heating system. He put together several cylindrical metal tanks in a glass-covered box.[16] This was better than keeping metal tanks outside, because it kept the water hotter for longer. But even under the most ideal conditions, it still took all day to heat up the water. At night, the water would quickly cool because the system was not fitted with any kind of insulation.

About twenty years later, William J. Bailey of Los Angeles solved this problem by dividing his Day and Night Solar Water Heater into two separate units. Bailey's heat collector had pipes attached to a black painted metal sheet placed in a glass-covered box – much like today. Water passed through narrow pipes, which reduced the volume of water exposed to the sun and heated it much more quickly. The water was then stored in an insulated tank that would stay hot for twenty-four hours.[17] This was a good system at the time, but it was still inefficient and relatively expensive. Shortly after Bailey began selling his device, local authorities in California discovered large amounts of cheap natural gas, which served as a strong competitor and eventually destroyed his business.[18]

In the early 1950s, when Tabor started looking into building a new device, he found several Bailey-type knockoffs in Israel. As a physicist, he knew the only substance that could capture and maintain a considerable amount of heat was polished metal, but the devices on the market only used the ordinary variety. Tabor had a solution. To make metal more efficient, he would blacken it without destroying the properties that allow metal to retain heat.

In 1955, Tabor sent his team to look at the various processes used to blacken metals, which are normally used for decorative or anti-corrosive purposes. Almost immediately they found two coatings that would yield the desired results. "Now I had luck because

I made a development which no plumber could make," says Tabor. "A physicist could make it because it required a special knowledge of physics. Simple physics, but nevertheless."[19]

Tabor and his team tested the device in the lab, and the contraption was immediately twice as efficient as anything created before it.[20] This innovation produced more hot water and gave the solar water heater the potential to produce electricity in significant quantities using a small turbine or engine.[21] Tabor had also done so without making the heater any larger. Its name: the Tabor Selective Surface. Or in Hebrew, the *dud shemesh* (pronounced *dood SHEMM-mesh*).

Tabor demonstrated his contraption to Ben-Gurion in 1955 and received the prestigious Weizmann Prize for Exact Sciences the following year.[22] But all this was not enough to get his innovation to spread. For that, he would need a lucky break.

IT BELONGED TO THE STATE

At first, Israel's big factories were not interested in Tabor's product. Despite his success at the conference, to the vast majority of people, harnessing the sun for mass distribution still seemed like an extremely kooky idea. But in 1961, Meromit-Olympia, an Israeli company that built and sold old, inefficient solar water collectors, approached the Israeli government to secure the right to use Tabor's innovation.[23] "It [the collector] belonged to the government, and I was a government servant," says Tabor. "[Those] days were different. Zionists were Zionists. It belonged to the state because I worked for them."[24] Three years later, Meromit began selling water heaters with Tabor's Selective Surface technology.

But over the course of the next decade, market growth for the solar water collector was slow and even encountered major opposition. The Israeli government did not encourage its citizens to adopt Tabor's invention. And the national electric company refused to give users a discounted price.[25] They did, however, encourage users to buy inefficient electric water heaters. "The electric company was actually opposed because they were threatened," says Lucien Yehuda Bronicki, the founder of Israel's Ormat Technologies, one of the largest geothermal companies in the world. "They saw themselves as a competitor so they lowered their prices so people wouldn't use it."[26]

The Housing Workers Union was also opposed to Tabor's device, mainly because it felt it was unsightly. Through the 1960s, the group built more than fifty-five thousand apartments around the country. It refused to allow Tabor's devices on any of their buildings and instead offered all their residents the electric water heater.[27] "When I created the *dud shemesh*, I thought of efficiency – who gives any thought to how it looks?" said Tabor. "Some people are opposed because they say it's ugly. Let's see them take a shower for a few days in cold water. We'll see what they say then. The design of the solar water heater is a compromise."[28]

But things changed after the 1973 energy crisis, a period during which the world's industrial powers faced major petroleum shortages. Six days after Syria and Egypt launched a surprise attack against Israel in what later was called the Yom Kippur War, the United States supplied Israel with arms to protect itself. This triggered the Organization of the Petroleum Exporting Countries (OPEC) to create an oil embargo against Canada, Japan, the Netherlands, the United Kingdom, and the United States. The result: a worldwide recession and massive inflation.

But there was an upside to the embargo, at least for Tabor's invention. In 1976, the Knesset, Israel's legislative body, passed a law requiring every building in Israel constructed after 1980 to have solar water collectors. The law has saved Israel and its citizens millions of shekels in energy costs.

Today, about 90 percent of all households in Israel use Tabor's invention – and many buildings throughout the country are powered entirely by solar energy.[29] Long before there was a global recognition of the importance of solar power, Israel's Harry Zvi Tabor led the first effort by a country to implement its use on a nationwide scale.

"Through his drive and creativity, Tabor turned what was at that time a specialized device into a standard appliance that's now installed in most of the homes across the country," says Amit Shafrir, former president of AOL premium services. The *dud shemesh* "provides an affordable source of hot water for generations of Israelis."[30]

In 2012, the Knesset's research center estimated that the *dud shemesh* saves Israel 8 percent of its energy consumption.[31] The report states that this savings is equal to the production output capability of a 900-megawatt power station. As Abraham Kribus, a professor of renewable energy at Tel Aviv University, puts it: "Without this invention, entire industries would not exist."[32]

NECESSITY: THE JEWISH MOTHER OF INVENTION

Kribus's statement is true not just in Israel, but elsewhere, too. Tabor's Selective Surface served as the scientific basis for a bevy of subsequent innovations in the field. "Everybody knows that Zvi Tabor is a solar power pioneer and the father of Israeli solar power energy," says Ormat's Lucien Yehuda Bronicki. What most people don't know is that "he is also the father of solar energy of the world."[33]

In the 1980s the Israeli company Luz used Tabor's surface as its model to set up the world's first solar power station (and one of the largest power stations in the world) in California's Mojave Desert. Luz proved that solar energy was reliable in producing electricity commercially.[34] "Almost every time I started digging into a new field of solar energy, there he was, right at the beginning.... Either Harry thought of it first, or he came very, very close," says David R. Mills, president of the International Solar Energy Society.[35]

Tabor passed away in late 2015, but he is widely remembered for his unique ability to harness the power of the sun "not in order to make money, but to improve the world," says Kribus.[36] On his ninety-eighth birthday, the Israel Energy and Business Convention, a prestigious event for leading Israeli entrepreneurs, recognized Tabor as the "Energy Man of the Year."[37] But for many scientists he was actually "the man of the century," says Amit Mor, CEO of Israel's EcoEnergy consulting firm. "There is no person in Israel or in the world who contributed so much to energy independence, sustainability and the energy field in general."[38] Shimon Peres, Israel's late president, agreed: "Dr. Zvi Tabor was a symbol of Israeli innovation who invented the modern solar water collector and inspired generations of scientists and entrepreneurs in the field of solar energy."[39]

Indeed, over the course of the last half century or so, interest in solar water heating has spread quietly across the globe. Governments are increasingly providing incentives for harnessing solar energy, because the price of renewable resources is falling as fossil fuels are becoming more expensive. Policy makers around the world realize they must try to mitigate climate change. With an increasing number of droughts, storms, heat waves, rising sea levels, melting glaciers, and warming oceans, Tabor's innovation will be in greater demand across the globe.

In other words, when he saw Tabor's invention on that sunny day in 1955, Ben-Gurion was right. Like a modern-day Joshua, the London-born Israeli scientist had figured out how to make the sun stand still for the sake of the Jewish state – and the rest of the world.

PART III

Technology for Good

CHAPTER 8

The Lame Shall Walk

Blessed are You, King of the universe, Who straightens those who are bent over.

~ Jewish daily morning prayer

Radi Kaiuf using a ReWalk exoskeleton (Mikhnenko773)

HE WOULD NEVER WALK AGAIN

It all started with a coupon in the mail. In 1996, Lily Goffer went to the mall in Nazareth, the largest city in the northern district of Israel; she was buying a pair of jeans for her husband. On a lark, she filled out a form to win a free all-terrain vehicle, and several weeks later, learned she had won.[1]

Her husband, Dr. Amit Goffer, had no interest in the machine. When it arrived, he sold it to a neighbor for half of what it was worth. But his children complained so much that he decided to make it up to them. One morning, Goffer rented a few ATVs and set off to ride across a dusty patch of wilderness not far from their home. The kids, he felt, would have a great time.[2]

On the outskirts of Sepporis, an idyllic biblical village, Goffer rode with his daughter, while his son took off on his own, kicking up dirt behind him as the machines growled along the dusty trails. But not long after the ride began, the brakes on Goffer's vehicle failed. The doctor went careening off the trail and crashed into a tree. His daughter emerged unscathed, but Goffer snapped his neck against the branches.[3]

Lying on the ground, he was terrified. "I couldn't feel anything," he says, "and I understood immediately what happened to me."[4] Prior to his accident, Goffer had founded a company that made MRI devices for operating rooms.[5] So he understood the science behind disability. As his children came running over, he told them to back away. "Don't touch me," he said, "I'm a quadriplegic."[6] He knew he would never walk again.

The next nine months were bleak. Goffer was paralyzed from his upper back down. He had slight movement in his arms, and eventually learned how to use an electronic wheelchair. That helped, but he constantly felt cramped and frustrated. "I couldn't sit for more than two hours."[7] Goffer recalls, "It was like being in a very big hole in the dark."[8]

One of his biggest challenges: going to the bathroom. For many confined to a wheelchair, accidents are common and bowel movements are irregular, which can lead to sepsis or even death. Many paralyzed people are forced to ask someone to insert two fingers into their rectums to stimulate the bowel. The process is painful and can take hours. Some ultimately choose to have surgery that creates a permanent opening between the colon and the surface of the abdomen, where stool collects in a bag.[9]

Despite his frustrations, Goffer was determined to retain some independence. At first, he wasn't able to brush his teeth. The doctors gave him a contraption to help, but he refused it. He relearned how to brush on his own. For months, Goffer didn't have enough strength to write, but eventually he relearned that skill, too.[10] "When you're at the bottom of such a hole," he says, "there's only one way to go. Up. You can't get any lower."[11]

Mentally, Goffer suffered the most. To help with his recovery, the doctors gave him a heavy regimen of painkillers and other medications. But the side effects clouded his mind. "My IQ went down," he says. "I felt stupid."[12]

He didn't give up. In January 1997, the hospital sent Goffer home, and soon, he stopped taking his medication.[13] It's one of the best decisions he ever made. As the haze lifted, Goffer began thinking about what he could do about his condition. "I became human again," he says.[14]

Having regained his ability to think, Goffer began to understand how paralysis stripped him of control. The more he thought about it, the more he became determined to create a way for the disabled to regain a sense of autonomy and dignity. "My motivation," he says, "was to . . . give to the disabled individual . . . a complete device that a person could [use to] go to the movies or theater or restaurant without asking first, 'Are there stairs?'" He also wanted to help the disabled look their loved ones at eye level – something most people take for granted.[15]

Given his condition, Goffer became obsessed with this dilemma. Life in a wheelchair, he felt, wasn't enough.

A REVOLUTION WITHOUT WHEELS

The first wheelchairs weren't chairs at all; they were wheelbarrows, an invention created in China during the second century CE. The first image of a modern wheelchair was engraved in China in 525 CE. For the next thousand years, there was no other record of a wheelchair outside of the country until an artist sketched King Phillip of Spain (1527–1598) using one to get around. Since then, inventors have tinkered with the idea and added amenities for comfort and mobility. But the basic concept has stayed the same.[16]

One of the few attempts to change the wheelchair occurred in the mid-1990s. That's when an inventor named Dean Kamen[17] partnered with Johnson & Johnson to create the iBOT, a wheelchair that could purportedly rise up on two wheels, go up and down stairs, and navigate over sand, gravel, and water. The iBOT never took off. Its $25,000 price tag was too steep, and the invention didn't live up to its promise: the stairs were too much of a challenge.[18]

As Goffer researched the history of the wheelchair, he couldn't believe humans had done so little to change it. Sure, we had found ways to help the paralyzed. We had learned a tremendous amount about the brain and done vital research on stem cells and spinal cord injuries. But neither has helped anyone walk again. Nor has it limited the complications associated with wheelchairs, including poor blood circulation, deteriorating bone density, increased urinary infections, loss of muscle mass, and pressure sores.

An accomplished academic who studied electrical and computer engineering in Israel and the United States,[19] Goffer was confident he could invent a new type of device to help the disabled. During the 1990s, the robotics industry witnessed several breakthroughs, including the first truly intelligent robots and the ability to synchronize their motion.[20] Goffer felt these advances could help him create a machine that would help a paraplegic walk again using a lightweight, motorized support suit with rechargeable batteries.

He started his research by determining how much energy it takes a human to walk and climb stairs. "I was afraid that the answer would be a cart full of batteries," he says, "or some kind of small truck driving behind a person." But Goffer determined it would only take a small battery.[21]

About a year after his injury, an idea came to him while he was surfing the internet: the disabled could perhaps walk again using a shell or exoskeleton. Animals, such as porcupines and scorpions, do it all the time. "How is it possible that no one ever thought of this?" he wondered.[22] He hurriedly began sketching out prototypes and thinking about how this concept could work.

In 2004, seven years after he first came up with the idea, Goffer finished building his first device: an exoskeleton that hugs users' legs, along with crutches to stabilize them as they walk.[23] Users wear a remote control on their wrists to control their movement. As they walk, a tilt sensor ensures the chest remains upright and balanced, allowing them to move without falling. The crutches help people go up stairs and stabilize their weight.

Goffer called his innovation ReWalk and decided to test it. He set up the device in his driveway. Two paraplegics and a quadriplegic volunteered as test subjects. His children strapped the first ReWalk on one of the paraplegics and plugged it in. His son stood near the chord, ready to unplug it in case the subject fell. His daughter controlled the tilt sensor. Goffer used his limited arm mobility to fire up the machine. And then it happened: the paraplegic took one step, then another, and then a few more. Goffer was so focused on watching the steps that he didn't notice the paraplegic was crying.[24]

IT WAS SO INSULTING

For the next two years, Goffer continued working on the device. He made sure it could work for up to four hours without recharging, far longer than most people walk on a regular basis. And while the initial ReWalk weighed more than fifty pounds, Goffer found a way to make it lighter and more user-friendly.[25]

At first, Goffer paid for everything related to his invention. But in 2006, he was accepted into Israel's prestigious Technion Incubator, which helps start-up and early-stage companies with funding, mentoring, and training, among other things. He also received a grant from an Israeli government program called the Tnufa Incentive Program. If a company is successful, the grant is considered a loan. If the company fails, the state assumes the loss. In both cases, the government doesn't take a share of the start-up. The major benefit of the programs is access. Tnufa plugged Goffer into a network of Israel's best and brightest with whom he could share ideas and receive advice.[26]

Yet the device didn't take off the way Goffer had hoped. Perhaps because of the failed iBOT, many of his contemporaries felt that ReWalk would never work. His biggest disappointment came in 2006 when he spoke at a robotics conference in Zurich. During his lecture, he showed video clips of a young disabled woman using ReWalk. Many attendees were either skeptical or convinced the clip was fake. Afterwards, Goffer sent another video to Dr. Zev Rymer, the chairman of the conference and a professor of physical medicine and rehabilitation at Northwestern University. Rymer sent Goffer back a terse note: "Can I get a video clip of how he [the test subject] walks without the device?"[27]

"It was so insulting," Goffer says. But he remained undeterred. Four years later, as he continued tweaking the device, Goffer finally gained some traction. In August 2010, he contacted the Veterans Affairs Rehabilitation, Research & Development National Center of Excellence for the Medical Consequences of Spinal Cord Injury in New York. The center was a leader in the field, and he wanted to show ReWalk to Dr. William Bauman and Dr. Ann Spungen, some of its top experts. "These things can't possibly work," Spungen recalls thinking. "We figured they were overselling their capabilities."[28] Goffer sensed her reticence, but traveled to New York anyway. He wanted to prove Spungen wrong.

They met in a small room where patients often watch football, play pool, and hang out. About twenty-five people – research staff, doctors, nurses, and patients – gathered to watch the live demonstration.[29] As a ReWalk test subject walked across the room, up and down a stairwell, and across a long hallway, Spungen watched skeptically. "I was convinced he was not really paralyzed," she says, "because he was walking so well." All twenty-five attendees followed the man down the corridors. As he walked down the hall, everyone – from the patients to the nurses – turned and stared. "It was like watching the Pied Piper," Spungen says. "Nobody could believe it."[30]

As the test subject took off the exoskeleton, Spungen saw his feet dangle and become flaccid, a clear sign of paralysis. Goffer's presentation was no hoax. Once she got over her shock, Spungen turned to Bauman, the center's director: "We gotta do this," she said.[31]

A DIFFERENT SORT OF MARATHON

Spungen's endorsement was a major turning point for ReWalk. But what really propelled the device was an extraordinary woman who proved that paraplegics can not only walk, but race, too. Her name is Claire Lomas, and she is a British chiropractor and avid horseback rider.

In May 2007, while competing in the Osberton Horse Trials, a high-level equestrian competition in the United Kingdom, her horse, Rolled Oats, clipped his shoulder on a tree, and Lomas went flying into its branches. As she lay on the ground, Lomas was unable to move her legs. Later, she learned she had fractured her neck, back, and ribs, and damaged her spinal cord. The doctors inserted titanium rods into her back to try to fix her spine, but the damage was done. She was paralyzed from the waist down. Her doctors told her that she would never walk again.[32]

Yet Lomas, like Goffer, was determined. Looking online, she discovered ReWalk. With the help of friends and family, she raised about $70,000 to purchase one of Goffer's devices.[33] She practiced with the ReWalk and regularly commuted more than two hours from her home in Leicestershire to East Riding of Yorkshire to learn how to use it properly.[34] After four months, she became so proficient that she focused on a new challenge: the London Marathon.

In May 2012, hundreds of people filled the streets to watch Lomas finish the course. Walking roughly two miles a day, she completed the 26.2-mile race sixteen days after she started.[35] As Lomas crossed the finish line, flanked by her husband and year-old toddler, the crowd thundered.[36]

STANDING UP AND FALLING DOWN

Today, ReWalk has been approved for sale in Europe and in the United States. There are roughly four hundred users around the globe, including a number of US military veterans and law enforcement officials. The company is publicly traded on the New York Stock Exchange, which has provided Goffer with millions of dollars for research and investment.[37] Over the next few years, the Israeli inventor hopes more people like Lomas will be able to use the device. The market's potential is huge: Goffer estimates there are approximately six million wheelchair users in the United States and Europe, about 250,000 of whom would be able to use his device.[38]

Yet ReWalk – and its competitors[39] – still have a number of critics. One reason is safety. It generally takes somewhere between twelve and fifteen sessions to learn how to use the exoskeleton.[40] Some patients, depending on their level of paralysis, never master the skill. The device can be risky. Paraplegics have very weak bones, so ReWalk encourages patients not to use the device on slippery, sloped, or uneven surfaces. Accidents, of course, happen, and some fear the device's risks don't outweigh the rewards. "All it takes is for one or two people to fall and seriously injure themselves for the FDA to shut the whole thing down," says Dr. Arun Jayaraman, a leading exoskeleton expert at the world-renowned Rehabilitation Institute of Chicago. "It has happened previously for other technologies."[41]

Another challenge is price. Because it costs $69,000[42] to $85,000,[43] purchasing an exoskeleton isn't possible for poorer patients. Health insurance providers in the United States have declined to cover it. (Experts say insurance companies are often slow to recognize new and useful technology.)

Some critics claim Goffer's device isn't therapeutic, but rather a mobility or performance aide. The difference sounds inconsequential, but it's not. As a mobility device, the benefits are intuitive, obvious, and universally received. Paraplegics are now able to use this device at home, outside, and at work. But critics say that to have the device recognized as therapeutic, Goffer would need to scientifically prove the medical advantages of the device outweigh the risks. He would also have to prove the benefits cannot be obtained by utilizing other, perhaps safer means – like walking on a treadmill or riding a stationary bike. "ReWalk is sold on the basis that it *should . . .* help with blood circulation, bladder function, bowel strength," says Rymer, the Northwestern professor. "There is no hard evidence that demonstrates that it has actually happened."[44]

Proving that ReWalk is therapeutic will be expensive and time-consuming, but Goffer remains optimistic. He thinks the device can eventually alleviate symptoms that are common among the wheelchair bound. Dr. Alberto Esquenazi, the chairman and chief medical officer of MossRehab of the Einstein Healthcare Network in Philadelphia, agrees.[45] He screened fourteen subjects, completed training for ten users of ReWalk, and determined that some users reported "improvements in pain, bowel and bladder function, and spasticity."[46] His study also determined that users "improved their physical endurance" with "no significant adverse side effects" and were willing to use the system on a regular basis.[47]

Based on this study and others, Goffer says insurance providers could save approximately $30,000 annually due to ReWalk's health benefits.[48] Jayaraman, the Rehabilitation Institute of Chicago expert, estimates the savings might even be higher, as regular exercise using the device could help patients as well.[49] If insurers would cover the device, Goffer and others in his field say, that would lead to more users, and likely more competitors, all of which would push costs down even more.

For all the excitement surrounding the product, however, there's still one person who can't benefit from it: Amit Goffer, the man who invented it.

THE LAST MAN SITTING?

When I meet Goffer near the elevator of his office in northern Israel, he is sitting in an electric wheelchair and has just enough mobility to shake my hand from side to side. He's spent hundreds of hours on this simple task, not to mention the time it took for him to relearn how to type or answer the phone. But to use ReWalk, patients need full control of their upper bodies, which Goffer doesn't have.

At sixty-two, he is overweight, because he sits all day. But as he ushers me into his office and begins to talk about his invention, his eyes widen with excitement behind his wire-rimmed glasses. Behind his desk, there's a photo of Goffer and his patients in New York's Times Square on the day his company went public, their hands raised in a victory pose.

As we speak, a man bursts in, using his ReWalk device to jog across the room. His name is Radi Kaiuf, and he was born in the Arab Druze village of Isfiya. In the spring of 1988, a few months before he was set to finish his service in the Israeli military, Hezbollah guerrillas shot him in the stomach during an operation in the Lebanese village of Maydun. "It's over," he recalls thinking before he lost consciousness. "I was shot in the middle of the body and I am going to die."[50] Under heavy fire, Kaiuf's fellow soldiers evacuated him by helicopter to Haifa's Rambam Hospital. For nineteen days, he was unconscious and barely clung to life. When he woke up, he couldn't move. The doctors told him his walking days were over.[51]

Like Goffer, Kaiuf became depressed. Wheelchair bound, he was often unable to work and tried to kill himself twice. But with the help of friends and family, he decided to look for help. He started going to therapy and physical rehabilitation, which gave him a major psychological boost. And over the next few years, he married, and his wife gave birth to four children.[52]

In 2007, he met Goffer at Tel Hashomer's rehabilitation center, and the two quickly became friends. During their first conversation, Goffer told Kaiuf that he had developed a device that would help the paralyzed walk again. "I didn't believe I would be able to stand up," says Kaiuf. "But after I tried it . . . I was amazed. My daughter was three years old back then. She looked at me and said: 'Dad, you are tall!' That made my day."[53]

Today, Kaiuf lives with his wife and children outside of Carmiel, in northern Israel, where he's able to take part in activities he never thought were possible. He's completed a scuba diving course and once even skied, using a chair-like device.[54] "There's no question," he says, "that I am a lot healthier with ReWalk than I would be otherwise."[55]

As Kaiuf and I say goodbye, Goffer tells me the former soldier often spends more time abroad than in Israel; he's practically become the face of the device. The idea of an Arab traveling the world praising an Israeli invention sounds like a fantasy. But Kaiuf is one of several Arabs who works for ReWalk, where Goffer says religious Muslims and Jews work side by side in peace. Little seems far-fetched in a place where everyone is focused on helping the paralyzed take their first steps in years.

Which is why Goffer hasn't given up on his dream of walking again. Before I leave his office, he tells me about his latest invention, UpNRide, a Segway-type device that helps quadriplegics move standing up.

Two months later, Goffer used his new device outside his home, in Yokneam. It was the first time he had stood in eighteen years.[56]

CHAPTER 9

GPS for the Brain

Against almost all odds, Imad and Reem Younis have built an amazing technology company that battles neurological diseases and saves lives. They are a shining example of what we can achieve when we work together in a country of different minorities, religions, and cultures.

~ Yoram Yaacovi, general manager, Microsoft Israel

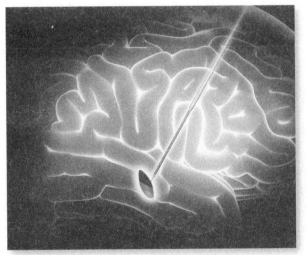

Placement of electrode for deep brain stimulation (courtesy of Alpha Omega)

LET'S DRINK TO HEALTH

As Charlene Lustig lay supine on the operating table, trying to relax, Dr. Kim Burchiel drilled two nickel-sized holes into her skull. The surgeon then placed two permanent electrodes into her brain. Under her skin, a small wire connected the two electrodes to a battery-powered generator in her abdomen, which pulsed like a pacemaker, disrupting her neurons.

For years, Lustig suffered from Parkinson's disease and consistently felt painful tremors across her upper body. She found it difficult to speak and lost movement on her left side.[1] The procedure, known as deep brain stimulation (DBS), was supposed to lessen her symptoms.

The only catch: to find the neurons, Lustig had to be awake for the entire surgery.[2] That's because Burchiel's team used a special medical device system that relies on microelectrode recorders and sound waves to guide them to the neurological target. The device graphically represented the sounds on a computer screen and served as a GPS for Burchiel and company to follow.

When the doctors completed the operation, Lustig's Parkinson's disease wasn't gone, but many of her symptoms disappeared. After the procedure, Lustig attended a party at her support group, where she and her friends celebrated with champagne. "It's just great to be independent again," she said. "Let's drink to health."[3]

Today, more than a decade after Lustig's procedure, deep brain stimulation is used to treat all kinds of neurological diseases, from obsessive-compulsive disorders to depression.[4] And clinical trials are testing the effects of the procedure on a variety of others, including Alzheimer's, Tourette's syndrome, chronic pain, post-traumatic stress disorder, epilepsy, and even schizophrenia.

More than 150,000 people have undergone deep brain stimulation, according to Hagai Bergman, one of the world's leading neurologists. And many have been treated using medical devices produced by Alpha Omega, the largest Arab high-tech company in Israel. "Alpha Omega," says Bergman, "is by far the most reliable and experienced company in the world in the area of multiple electrode data acquisition."[5]

Founded by Imad and Reem Younis, a married couple from Nazareth, the company is well-known among neurologists across the globe. Given the obstacles the Younises had to overcome – from breaking societal norms to being Arab minorities in a predominantly

Jewish country – the company's rise is every bit as remarkable as its innovation.

THE AMAZING BRAIN

Since the 1960s, researchers have used electric stimulation to locate and distinguish specific sites in the brain. In more recent decades, scientists began using neurostimulators, often referred to as "brain pacemakers," to treat movement and psychiatric disorders using electrical impulses. But it wasn't until 1987 when the French neurosurgeon Alim-Louis Benabid used deep brain stimulation to successfully target essential tremor, the most common movement disorder, that researchers realized the full power of the procedure.[6] Soon afterwards, scientists around the world began racing to map out the brain and use deep brain stimulation to reduce the effects of various incurable diseases.

As the race ensued, Imad and Reem met and fell in love. They were in college and studying engineering at the Technion, the world-renowned technology institute. But when they graduated, both struggled to find jobs. At the time, most of Israel's high-tech industry centered around the military and security, and few were willing to hire Arabs.

Imad found his first job at the Technion's medical school. There, he was responsible for helping scientists secure the tools and equipment needed to conduct their research. When researchers could not find off-the-shelf products for their research, Imad and his colleagues helped develop custom replacements. His position also gave him a deep understanding of medical trends, as well as potential business opportunities.[7] Later, Reem found her first job working as an engineer at a Nazareth-based construction company.[8]

The jobs were fine, but like many Israeli-Arab engineers, both Imad and Reem wanted more.

"We had conversations with friends, engineers who finished the

Technion…and [came to the conclusion] that we live in the country of high-tech but with no high-tech in the Arab community," recalls Imad. "There was nothing."[9] So in 1993 the couple decided to start their own company. "We didn't have money," Reem says, "so we sold our car," a Volkswagen Jetta, and cashed in four gold coins they had received for their wedding.[10] And with that, Alpha Omega was born.

LOVE THY STRANGER

From the beginning, both Imad and Reem's families were against the decision. "They thought we were crazy," Reem recalls. "They said, 'How do you leave a steady salary? Two engineers who graduated from the Technion? How could you take such a decision?'" Reem recalls.[11]

And maybe they were crazy. Like many entrepreneurs, the Younises created their company with no product, no idea, and no problem to solve. They simply began with the decision to start. The couple had a solid background in research and development, and as graduates of the Technion, a strong network of scientists, engineers, and professors. They started with subcontractor work, helping scientists and corporations outsource their R&D projects. Which is how they came up with the name for the company. "We could do anything from A to Z," Imad says. "Just give us the specs."[12]

But it wasn't until the Younises began working with Hagai Bergman, the acclaimed neurologist at the Hebrew University, that they developed their future niche. Imad met him in 1983, just after he graduated from the Technion, while Bergman was completing a medical degree and a PhD. The two initially bonded over a shared interest in medical device tools and brain neurons. As the holiday season approached, the Younises invited Bergman and his family to spend Christmas at their home in Nazareth – the biblical birthplace of Jesus.[13] One of the most impressive Christmas festivals in the world takes place here ever year. Residents light large Christmas trees, while bands perform in the streets. "For my kids," Bergman says, "Imad is Santa Claus."[14]

Because Imad was born Catholic and Reem Greek Orthodox, the Younis family celebrates Christmas twice a year.[15] The Bergmans did, too. "We were the only Jewish people in the world that have done two Christmases a year," Bergman says. "I am very proud to be a family friend of Imad, Reem, and their kids. I really hope that their work can show the world that Israelis and Palestinians can do better things together and not just fight and kill [one another]."[16]

In Alpha Omega's early years, Bergman sent the company a large number of contracts. In 1990, he was the first scientist to discover that doctors could treat Parkinson's via deep brain stimulation.[17] But finding the exact point to target was incredibly challenging. The Younises began to develop proprietary tools to solve this problem. Alpha Omega devices act as a GPS inside the brain that guides doctors to the required location so they can implant a permanent electrode.

After he saw what the Younises created, Bergman began promoting their equipment all over the world. The Younises quickly realized that most of their work came from neurologists. They began selling their machines in Israel and eventually expanded into the European and American markets as well.

Imad says he entered the field of neuroscience in the early 1990s and got hooked because it's so rewarding. "Every time I see our devices," he says, "I am struck and say, 'Wow, this device really helps patients.'"[18] As for Reem, helping those with Parkinson's is personal. Her father had this terrible disease but wasn't able to benefit from Alpha Omega's devices. He died more than a decade ago, but Reem is thankful she's able to help others.[19]

In 1993, Bergman introduced the couple to Benabid, the godfather of deep brain stimulation.[20] Benabid was working with Medtronic, the US-based medical device, and looking for someone to help him create equipment that records electrical activity in the brain. He quickly invited the Younises to test their equipment in Grenoble, France.[21]

Within a few weeks of their initial call, the Younises flew to Grenoble to attend one of Benabid's surgeries to understand his needs. It was the first of many visits and a working relationship that continues to this day. "They were responsive, which is not always the case for commercial companies," recalls Benabid. "They are the Rolls Royce of deep brain stimulation equipment."[22]

WE ARE BOTH ISRAELIS AND PALESTINIANS

In 2003, the Younises moved to the United States to be closer to their largest prospective client base. They started off by driving across America and pitching their product wherever they went. They settled on Atlanta, but didn't stay there for long. After two years, they decided to move back home. "We always had Nazareth on the brain," says Reem. "The only reason we came back was to live in Nazareth... to impact Israel. We wanted to play a role in making Nazareth a better place to live in."[23]

The challenges facing Nazareth – and Israel's 1.7 million Arabs – are significant, especially in the tech sector, where Israel's Arabs are on the periphery. "We are 20 percent of the [Israeli] population," says Reem. "We also need to be 20 percent of the Israeli high-tech scene, but we are not."[24] Arab numbers are commensurate to their percentage of the population in the country's top universities. But only 2 percent of Israel's technology workers come from this demographic, making them marginal participants in Israel's technology boom. "Israeli tech needs peace and education," says Yossi Vardi, considered Israel's unofficial innovation ambassador. "It also needs to become more inclusive [of Arabs]."[25]

But with the appetite for highly educated, capable programmers on the rise, the number of Israeli Arabs entering the technology field is increasing. In 2015, there were reportedly about 2,000 Arab tech engineers in Israel, a figure that increased from 350 in 2008.[26] And as hundreds of millions of Arabic-speakers make their way onto the internet, multinational companies in Israel – from Intel to Microsoft – are increasingly hiring more of them. Those who don't take jobs with tech giants tend to migrate to Arab-focused start-ups, generally backed with venture capital funds that specialize in this market.

Nevertheless, a large disparity remains. Imad believes there are two primary reasons. First, the vast majority of Israeli Arabs do not live in Tel Aviv, the heart of Israel's technology sector, but rather in the north and interior of the country, in their ancestral villages and towns. Second, most Israeli Arabs do not serve in the military; doing so, many believe, would be akin to taking up arms against fellow Palestinians and neighboring Arab countries. And many – including Imad and Reem – fundamentally oppose Israel's presence in the territories and any institution that keeps Israel there.

This lack of military service leaves Israeli Arabs at a disadvantage. IDF service is one of the major ways Israelis enter the technology sector. Elite intelligence units, for instance, provide trainees with exceptional technological skills along with highly specialized training and the camaraderie that eventually helps them form a strong social network. In the United States, where someone went to school is important. But in Israel, it's a person's military unit that is often considered defining.[27] Every Israeli job applicant is asked, "Where did you serve in the army?" Serving in particular units such as 8200, the Israeli equivalent of the National Security Agency (NSA), improves an applicant's ability to secure a job. It's so important that there are many job offers on the internet and in want ads in Israel that specify they are meant for alumni of special units of the IDF.

Given this reality, both Imad and Reem see it as their mission to be leaders of their community, to teach by example and do what they can to help their Arab neighbors achieve success. Both Younises are involved in several Arab and Jewish nonprofits, whose goals include higher learning for disadvantaged youth, Arab high-tech initiatives, and peaceful coexistence between Arabs and Jews.[28] "Yes, there are things the city can do and things the Israeli government should do, but I as a person who lives in Israel have to make a difference too," says Reem. "I think Imad and I are role models for younger people to realize that they can make a change, that they can dare go out and do things that haven't been done before."[29]

Imad agrees. "There is discrimination," he says. "The state [Israel] has now woken up and is making serious efforts to fix it.... On the other hand, we Arabs...have been walking around with feelings of inferiority since our childhood."[30]

The Younises place great importance on encouraging their employees to lead. In recent years, four engineers have left Alpha Omega to start their own ventures, two as direct competitors. The Younises have supported these decisions because of the positive impact they believed it would have on Israel's Arabs.

Many Alpha Omega employees graduated from the Technion and Tel Aviv University, two of the premier schools in Israel for engineering. Alpha Omega also has a policy of hiring employees straight out of the top universities without any real-world experience "because there are many good Arab engineers who have not been hired by 'Jewish' companies," says Imad.[31]

Yet the company employs a lot of different types of people: Catholics, Protestants, Orthodox Christians, Protestants, Muslims, and Jews. "Imad and Reem Younis represent the rich diversity of the country's high-tech and start-up culture," says Israel's president, Reuven Rivlin. "They bring together all the communities in Israel with a shared vision for the future."[32] And the company's workers share this sentiment. "An engineer's an engineer," says Samer Ayub, one of Reem and Imad's employees. "We work together professionally and objectively."[33] That type of sentiment is common at Alpha Omega. "When we employ people from different cultures, we can go even farther because each one thinks differently," says Imad. "And that can create innovation. We have the same father [i.e., Abraham]. We can work together to achieve common goals."[34]

This is why Imad and Reem don't see themselves as just Israelis or Palestinians. "We present ourselves abroad as both," Imad says. "This is what we are."[35]

A DRIVERLESS CAR FOR THE BRAIN

Today, Alpha Omega's devices are used in more than a hundred hospitals and five hundred labs around the world.[36] The company's sophisticated machinery is manufactured locally in Nazareth, but marketed by their offices in the United States, Germany, and Israel, as well as representatives in China, Japan, and Latin America.[37] Its sales have grown at a rate of 15 to 24 percent annually over the last few years.[38] The company's revenue represents the majority of Israeli Arab high-tech exports internationally.[39]

The company is only getting started. Bergman and the Younises are now collaborating on what might be one of the biggest leaps in the history of deep brain stimulation. In 2015, they created a tool that does not need human intervention to place an electrode in the brain. "You push the button and the system goes," says Bergman. Likening it to a driverless car, Bergman says he dreams of creating devices that will replace humans for most surgery-related functions. "People ask me, do you think that an automatic navigation system will be better than you? My answer is no." Bergman also believes that "there is no way that a machine will be better than the best human . . . [but] if you don't take the best human expert – you take the average one – then automatic systems will do much better."[40]

Experts say this type of technology is best suited to the developing world, where there is a great need but also a shortage of electrophysiologists. For patients who don't have access to excellent healthcare, this type of solution could mean the difference between a normal life and one filled with sustained suffering. "We are still at the beginning," says Imad. The goal is to "make the targeting easier, more efficient, more accurate, and also to make the therapy more efficient."[41]

So far, researchers have tested the Younises' technology in about twenty cases in Jerusalem, and more than fifteen times in the United States. "Alpha Omega is in a position superior to all of its competition," Bergman says. "To the best of my knowledge none of the competing companies is even thinking about it."[42]

Being on the vanguard of their field is rewarding for the couple. What's more rewarding, however, is knowing their company has helped tens of thousands of people. As Reem puts it, "We return people back to life."[43]

CHAPTER 10

Golden Firewall

For I, says the Lord, will be unto her a wall of fire round about, and I will be the glory in the midst of her.

~ Zechariah 2:9 (2:5 in Christian Bibles)

Gil Shwed (courtesy of Check Point)

SHUTTING DOWN THE ROCKET KITTEN

On November 9, 2015, not long after six in the evening, Yaser Balaghi, a senior Iranian cyber expert, was surfing the web on his smartphone when he read the news. Western security experts, it seemed, had finally figured it out. For years, Balaghi and several of his colleagues had used the internet to attack more than sixteen hundred high-profile people around the globe, including members of the Saudi royal family, Israeli nuclear scientists, NATO officials, journalists, Iranian dissidents, and human rights activists. But the cyber expert couldn't help but smile as he read that security personnel on three different continents had given his group a name: Rocket Kitten.[1]

For more than two years, Check Point, one of the world's top cybersecurity companies, had tracked the gang, which was affiliated with the Iranian Revolutionary Guard. Among their many schemes, the hackers seduced victims to open emails that automatically downloaded spyware, allowing them to steal information directly from their computers. But Balaghi left a back door open that allowed Check Point's engineers to find a database of his team, their usernames and passwords, their email addresses, the webpages infected with their malware, the servers from which they carried out their attacks, and a list of everyone they had targeted.[2] Unlike other criminals, Balaghi didn't live in the shadows – he has a public internet website and teaches at a number of prominent Iranian universities. His hacking courses are available online.[3]

Before they released their report on Rocket Kitten, senior Check Point executives got in touch with European, American, and Israeli national security officials to share their findings.

The damage was bad, but it could have been much worse. What saved countless people from being hacked was the computer firewall, an invention created by Check Point's chief executive, Gil Shwed.

WELCOME TO THE 8200

Most people have never heard of Gil Shwed, but if you use a computer, there is a good chance you've used one of his company's products. Born in 1968, Shwed was raised in Jerusalem's bucolic Ein Karem neighborhood, the purported birthplace of John the Baptist. He was raised in a middle-class family, and his father was a systems analyst at the Israeli Ministry of Finance.[4] At the age of ten, Shwed enrolled in a weekly computer class, and quickly began to learn on his own.[5] Two years later, he got a job working at a software company, and at fourteen he asked his parents if he could take classes at Hebrew University. "My parents were supportive," Shwed recalls. "But they did a very good thing for me, which was they didn't push me. The only thing they pushed me to do was balance my life."[6]

As a teenager, Shwed also worked two jobs, one at the Hebrew University as a computer systems administrator, and another at EMET computing, a company that specializes in architecture and infrastructure solutions.[7]

At eighteen, however, the young Shwed was required to do his military service. He was drafted to the IDF and joined one of the most elite units, the 8200. This group, which is similar to the US's NSA, focuses on signals intelligence and decrypting code. During his service, Shwed developed a network of computers that allowed some users to access classified material, while denying others.[8] "I was exposed to a lot of security issues where there was sensitive information, which was classified and only accessible by certain ranks," says Shwed. "I got to understand the different issues where everyone had to work on the same network but with different rights."[9]

During his time in the military, Shwed also realized what he wanted to do with his career. "Since the early days in the army I had an idea to create something," he says. "It was never very exciting working for someone else, which is how I spent most of my teenage years. I had this idea to create a product based around providing security for computer networks, but I evaluated it with my friends and decided there was no market for it [yet]."[10]

In 1991, he left the IDF, and against his parents' wishes, decided to skip college.[11] Instead, he began working as a software developer for Optrotech,[12] an Israeli start-up. It was one of the best decisions of his life. Not only did he learn how to create, package, and market new products,[13] he also met Marius Nacht, a talented programmer.[14] The two clicked, in part because of their similar military backgrounds. Nacht was a graduate of the elite Talpiot program, where participants pursue higher education while serving in the military and then utilize their expertise for research and development for the IDF's technological needs.[15] Shwed shared with Nacht his idea of creating protection for networks. The internet was still small, and mostly used by governments and universities. But they both knew that it was only a matter of time before the web went global. "I thought that the internet would be something huge. A revolution," says Shwed. "I didn't realize to what extent."[16]

STARTING FROM SCRATCH

In the early 1990s, as the web was getting more popular, Shwed discovered a number of forums that focused on internet protection.[17] "It was pretty clear that companies wanted to connect to the internet but were concerned about security," says Shwed. "We knew eventually people would realize they had to have it."[18] He sent several emails to companies to understand their security concerns, determine what products they might purchase, and gather intelligence on the potential competition. The young security expert realized this was a big opportunity.

Shwed contacted his friend Shlomo Kramer from the 8200. He pitched him the idea of creating a company that focused on internet security and firewalls. Kramer agreed, and Shwed was elated.[19] In February, Shwed and Nacht attended a computer developers' conference in San Diego to continue their market research. The conference admission cost was $2500, half of Shwed's life savings.[20] But he had a feeling the money would be well spent.

He was right. The two young men left the conference shocked. "Most people didn't see the internet as a mass market problem," recalls Shwed. And Nacht remembers thinking that "these were happy-go-lucky guys who had fun developing tools."[21] Most people were not focused on how to protect internet data. The two returned to Israel, briefed Kramer, and started preparing a business plan.

The three young engineers soon quit their jobs to focus on their start-up. They began working at Kramer's grandmother's apartment, spending twelve to fourteen hours a day writing the software code. The goal was for the program to function like airport security. It would check a computer's Internet Protocol (IP) address[22] to either permit or deny access. It would also allow for inspection at a single point of entry.[23] That way the system successfully screened all incoming data. "I started from scratch," says Shwed. "I didn't take a single line of code from the army. The idea was the same, but I waited for the market and built a company around it."[24]

A few months later, they decided to speed up the process and began working in eight-hour shifts. They ate a lot of pizza, drank a lot of Coke, and took turns refilling the printer.[25] They also spent their time calling and trying to meet with potential investors. "We were just crossing our fingers," Nacht says, "that nobody would come up with a similar idea."[26]

HOW DO WE PULL IT OFF?

Less than six months after they began coding, the three young men secured seed money to start their firm. They decided to call it Check Point. In June 1993, BRM Technologies, a Jerusalem-based software company, gave Shwed $250,000 in return for partial ownership. "Gil had a strong knowledge of what he was talking about," says Nir Barkat, BRM's founder and present mayor of Jerusalem. "Not everyone sees opportunities like he does. He seems like a guy betting double or nothing. The reality is that he's not. He understands the market."[27]

In September, the trio finished writing the code and had a fully functioning product. "It was a new market at the end of '93–'94, and nobody knew how to make a business out of it," says Shwed. They began to test the product at night on various businesses around Israel. In one harrowing instance, "within one hour someone tried to break into the system, even though it was the first time these companies had ever been externally linked," recalls Shwed. "The alarm sounded and we thought it can't be possible, but two weeks later the police were able to make an arrest. It was [a] good confirmation for us."[28]

But the big challenge for Shwed and his colleagues was how to sell the product. "We're sitting here in an apartment in Ramat Gan, and the customers are in the US and all over the world," says Shwed.[29] "How do we pull it off?" The three knew that their product needed to be sent and sold about ten time zones away. "It needs to be able to sell itself and be easy to install," says Shwed.[30]

Soon, they traveled to the United States and met with about twenty companies to try to sell their system, the FireWall-1. Among them were State Street Bank, Goldman Sachs, and National Semiconductor. The trio stayed at low-cost hotels and often wore all black to meetings because it made them look uniform and allowed them to travel with fewer outfits. During the pitches, the team installed a trial copy of their FireWall-1 to show how simple their product was. "Customers were saying, 'Firewalls are so complicated,'" recalls Shwed. "So we'd say, 'Let's just install it right now.'" The companies were surprised, as messages would quickly pop up showing that hackers had begun pinging their networks to look for vulnerabilities.[31]

It was immediately clear to technology experts that the FireWall-1 was revolutionary. Not only did it extract information about the origin, destination, and purpose of data that was about to be installed onto the network or computer, but Check Point's user interface was highly intuitive. Their system didn't require an IT person to install it, and with a bit of training, anyone could use it.

With part of the capital they got from BRM, Shwed hired San Francisco–based venture capitalist David J. Blumberg to help them secure US business. It was critical to "penetrate the US market first and then scale the rest of the world," says Shwed. "It is not easy working the other way around." They decided to distribute the product rather than try to sell it directly.

At first, Check Point faced major challenges. Getting customers proved difficult in part because only big companies had a dedicated internet connection, and security was not their top priority. Check Point also had an image problem. Rumors began circulating that the company was actually a Mossad front. On one occasion, Blumberg did a pitch at the NSA while Nacht was forced to wait in the visitor parking lot out of suspicion that he worked for Israeli intelligence.[32] The company also didn't have a US presence to help them sign up clients. Shwed looked in the yellow pages and found an answering service in Boston. "It took mail and faxes and forwarded them to us," recalls Shwed. "I had never been there. The phone machine said, 'Gil is not here.'"[33]

FOUR THOUSAND ATTACKS A DAY

Despite these initial setbacks, three crucial events took place in 1994 that shaped Check Point and propelled Shwed's innovation. In late March, the trio took their product to the NetWorld+Interop show in Las Vegas for the firewall's public debut. Being cost conscious, they shared their booth with another company and didn't bring promotional brochures. "We put out a press release, but back then, we didn't even really know what a press release was," says Shwed. "That Las Vegas show gave us a great feeling – it was the best single moment we shared, and gave us the recognition that we were on the right path."[34] Their firewall was so successful it won the best-of-show award.[35]

Later, Check Point made its first huge sale to Sun Microsystems. The computer giant was unable to break into the firewall market, so it agreed to bundle the FireWall-1 as part of its value proposition. As a result, Check Point's sales that year rocketed to $800,000.

Later, in February 1995, Check Point was featured on *60 Minutes*. The producers of the show wanted to find out if Shwed's product was as good as he claimed. Check Point agreed to let its company computers come under attack from hackers live on camera. "I was not happy to participate," recalls Shwed. "It is nice to show your parents and friends, but customers don't buy it because you were in the media."[36]

To initiate the cyber-duel, *60 Minutes* approached a member of Masters of Deception, a famous hacker gang in New York in the late 1980s. With the cameras rolling, Mike Wallace and Check Point's David Blumberg sat in one room, while a hacker, who went by the name Noam Chomsky, sat in another, wearing a felt hat and a bandit mask. "He looked like Zorro," says Blumberg. "I wore that outfit for Halloween last year."

Before the hacking began, David Blumberg's phone rang. It was Shwed, who sounded panicked. Hackers were bombarding Check Point. During the previous twenty-four hours the FireWall-1 had been attacked more than sixty thousand times. "Every hacker asked all of his hacker friends, 'Have you ever heard you can break Fire-Wall-1?'" recalls Shwed.[37] The day before the *60 Minutes* episode aired, someone leaked that the dual was taking place to a hacker conference taking place at New York's Citicorp Center.[38] Many of the participants tried to breach the system, but all of them failed. By the end of the show, Check Point became a household name.

The amount of cybercrime that takes place around the world is staggering, making Shwed's innovation indispensable. More than 1.5 million attacks take place each year. That means there are four thousand every day, 170 every hour, or three every minute.[39] In 2014, hackers stole the personal information of roughly 47 percent of the American adult population.[40] And in 2013, cyber criminals managed to successfully breach 43 percent of American companies.[41] MacAfee, the world's largest dedicated security technology company, estimates that the global cost of cyber-related crime is more than $400 billion.[42] "The firewall is the lifeblood of cyber security," says Yoav Adler, head of innovation and cyber-technology at Israel's Ministry of Foreign Affairs. "This extraordinary innovation was the first of many Israeli innovations that secure global communication."[43]

Today, Check Point's firewall protects more than 100,000 businesses, including 94 percent of Fortune 100 firms, 87 percent of Fortune 500 firms, and nearly every government around the world.[44] The company's market cap is more than $15 billion,[45] and it has over twenty-nine hundred employees worldwide in offices located in Australia, Belarus, Canada, Israel, Sweden, and the United States.[46] "In the age of digital transformation, life without the firewall is inconceivable," says Orna Berry, a former chief scientist of Israel.[47]

Perhaps just as importantly, "Gil Shwed [has] had a fundamental impact on Israeli society," says Charlie Federman of Israel's BRM Capital, the original company that funded Check Point. "[He's] changed the Jewish mother's dogma for the last 100 years that their sons and daughters should be doctors and lawyers.... Gil has revolutionized them to become software designers, engineers, and entrepreneurs."[48]

Many affectionately call the creator of arguably the most successful internet security company in the world "Gil Bates." Despite this success, hackers continue trying to burrow their way into the computers of governments, businesses, and individuals alike. "I view internet security as a proactive, positive thing as opposed to a negative thing about fighting crime," says Shwed.[49] "We don't look at it like we're the police."

And what would have happened if Gil Shwed had followed his parents' advice and stayed in school? He might never have created the firewall, an internet security tool that has surely made the world a better place.

CHAPTER 11

Swallow the Camera

And you shall have great sickness by disease of your bowels...

~ II Chronicles 21:15

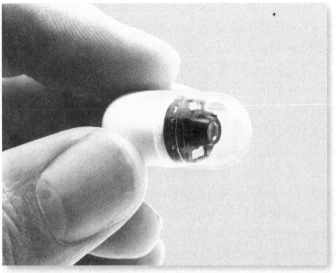

PillCam (Getty Images)

A CAMERA IN A CAPSULE

The venture capitalists couldn't stop laughing. "Seriously?" one of them said. "Do you really think it's possible to see anything with this camera? You have to put windshield wipers on it."[1] It was the mid-1990s, and Gavriel Iddan was meeting in a boardroom with a group of prospective investors. Their idea: an ingestible camera and radio transmitter, roughly the size of a multivitamin, which can travel through the gastrointestinal tract to take photos of your insides.

At the time, doctors were still relying on endoscopes to visualize the colon and small intestine — the coiled fifteen feet between the stomach and the large intestine. These endoscopes were long, thin, and generally flexible tubes with high-definition video cameras at the tips. But they couldn't display the whole organ; they could only see a portion of the small intestine, which often led to unnecessary surgeries. In order to see anything, the doctors had to perform a colonoscopy, an uncomfortable procedure. During an exam that lasts up to an hour, physicians pump air through the anus to inflate the colon for better viewing and insert a six-foot tube through the rectum.[2] Patients are normally given sedatives to relieve discomfort.

In the United States alone, roughly 19 million people have small intestine disorders – from celiac disease to small bowel cancer.[3] Three million people suffer from gastrointestinal illnesses that are serious enough to send them to the hospital. In more than a third of these cases, doctors never discover the cause.[4]

Iddan knew his idea could better diagnose these diseases.[5] As the tiny camera made its way through a person's insides, it took tens of thousands of images, providing a fuller, more comprehensive view of the gut. The capsule, he posited, would also make the experience far more comfortable for patients.[6]

Unfortunately, most venture capital firms were skeptical; they worried the product would be impossible to create. Iddan was undeterred. He believed his device could save the lives of millions of people and ultimately change the world. All he needed was the funding.

To find it, he turned to an unlikely source.

ROCKET MAN

It began with a conversation with his neighbor, a leading gastroenterologist named Eitan Scapa. The year was 1981, and Iddan was living in Boston and working for a company that develops X-ray tubes and ultrasonic probes, which generate imaging capabilities.[7] He and Scapa, who is also Israeli, had become friendly and often swapped stories about their jobs. One day, Scapa mentioned the limitations of fiber-optic endoscopes. Iddan – an engineer by training – suggested there had to be a better solution.

"If you're such a smart scientist, why don't you find it?" Scapa said. "Just give me a few days."[8]

Iddan didn't have a plan, but he couldn't get the idea out of his head. He knew next to nothing about gastroenterology, so he began by learning about the history of endoscopes. The field of endoscopy – Greek for "looking inside" – was created by Philip Bozzini, a German inventor, in 1806. Bozzini built a rigid tube-like device called a Lichtleiter, or light-guiding instrument that enters the body through an opening, such as the mouth or anus.[9] Since then scientists had improved the device, by adding magnification and more flexible rods. But modern endoscopies were still only able to diagnose the upper part of the intestinal tract.[10] Other devices weren't much help. X-rays did not provide doctors with useful images, nor did ultrasounds. The more Iddan read, the more he was certain he could create something better.

At the time, Iddan didn't know much about the small intestine. But he did know an awful lot about two things: rockets and cameras. Before working for the company in Boston, he had worked at Rafael, Israel's premier defense contractor. There, he helped develop the eye of a rocket, a camera that helps it hit the target. Among other things, he had also worked on an infrared homing device for air-to-air missiles.[11] As he thought about the endoscope, he started imagining a missile sensor that was small enough to fit inside the body. The only problem: the technology didn't exist. He dropped the idea.

Ten years later, in 1991, Iddan visited Scapa in the United States, and he once again challenged Iddan to find a way for doctors to get a better view of the small intestine.[12] But Iddan knew there were major obstacles. "It was still utterly hopeless," Iddan recalls. "Batteries lasted ten minutes, and we needed one that would last ten hours. And even if it did, what doctor would stay next to a patient for eight hours, watching a monitor while the capsule moves through?"[13]

Nevertheless, Iddan dived back into the challenge. He was now working at Rafael full-time, so he approached his superiors to get their support to work on the project. They told him his ideas were great for Hollywood movies, not the Israeli military. But they did let him use their labs.

In 1993, he carried out a series of important experiments. He started by building a transmitter and a camera smaller than a dime, because the technology had improved. He then inserted it into a frozen chicken.[14] Iddan was able to see the chicken's intestines, and the video image was remarkably clear. The same thing, he hoped, would work for humans. Next, Iddan started tackling the battery-life issue. He found what he was looking for at NASA, which had succeeded in building extremely small batteries that can last at least ten hours.[15]

A year later, Iddan applied for Israeli and US patents. Now, with all the components in place, he needed to start a business. His first step: raising money.

A MISSILE THAT DOESN'T EXPLODE

When Iddan approached Gavriel Meron in 1995 to be his partner, Meron was the CEO of Applitec, an Israeli company that was providing video cameras for endoscopy.[16] Even though the two were friends and colleagues, Meron didn't immediately commit to leaving his high-powered position. He initially tried to convince the leadership at Applitec to invest in Iddan's idea. But when it became clear Applitec was not interested, Meron knew he had to choose: stay at his comfortable job or gamble on his gut.[17] "It was an interesting idea with a lot of technological risks,"[18] Meron says about Iddan's venture. He wasn't looking to make a professional move. But the idea compelled him. He went for it.

Meron quickly started working on an investment plan. But venture capital and private equity firms began to shun him. Two years later, he and Iddan approached Rafael Development Corporation (RDC) – a joint venture that included Rafael, Elron Electronic Industries, and the Discount Investment Corporation. Unlike the other potential investors, RDC liked their idea, and the group invested $600,000. In return, Iddan and Meron gave away 10 percent of their company, Given Imaging.[19] The only problem: Iddan and Meron didn't know if their idea worked on humans.

To figure it out, they approached a United Kingdom–based scientific team headed up by C. Paul Swain. He had expertise in anatomy – and the small intestine in particular. In the fall of 1999, they performed their first human experiment. Scapa, Iddan's former neighbor, oversaw the procedure, while Swain ingested the pill.[20] They waited a few minutes and then suddenly saw some blurry images. The researchers were confused. Iddan was holding an antenna that received information from the tiny camera and beamed it onto a grainy screen. He kept moving around the antenna, but the image quality did not get any better. Based on the capsule's signal, however, the team figured out it had successfully traveled through the small intestine. They were so happy, Swain agreed to ingest another pill. By holding the antenna in different positions, the team was able to view higher quality images and finally see the small intestine. Iddan and Swain likened the experiment to "swallowing a missile that doesn't explode."[21]

In 2001, after Iddan and Meron successfully conducted clinical experiments proving their product was safe and effective, health authorities in Europe and in the United States approved the device for sale. That same year, Given Imaging was set to go public on the NASDAQ stock exchange. Then came the September 11 attacks on the World Trade Center and the Pentagon.[22] "I thought the IPO was all over, that we didn't stand a chance," says Iddan.[23] Weeks later, however, Given Imaging became the first company to go public on the exchange. The economy had crashed, but Iddan and company managed to raise $60 million. "After those tragic deaths, my big hope is that our pill will save many thousands of lives," says Iddan. "That it will be what the Bible calls beating swords into ploughshares."[24]

EASY TO SWALLOW

Even though Iddan's invention has clear advantages over the traditional endoscope, doctors didn't initially take to the idea. Their equipment wasn't perfect, but it was good enough, and many medical practices didn't want to spend the money on something new. Some were also afraid to use a pill that would enter a patient's body and disappear, causing an unknown series of complications.

Eventually, they came around. The evidence of the superiority of the PillCam was too strong. The traditional endoscope has the potential to tear the gastrointestinal wall, which can lead to life-threatening infections. According to Mark Pochapin, director of gastroenterology at NYU Langone Medical Center, endoscopic procedures also miss as many as 10 percent of large polyps (some of which develop into cancer). "Colonoscopy is a wonderful procedure and has been shown to save lives," says Dr. Pochapin. "But we want[ed] to do better."[25]

They have done better. Iddan's invention allows doctors to see the entire small intestine and provides detailed images. "Until the invention of the PillCam, the small intestine was a gastroenterological black box," says Eric Goldberg, director of capsule endoscopy at the University of Maryland School of Medicine.[26] For patients, it is also a far more comfortable experience than an endoscopic procedure.[27] The PillCam is minimally invasive and there is no recovery time. And while the capsule is in the body, patients can go about their normal routine, save for any strenuous activity.[28]

Using the PillCam is also cheaper; it costs patients about $500 compared to $800–$4000 for traditional endoscopies.[29] In theory, the pill is also reusable. "But who would want to dig through their feces to 'rescue' [it]?" says Meron. "The price is low enough that I don't think anyone would bother."[30]

In fact, the only drawback to the PillCam is that unlike the endoscope, which can remove polyps, capsule imaging can only identify them. When a doctor discovers a problem, he or she must perform a separate procedure to take care of it. There are also rare instances in which the PillCam gets stuck in the intestine and surgery is required to remove it.[31]

Today, capsule imaging is the most common way to conduct an endoscopy. And though there are now competitors, PillCam controls 90 percent of the market share. More than two million patients have ingested a PillCam device since 1998, and more than five thousand medical facilities in more than seventy-five countries are using it.[32] "I anticipate all academic hospitals using it, then most GI practices within about five years," says Ira Schmelin, a gastroenterologist at Noble Hospital in Massachusetts. "It's definitely a lifesaving tool that will find cancers."[33]

Despite the early skepticism of venture capital and private equity firms, Iddan has helped millions of people around the globe – simply by following his gut.[34]

CHAPTER 12

Eye on the Spine

It shall be health to your navel, and marrow to your bones.

~ Proverbs 3:8

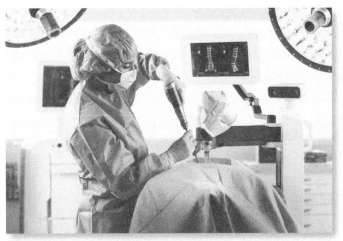

Robotic spinal surgery aid (courtesy of Mazor Robotics)

RISKY SURGERY WAS THE ONLY HOPE

It was pitch black outside, and the sounds of chirping crickets accompanied Floyd Goodloe as he rode his horse through the dusty canyons of Capitan, New Mexico. It was 1998, and Goodloe, a cattle rancher, was bringing his cows home from the pasture. But as he galloped near a rocky patch, something scared his horse, and the stallion tossed him to the ground, then kicked him into a nearby wall. Shaken, the then forty-something cowboy stood up and could hardly walk. Somehow he managed to drag himself home.

Over the next few months, Goodloe's condition didn't improve much. He waited patiently, gritting through each day with physical therapy exercises and chiropractic adjustments, hoping his body would eventually recover. It didn't. He thought about back surgery, but the risks seemed too high. Over the next fifteen years, Goodloe's pain worsened until he could no longer walk comfortably or ride his horse. Numbness spread out over his legs, and fearing he would no longer be able to make a living, Goodloe finally decided to see a doctor to get an MRI.[1] His doctor, George Martin, diagnosed him with spondylolisthesis, or a shift in the last two segments of the spine. His condition, the doctor said, would never improve without surgery.

But much had changed in the medical field since Goodloe's injury. Martin suggested Goodloe consider a new medical procedure created by an Israeli-based robotics company to try to reduce his pain. Little did he know, halfway across the world, a man named Moshe Shoham had developed a procedure that relied on artificial intelligence to help doctors carry out surgeries that had previously been unthinkable.

A NERVE-RACKING EXPERIENCE

Moshe Shoham was born in Haifa in 1952.[2] As a child, he was obsessed with building things. He spent hours assembling model airplanes and once created a contraption that would count the number of people who came in and out of a room. When the last one left, the device would sense a lack of motion and shut off the light.[3] "When we were growing up we didn't have a lot," says Shoham. "My mother would create all our toys by reusing things around the house. The lesson was, make do with what you have."[4]

For college, he enrolled at the Technion and studied mechanical engineering, before moving on to obtain his PhD in the same field.[5] When he was in school, he also worked at the prestigious Israel Aircraft Industries (IAI), the country's premier aerospace and aviation manufacturer, where he helped develop missile technology.[6] After graduating in 1986, he became an assistant professor at Columbia University in New York and headed the robotics lab. After four years, he returned to the Technion, where he went on to run the school's Center for Manufacturing Systems and Robotics.[7] By the late 1990s, the robotics industry had matured to the point that Shoham believed he could make a significant contribution by using artificial intelligence to improve medical devices.[8] He began looking into the spine because of its critical role in human mechanics; he hoped that the latest in robotic technology could help doctors in the operating room. In 2000, he approached the Technion's incubator – whose mission is to provide start-ups with operational support, management training, and office space – and started his company.

One of the first things he learned was that spinal surgery can be a nerve-racking experience for doctors, who often place large screws into small slots in the vertebrae by hand. If the doctor is slightly off, there is a high risk of paralyzing a patient for life. These types of procedures often require extensive tissue dissection and can result in blood loss and infection. The more accurate a procedure, the higher the probability a patient will have a swift and healthy recovery. Shoham learned that subminimal nerve damage during spine surgery took place about 2 to 3 percent of the time, and that, he felt, was unacceptably high.[9]

As he began developing a robot prototype, Shoham decided he needed to bring someone into the company who could help run it. As an academic, he didn't have these types of skills. The professor put out an announcement in the paper in November 2000. Soon, he got a call from Eli Zehavi, the chief technology officer for Elscint, a medical imaging company. Zehavi had heard about the position from a friend who knew Shoham.[10] "Just by listening to his voice," Shoham says, "I knew this was the person I would like to work with."[11] The engineer felt Zehavi had the requisite skills to take a prototype and turn it into a working product. A few days later, Shoham extended his new friend the offer. "Moshe, I'm coming," Zehavi told him. "I am joining to develop a tool to conduct better surgery."[12]

THE THREE MUSKETEERS

Shoham and Zehavi started with little more than an idea. Their robot was able to move, but it couldn't help with a medical procedure of any kind. They also had no way to see inside the spine without cutting someone open. They hoped some existing software could help, but they were wrong.

About fifteen years ago, spinal surgery was a lot like grasping in the dark. Doctors had to open up the spine to even understand what procedure was necessary. Within three months of starting the company, Shoham and Zehavi concluded they would have to create their own imaging software. They began developing a method whereby doctors can take a CT image before surgery and create a three-dimensional blueprint of the spinal column. This gives them the ability to plan the operation with a high degree of precision. They also started developing a robot that looks like a soda can and has the ability to insert a spinal implant, while the surgeon examines and approves the system's recommendations. The doctor then implants the appropriate surgical instrument through the robot, reducing the danger of damaging the nerves and vital organs.

To develop all of this, however, they needed to raise money. Throughout 2002, Shoham and Zehavi met with more than twenty-five venture capital funds. The two founders eventually took money from the Shalom Equity Fund and Johnson & Johnson, both of which felt the duo needed a CEO with more experience. Eventually, they found Ori Hadomi, who had served as the CFO and vice president of business development of DenX, a company that specialized in image-guided dental surgery.[13] A few months later, Hadomi joined the team.

It was one of the smartest decisions Shoham and Zehavi ever made.

CHILLS DOWN THE SPINE

The Mazor team spent the better part of 2003 and 2004 putting together a working system, one that included the robot's algorithms and kinetic movement as well as the imaging system.

In early 2004, Mazor began by testing its product on cadavers at the Sheba Medical Center in Israel and the Cleveland Clinic in the United States.[14] The team set out to prove its invention could reduce operating room time, minimize invasive surgeries, reduce the risk of infection and blood loss, and expedite recovery. The system wasn't meant to replace surgeons, but to help them achieve a better result.

By the end of 2004, Mazor not only had a fully working product called SpineAssist, but health authorities in Europe and the United States had approved it for sale.[15] "I was really astonished," says Shoham. "We got it quite early."[16]

In Mazor's unique imaging system, a patient undergoes a CT scan of the spine prior to surgery. On the day of the procedure, doctors take another two X-rays of the spinal column, one from the back and another from the side. A medical specialist then merges the two sets of images using SpineAssist's algorithms to create a three-dimensional blueprint. This allows the surgeons to accurately see the spine in a way that was never possible before. Doctors mount the SpineAssist platform on a patient's back, which allows the medical team to drill optimal holes in the vertebrae. This system attaches directly to the patient's body and directs surgeons to the exact spot they need to operate or insert an implant. The holes can be placed within one millimeter– about one-fifth of the width of a human hair– of the desired location.[17] Given this accuracy, surgeons can reduce the chances of damage to the spinal cord and blood vessels during the operation. "With the robot we can be very precise," says Dr. Andrew Cannestra, a Baptist Health neurosurgeon who specializes in minimally invasive procedures. "It's difficult to get the screws into the bone because there's just not that much real estate.... The robot allows us to put the largest screw possible into the smallest space."[18] The system also has the added benefit of lowering radiation exposure during the surgery for both patients and the surgical teams.

Using the robot, Mazor said surgeons could suddenly carry out procedures they previously would never have attempted – from spinal fusion to biopsies for suspected tumors. Medical procedures would never be the same, Mazor posited. The only problem: marketing.

A MIRACULOUS RECOVERY

After Mazor got its requisite medical clearances from the United States and Europe, Hadomi was certain he would sell his product in the States without much difficulty. He was wrong. "We had real growing pains," Hadomi recalls. "Even when I thought we were right before the product launch, it took many years before we took off [in the market]."[19]

Instead, Mazor started gaining traction in Germany. At first, "I lowered their expectations," says Hadomi. "After your first ten procedures…you are going to hate us. After the next twenty, you will sweat. It will take you another thirty or forty surgeries until you will have a product you can work with."[20] Hadomi and his team knew they were going to need to make corrections and improvements along the way, as is standard with any new medical device. Four German hospitals were keen to be part of the process because Mazor gave them a steep discount. They also got bragging rights that they were the ones who got to help perfect the product. Over the next few years, the Mazor team produced a better instruction manual and upgraded the operating system to become faster and more ergonomic. They also tried to make the machine fun to use. The new Mazor robots were a shade of kryptonite green, and the tools were the colors of the rainbow. "People don't like to work with products that are not fun," says Hadomi. "Users need to feel that their life is much better from the moment the robot arrives in the operating room."[21]

In 2007, the company accomplished two major goals. First, Mazor went public on the Tel Aviv Stock Exchange.[22] And then the North American Spine Society approved the company's SpineAssist system. This wasn't just an important seal of approval. It also enabled doctors to receive a reimbursement from insurance companies of $230 per procedure. This amount was low, but Mazor was now in the system. And while the reimbursement did not fully cover a hospital for the use of the robotic surgery, it did serve as an incentive.[23]

By July 2010, twenty-five hospitals around the world had purchased the Mazor system. This was also the year Mazor decided to try to penetrate the American market. At the time, hospitals had used the SpineAssist in more than fourteen hundred spinal procedures.[24] Six months later, the number of patient procedures jumped exponentially.[25]

Mazor has continued to win over doctors and patients, one procedure at a time. More than a decade after Mazor received permission to sell its product in the United States and Europe, surgeons all over the world are performing over a hundred operations a week using its technology.

And no patient who has undergone a procedure with Mazor's robot has been crippled or experienced any kind of nerve damage. "This is a major source of pride for me," says Shoham. "The fact that not a small number of people are able to walk on their feet as a result of our robot is amazing, and I feel tremendous satisfaction."[26]

Goodloe, the cowboy in New Mexico, is one of them. "When I started coming to after surgery, all I could think about – even though I could hardly talk – was that my legs didn't hurt anymore," he recalls. "The recovery has been miraculous."

Two days later, the cowboy left the hospital with a prescription for pain medication. He hardly took any.

"I noticed how much taller he was," says Goodloe's wife, Connie. "I was just so overwhelmed. It's just like an answered prayer."[27]

PART IV

Small Nation, Big Vision

CHAPTER 13

A Better Band-Aid

The Israeli Emergency Bandage helped save the lives of my con-stituents when a gunman opened fire in my hometown of Tucson, Arizona. Today, many loved ones and their families are alive and together because of the incredible contributions made by former Israeli military medic Bernard Bar-Natan.

~ Gabrielle Giffords, personal correspondence

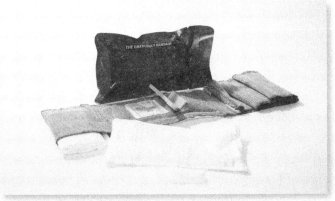

Emergency Bandage (courtesy of Persys Medical)

IT COULD HAVE BEEN WORSE

On a clear, cold morning in early 2011, about thirty people gathered in the parking lot of a supermarket in Tucson, Arizona, where Congresswoman Gabrielle Giffords was set to speak. Just after ten o'clock in the morning, however, as Giffords addressed those in attendance, a twenty-two-year-old paranoid schizophrenic named Jared Lee Loughner drew his Glock semi-automatic pistol and shot Giffords just above her left eye.[1] Loughner then fired thirty-one shots into the crowd, killing six people, before several bystanders wrestled him to the ground. Minutes later, ten Pima County sheriff's deputies arrived. As they arrested Loughner, what they saw was a parking lot drenched in blood, something that looked more like a plane crash than the scene of a crime.

The carnage could have been much worse, and what mitigated it was an inexpensive first-aid kit the medics used to treat the victims. One of its critical components was a special bandage developed thousands of miles away by an Israeli medic named Bernard Bar-Natan. It's called the Emergency Bandage, and it consists of a sterile pad that medics apply to a wound to stop the flow of blood. What differentiates it from traditional bandages is a built-in handlebar that can provide up to thirty pounds of pressure to stanch the bleeding, even on traumatic head injuries.

As the paramedics arrived, they rushed to help Giffords and immediately wrapped the Emergency Bandage around her.[2] It not only saved her life, it saved many others as well.[3]

THIS IS ABSURD

The son of Holocaust survivors, Bernard Bar-Natan grew up in Brooklyn in the 1960s and lived what he calls the life of an ordinary Jewish kid of his generation. He played stickball, went to the movies, and built model airplanes.[4] As he grew up, he felt the pull of his ancestral homeland, and in 1979, shortly after graduating college, he decided to move to Israel.

After a few years, he was conscripted into the military. During his service, Bar-Natan's close friends encouraged him to do something other than grunt work. So in the spring of 1984, when an IDF official came to his unit and said they needed ten radio guys and twenty medics, he chose the latter. Months later, he began his training at the Tzrifin military base in the center of Israel near Ben-Gurion International Airport. It was unseasonably hot, and there was no air conditioning, so as Bar-Natan and his classmates spent days placing tourniquets on each other's arms and safely inserting IVs, everyone was uncomfortable. "It got to be annoying after a while," he says. "[But] it was better than...being in combat in Lebanon."[5]

A bandage was among the first items Bar-Natan used, and he was taken aback when he discovered that the ones the IDF issued were made as early as 1942. They all had a pad in the middle and gauze strings on each side. They had not been modified since the World War II era. "The gun they gave me is not from 1942," Bar-Natan thought, "so why is the bandage the same?"[6]

It needed to be improved, but so did other things. As Bar-Natan's instructors taught him about the importance of sterility and hygiene, the American was shocked to hear them advise him to take a stone from the field and tie it on top of a wound to apply pressure. "Where do I sterilize it?" he thought. "This is absurd."[7]

Bar-Natan knew there had to be a better way. After he finished his military service in the mid-1980s, he started working on his own version of the bandage. As he bounced from job to job, he kept thinking about it, tinkering with it, modifying it, experimenting with different fabrics and weaves. "It could sit on that kitchen table for two months," Bar-Natan says. "I wouldn't touch it, but at the same time it wouldn't leave me alone, it was always there." Eventually, he went to meet a tailor who owned a store on Jerusalem's King George Street.[8] With the tailor's help, Bar-Natan began thinking of ways to automatically apply pressure to the wound without using a stone. He came up with a novel idea: a bar that allows users to wrap the bandage around the wound and then change direction to create pressure — using only one hand.[9]

By the early 1990s, Bar-Natan had a prototype, but he didn't have a business plan or a way to mass-produce his product.[10] To come up with both, he turned to the Israeli government for help. In 1993, he secured a spot in Jerusalem's Har Hotzvim technology incubator.[11] The Israeli government provided a grant to participants that covered 80 percent of his expenditures – from subcontractors to attorneys.[12]

By the end of his two years at the incubator, Bar-Natan had filed his first patent request, set up the business, and attracted some outside investors. He then turned to an unlikely group to help him make the bandages: Bedouins in northern Israel.[13]

EATING FROM THE SAME PLATE

Ahmed Heib met Bar-Natan for the first time in 1996 when he picked him up at the Rosh Pina Airport, a small strip just north of the Sea of Galilee. An acquaintance in the garment industry made the introduction, thinking the two could help each other: Bar-Natan needed to produce his bandage in large quantities, and Heib owned a factory.

Their initial meeting was awkward. On the surface, the two had little in common: Bar-Natan was a cosmopolitan Jew from Brooklyn, while Heib was a Muslim who grew up in a rural backwater, infamous for its crime and gangs. "He didn't know who this Ahmed guy [was]," Heib says. "To tell you the truth...he was afraid. But it only took him a few days to understand who he was dealing with."[14] Bar-Natan seconds Heib's assessment: "I thought tailors were only called Mr. Cohen," he jokes.[15]

With his low-cost business model and deep knowledge of tailoring, Heib turned out to be the perfect partner for Bar-Natan. He initially worked with him through his small factory on the first floor of his house in Tuba-Zangariyya, a town of roughly six thousand — mostly Muslim Bedouins — near the Jordan River.

The more Bar-Natan and Heib worked together, the more they developed a friendship — especially after two of Heib's children died at birth. "He is a dear brother," Heib says of Bar-Natan. "He was here and so was his wife, Lila. They were with us in sad times and good times. They were at the weddings of our three daughters."[16] Bar-Natan feels the same way. "We eat from the same plate," he says. "If I didn't do my job, he wouldn't have work. And if he didn't do his job, I wouldn't have what to sell."[17]

Roee Madai, a Jew of Yemeni descent and the president of Bar-Natan's company, has an equally good relationship with Heib. "This morning I spent maybe half an hour with him on that phone and maybe today or tomorrow I'll go to have dinner with him after the Ramadan," he says. "I love the guy. I believe in him. I trust him. He knows that his business relies on me, and I know that my business relies on him. We keep each other, we protect each other. If he has problems, I will solve them. If I need his assistance, he will do that."[18]

As Bar-Natan's company grew, Heib's business did, too. He expanded his factory to three floors capable of producing millions of bandages a year. All fifty of his employees are women. "I know that if I didn't have this factory here, these women would not be working," Heib says. "Their kids would not have much."[19]

Arij Kabishi, a Druze woman who is in charge of quality control at his factory, agrees. "I feel like I personally took part in the creation of this," she says, "…and [in] saving lives."[20]

WHOEVER SAVES A LIFE SAVES AN ENTIRE WORLD

At first, the company was so small, it felt as if they weren't making much of an impact. But starting in the late 1990s, Bar-Natan began traveling to medical exhibitions all over the world. There, he met with military representatives from NATO, the United States, and Israel, among others. Bar-Natan had a theory that if the military – any military – bought the bandages, they would do so in bulk, and this would eventually help the company reach the civilian market as well. To prove that the bandages worked, he began giving them away.

At first, few seemed interested. But Bar-Natan's persistence eventually paid off. "Militaries are more concerned to get the best quality and the best product," says Madai. "They don't tend to change it unless there is something really egregious." In 1998, a European medical equipment distributor sold the bandage to Belgian and French NATO forces operating in Bosnia.[21] "The bandage performed well,

[and] they were pleased," says Bar-Natan.[22] Before long, the sales pitch became self-evident: regular bandages cost around $6.50; the Emergency Bandage is two dollars cheaper — and it works better.

Soon, more sales began to trickle in. After Bar-Natan gave them to the 75th Rangers regiment and the 101st Airborne as they were deploying to Iraq and Afghanistan, word spread, and the Navy Seals, the CIA, and the FBI began purchasing the bandage as well.[23] Every year, Bar-Natan's market share grew. Today, the Australian military, the New Zealand military, and most of NATO have adopted it. It's also standard issue for the US Army, the Israel Defense Forces, and the British Army.[24]

Ultimately, Bar-Natan's theory proved correct, and more civilian institutions wound up purchasing his product. Which is how Congresswoman Giffords and those whom the medics treated on that tragic day in Arizona were saved. "I've thought often of that [Talmudic] saying, about 'whoever saves a life, saves an entire world,'" says Bar-Natan.[25] "My day will come. And, if you believe in a heavenly court, I hope that, when I get there, they'll say, 'You're the guy with the bandage? You can come in.'"[26]

CHAPTER 14

Working for Tips

This is My covenant, which you shall keep, between Me and you and your seed after you: every male among you shall be circumcised.

~ Genesis 17:10

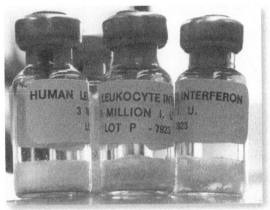

Vials of interferon (National Institutes of Health)

AN ANCIENT COVENANT

The rabbi was fifteen minutes late, just enough time for my fears to spiral. Would he do a good job? I wondered. How much would it hurt?

Eight days prior, my wife had given birth to our first child, a boy. Now, he would not only receive his *brit milah*, the "covenant of circumcision," but also his name.

It was early February 2011, and I was standing in my living room, sweating through my white button-down shirt. The room was hot and loud, as dozens of friends and relatives chatted, munching on carrot sticks and chocolate chip cookies. But when my in-laws brought the baby downstairs, everyone hushed. I saw my son – his tiny hands, his long lashes, and his dark, penetrating eyes – and suddenly couldn't breathe.

129

The rabbi smiled at the guests and announced he was prepared to start the ceremony – the same ceremony my people had been carrying out for thousands of years. I sat next to him at the front of the room. I had volunteered to hold my son as he went through this ritual. If he was going to experience this, so would I.

One by one, from the back of the room, my friends and relatives passed my son forward. The closer he came, the more nervous I felt. When he arrived on my lap, the rabbi looked at me and asked if I wanted to conduct the circumcision. The guests laughed, and I assured him he was far more capable.

I took a deep breath and pinned down my son's chubby legs as the rabbi removed his diaper. I watched the rabbi's hands as he began to use a circumcision clamp and an *izmel*, a specially designed knife that can cut using either side. Soon he began separating the baby's foreskin. I glanced over at my wife, who was standing nearby. She looked like she was about to cry and vomit simultaneously. I felt the same way, but I knew I had to focus. On the rabbi. On my son. On making sure I was there for both of them.

The rabbi flicked his wrist, and I saw blood and heard the baby scream. I wanted to scream, too, but instead I whispered; leaning into the rabbi's ear, I told him the name of my son. Eiden Corbett Jorisch.

He said it aloud and the room erupted in celebration. The party continued as my wife and mother-in-law took the baby to a quiet room. The rabbi gathered his things, spent a few minutes with the guests, and then slipped out quietly.

It never even occurred to me to ask what he did with the foreskin. It never occurred to me to ask about Michel Revel, the revolutionary scientist leading the fight against multiple sclerosis (MS).

AN IMMUNOLOGICAL PAUL REVERE

Born in Strasbourg, Germany, in 1938, Revel relates that one of his earliest memories was fleeing the city with his parents. In June 1940, the Nazis invaded Alsace-Lorraine, a fertile region in central Europe that France and Germany had been fighting over for hundreds of years. To escape the German death camps, Revel's father served as a physician in several small villages in the French Alps, where the locals hid him from the Nazis. He also joined the underground resistance, and led a chapter of the Oeuvre de secours aux enfants, a group that saved thousands of Jewish children during the Holocaust.[1]

After the war, the Revels remained in France. As he grew up, Michel became close with his maternal uncle, André Neher, a well-known professor and philosopher at the University of Strasbourg. "He influenced me very much," recalls Revel. "He was a source of inspiration because of his humanitarian view of Judaism."[2] In 1963, the young student completed a medical degree and doctorate in biochemistry at his uncle's university.[3] He received a license to practice medicine, but decided to focus on research. "I studied medicine mostly because of my father, but I found I didn't have a bedside manner," he says. "The work that was involved with patient care – it really wasn't my kind of job."[4]

After finishing his graduate studies in France, he moved to Boston to do a one-year postdoctoral fellowship at Harvard Medical School and the Beth Israel Hospital, before returning to France. But after the 1967 war between Israel and its neighbors, Revel and his Strasbourg-born wife, Claire, decided to make aliyah. "The Six-Day War, which almost destroyed Israel, was a great shock to [those of] us who were educated after the Holocaust," says Revel.[5]

In 1968, he became a professor at the Weizmann Institute in the Department of Molecular Genetics. Soon, he became fascinated by interferon, a protein cells release as an early warning system to alert the body of an impending attack from viruses and other microorganisms that cause disease. Think of it like an immunological Paul Revere. Interferon acts as a messenger to alert the immune system, letting it know it should produce more proteins to fight the virus.

The cells respond by resisting the incoming invasion. When the body successfully fends off an attack, its cells stop producing interferon.

In the late 1950s, two researchers at the National Institute for Medical Research in London discovered this remarkable protein. It was named for its ability to *interfere* with a virus's ability to multiply within a host cell. The human body, they discovered, produces three kinds of interferon – alpha, beta, and gamma. Each is produced by a different kind of cell, and each is effective against different kinds of viral infections.

Beyond that, however, interferon largely remained a mystery because the human body produces it in such minute quantities – researchers simply didn't have enough to conduct serious clinical trials.

And as Revel studied this remarkable protein, he suspected it could help fight some of the world's most debilitating diseases.

THE LUBAVITCHER REBBE TO THE RESCUE

To study interferon, Revel and his fellow researchers needed a large amount of it. "Back then, you couldn't just order proteins," says Revel. "You had to make them yourself."[6] In the late 1970s, a liter of human interferon was valued at $1 billion, because of the complexity and cost of isolating it.[7] One of the few places in the body that contains interferon in relatively higher amounts is the foreskin of a young baby. Given the number of ritual circumcisions that take place in Israel each year, Revel's team believed it would be relatively easy to secure the necessary amount.

They were wrong. They approached a number of *mohalim*, Jews trained in the practice of ritual circumcision, and asked them to provide foreskins. But these men resisted because they traditionally bury the foreskins after the ritual.

Fortunately, one of Revel's young researchers, Dr. Dahlia Gur-Ari Rothman, was related to Menachem Mendel Schneerson, one of the greatest rabbis of the twentieth century. Schneerson was

the head of Chabad Lubavitch, a Hasidic movement that has syna-
gogues all over the world. In the late 1970s she traveled to his home
in Brooklyn and told him about Revel's research.[8] He quickly agreed.
"The Lubavitcher Rebbe actually gave his blessing… and it worked
wonders." Revels says. "The *mohalim* accepted not to throw away
the foreskin but to put it in a petri dish."[9]

Soon, six Israeli *mohalim* provided Revel and Rothman with
twenty foreskins. "She [Rothman] would take it back to the lab…
and measure how much interferon they produce," recalls Revel.[10]
"We had to try many. Some foreskins had high levels of interferon,
others low."[11]

Revel and his team ultimately obtained enough raw material
to produce interferon beta in sufficient quantities for scientific
research.[12] Most of it, however, came from one source: foreskin
number 15.

Though Revel didn't know it at the time, a small piece of skin was
about to play a big role in the fight against a deadly disease.

FLYING WITH CHINESE HAMSTER EGGS

By the late 1970s, Revel – and others around the world – became
increasingly convinced that interferon could help play a major role
in fighting deadly diseases. Some thought it would be a miracle cure
for cancer. Others believed it would be used to treat herpes and
wart-like growths on the larynx.[13]

But in order to test out these theories, Revel needed to protect
his intellectual property and secure a pharmaceutical company that
would help him produce interferon in massive quantities.[14] His only
condition: that the plant be located in Israel.

Revel contacted three companies in Europe and the United States:
Cetus, Roussel, and Meriex. Initially, no one seemed interested;
Israel, they felt, was too far away.[15] But in 1979, Revel approached
a small Swiss pharmaceutical company called Serono.[16] Its chief
executive, Fabio Bertarelli, was interested in Revel's research and its

potential to change the medical field. In their first conversation, he agreed to set up a factory in Israel (Bertarelli was already involved in the Israeli pharmaceutical market).

That same year, Weizmann and Serono launched a joint project, and the factory began producing interferon from foreskin.[17] Soon, however, they realized this method was too cumbersome and expensive. Revel and his team decided to search for a more effective way to secure interferon. After a lot of experimentation, they found what they were looking for: the gene for interferon beta.[18] Once they identified it, they needed a host organism that would reproduce it in massive amounts.

They discovered it in an unusual place. In 1975, while he was on sabbatical at Yale University, Revel learned that the ovaries of Chinese hamsters can host and multiply cells of foreign bodies without changing their makeup. Elated, he asked for and received permission from Yale to take a set of Chinese hamster ovary cells from its lab and bring them back from the States. Packing them into a special container filled with liquid air, he placed the cells in his carry-on luggage for his flight back to Israel.[19] But during his layover in Zurich, customs officials searched his bags and forced him to put the container through the X-ray machine.

He agreed, and nervously watched the vacuum-sealed canister move along the conveyer belt. Suddenly Revel saw smoke and vapors rise from the machine. The security officials were worried Revel had an explosive device. The Israeli scientist, however, feared something had happened to his precious cells. Irritated, the security officials asked him what was in the container. When he explained who he was and what he was studying, they relaxed. Before they let him go, however, they asked him if the cells were worth any money.

No, he said, smiling.[20]

THE SLAVE DRIVER

In 1980, Revel started experimenting with the interferon he successfully produced from the Chinese hamster ovaries. This was the first time anyone had used mammalian cells to produce a human protein. And Revel's interferon beta was identical to the natural protein found in the human body.[21] "This technique is now used worldwide for the biotechnological production of drugs," he says.[22] It's also the primary way to produce interferon beta today.

That same year, Revel managed to woo a young scientist, Menachem Rubinstein from the Roche Institute in New Jersey, to join his department at Weizmann. Rubenstein became critical to Revel's success. Rubinstein had developed a unique way to purify interferon. But the decision to join Revel's department was not an easy one. The reason: Revel's colleagues recognize him as highly demanding. "For me it didn't matter because I was independent," Rubinstein recalls. "But [to] people who worked with him, he was a slave driver."

It took Rubinstein a year to perfect a special method that allowed him to separate the various proteins and sugars in interferon. "It is a demanding procedure . . . to get the kind of purity the FDA requires to inject into patients," he says.[23] Revel and his team called this synthetic interferon beta-1a, and Serono gave it the commercial name Rebif.

With the methodology to purify interferon beta now in place, Revel and company handed over their scientific operation to Serono. The company began to produce large amounts of the new drug to start clinical trials and determine what disease would respond best to it.

In 1982, Serono's and Revel's teams got lucky. Prior to FDA approval, Lawrence Jacobs of Roswell Park Memorial Institute published a paper regarding a trial he conducted on ten patients using interferon beta, which he produced on his own. "Today no one would dare [conduct this type of study]," says Rubinstein, because this would not meet US federal scientific safety standards.

Jacobs was able to show that the patients who injected themselves with interferon slowed down the deterioration of their bodies that was being caused by multiple sclerosis.[24] "On the basis of this publication," says Rubenstein, "the company [Serono] went into production."

Revel and his team knew that interferon beta was able to bolster the immune system. Now, they hoped it could perhaps stop the auto-immune attacks that cause MS. Revel convinced Serono to conduct clinical trials. He wanted to test his theory.

After decades of research, his chance to change the world had finally arrived.

THE CONSEQUENCES WILL LAST A LIFETIME

In patients with autoimmune disorders, the immune system works overtime, attacking both the invading virus and the body. In the case of multiple sclerosis, the cells in the brain and spinal cord are affected, as the nerve's protective sheath gradually erodes. Patients get progressively worse. Those who suffer from this horrible disease – about 2.5 million worldwide – gradually experience extreme fatigue, slurred speech, difficulty controlling their bodily functions, trouble thinking and speaking, and in extreme cases, complete paralysis.[25]

Revel hoped to eliminate, or at least limit, this slow deterioration. From the early 1980s through the mid-1990s, Serono tried to prove Revel's theory that Rebif could help those afflicted by MS.

Serono devoted tremendous efforts to building a factory that was both advanced and capable of producing the volume necessary to treat hundreds of thousands of people. Once they developed the capacity for the drug, the company conducted clinical trials to prove it was safe and effective. Serono was able to scientifically demon-strate that Rebif decreased the frequency of MS attacks and delayed the accumulation of physical disabilities.[26] According to Rubinstein, doing so took about fifteen years and cost more than $2 billion.[27]

The earlier a patient is diagnosed with MS and starts taking the appropriate drugs, the better the chances of slowing its progression. Patients inject Rebif three times a week in prefilled electronic syringes. Clinical trials demonstrate that taking the drug reduces MS attacks by more than 50 percent.

In 1998, European health authorities gave permission to distribute the drug. A few years later, the United States, Canada, and ninety other countries did the same.[28] Today, Rebif is one of the most popular MS drugs in the world, and its sales exceed $2.5 billion dollars annually.[29] Approximately 600,000 people have used Rebif and the related drugs that use his patent.[30] "What touches me most are individual patient testimonies," says Dr. Bernhard Kirschbaum, former executive vice president for research and development of Merck Group. "Rebif has made a very important contribution to improve the lives of hundreds of thousands of MS patients."[31] The other popular drug for the treatment of MS is Copaxone, which was also developed by Weizmann Institute's Ruth Arnon and Michael Sela. Copaxone and Rebif together treat a large number of multiple sclerosis patients around the world.[32]

Like most medications, Rebif isn't perfect. Side effects include flu-like symptoms,[33] and interferon beta does not work for every MS patient, nor do scientists consider it a cure. "My patients have 50 percent less relapses, meaning fewer days when they are incapable of work, less neurological regression," says Dr. Wolfgang Elias, a leading neurologist in Hamburg, Germany. "I think the ghost of MS lost a lot of its horror through these possibilities."[34]

Today, Revel is nearly eighty years old and considered "a living giant in the scientific community," says Dr. Tamir Ben-Hur, head of the Department of Neurology at the Hadassah Medical Center. "He has changed the course of history through his work on interferon proteins by altering the way doctors treat multiple sclerosis."[35] But he isn't finished with his research. Decades after he began searching for a way to make the world a better place, he has not given up. Despite his success, he's still trying to discover new drug compounds to help fight MS and other devastating neurological diseases.

By the time my son is grown, I hope that's the case. If it is, we will have people like Revel to thank.

CHAPTER 15

A Higher Calling

Every moving thing that lives shall be for food for you; as the green herb have I given you all.

~ Genesis 9:3

Cannabis leaf (Lode Van de Velde)

WHAT IS THAT SMELL?

On an ordinary morning in 1963, Raphael Mechoulam walked out of the National Police Station in Tel Aviv with eleven pounds of Lebanese hashish tucked away in his bag.[1] The fastest way to get back to his hometown with no car was public transportation. So he hopped on a bus, and for the next hour or so, held his package closely as the vehicle rumbled over the road.[2] Some passengers stared at him. Others sniffed the air or asked, "What is that smell?" Finally, when the bus arrived in Rehovot, a small dusty town on the outskirts of Tel Aviv, he stepped off, package in tow. It was time to make his delivery.[3]

Mechoulam isn't a drug dealer or an undercover cop; he's a scientist. And the hashish the police gave him played an instrumental role in expanding the way we understand marijuana. Some fifty years ago, Mechoulam was the first to isolate, analyze, and synthesize THC, the main psychoactive ingredient in cannabis. Today, roughly 147 million people use the drug to reduce pain associated with cancer, AIDS, and multiple sclerosis, among other diseases.[4] Experts believe these numbers will grow exponentially in the coming years, and Mechoulam is now widely recognized as the godfather of medical marijuana, the high priest of his field.

SCIENTISTS KNEW NEXT TO NOTHING

Mechoulam's journey to become a leading marijuana scientist and "the father of cannabis and endocannabinoid research," as he is called by many (including Dr. Nora Volkow, the director of the US National Institute on Drug Abuse), was an unlikely one.[5] Born in 1930 to a prominent Jewish family in Bulgaria, he came of age at a time when Hitler's regime was taking over Europe and exterminating Jews. When World War II broke out, Bulgaria passed anti-Semitic laws, and Mechoulam's family was forced to flee. They moved to the Balkans and wandered from one village to another to escape the looming threat.

After the war, in 1944, as a communist government came to power in Bulgaria, the young Mechoulam began studying chemical engineering. In those days, however, his family felt the country still wasn't safe for Jews, so in 1949 they fled to Israel. After a short stint as a land surveyor, Mechoulam was drafted into the Israeli army, joined a research unit, and worked primarily on insecticides. It was in the military that he found his calling. "I found the independence of research to be an addiction from which I do not want to be cured,"[6] he says.

In 1956, after three years of military service, Mechoulam began his doctorate in chemistry at the prestigious Weizmann Institute of Science – one of the top-ranked research institutions in the world.[7]

Four years later, the Weizmann Institute appointed him a junior faculty member in the Department of Chemistry. As he began looking for a research project, the young professor was surprised to learn that scientists had yet to discover the psychoactive and non-psychoactive ingredients in cannabis. Morphine had been isolated from opium over 150 years ago, and cocaine from coco leaves some five decades earlier. But when it came to pot, scientists knew next to nothing.[8]

The reasons vary. In most universities, researchers couldn't follow the security regulations, and pharmaceutical companies didn't want the presumed notoriety of trying to profit from marijuana.[9] The active parts of cannabis also weren't available in pure chemical form. Crude plant extracts are complicated mixtures, and so the research was difficult to reproduce and interpret. Opium and coca, on the other hand, are easily distilled.

Mechoulam was nevertheless determined. After securing the hashish from the police, he began conducting extensive tests on it. In 1963, he had a breakthrough: he discovered the exact chemical structure of the active compounds in pot. One of them, cannabidiol (CBD),[10] does not cause a "high,"[11] but Mechoulam determined it reduces sugar levels in diabetes-prone mice and redirects inadequate blood supply to the heart.[12] Today, children with epilepsy who experience numerous seizures daily are treated with cannabidiol, and doctors prescribe high doses of this chemical substance to treat schizophrenia.[13]

Mechoulam wasn't finished. In 1963, the professor started looking for colleagues to help him identify cannabis's other active ingredients. He convinced two people to assist him: Yehiel Gaoni, an organic chemistry expert, and Habib Edery, the head of pharmacology at the Biological Research Institute, Israel's government defense research institute.[14] After extensive testing, the three professors used their hashish to identify tetrahydrocannabinol (THC) as marijuana's active ingredient. This compound is responsible for the high that makes the drug so popular. Using chromatographic separations, a scientific method used to separate various compounds, they were able to synthesize THC, a leap that better enabled scientists to study cannabis.[15]

That same year, they tested the subject on monkeys. Edery had access to them through his lab. Scientists consider rhesus monkeys to be aggressive animals. But when Mechoulam's team injected them with THC, they became calm.[16]

Next, they turned to humans. Not long after the monkey experiments, Mechoulam invited ten people to his Jerusalem home for a small party.[17] His wife Dahlia prepared a "very tasty cake" and laced each piece with THC.[18] "That," recalls Itai Bab, a professor of oral pathology at the Hebrew University of Jerusalem, "was the real test of THC."

In the initial experiment, five people, including Mechoulam's wife, consumed the THC-laced pastry. Five others ate the baked good without the infused cannabis. Mechoulam says he didn't participate in the experiment and has never tried the drug.[19] "None of us had ever used cannabis before," he says. "Everybody was affected differently. She [Mechoulam's wife] dreamed a bit, and she hasn't touched marijuana since. Another person didn't feel high, but he couldn't stop talking... another had an anxiety attack."[20] Some felt strange, like they were in a different world, and others just wanted to relax, or could not stop giggling.[21]

In other words, they found that marijuana works exactly as it has since the beginning of recorded time.

HOLY SMOKES

Not long after Mechoulam's human experiments with THC, the Israeli scientist applied for a grant with the US National Institutes of Health (NIH). The response was not exactly welcoming. "Cannabis is not important to us," he recalls an NIH official telling him. "When you have something relevant, call us... marijuana is not an American problem."[22]

"How little did they know!"[23] Mechoulam remembers thinking. At the time, not a single US lab was working on cannabis. But a year later, the NIH decided to fund Mechoulam's research. The professor soon found out why. Dan Efron, the head of pharmacology at the National Institute of Mental Health, came to see Mechoulam at his Jerusalem lab. "What happened, all of a sudden, that you have great interest?" Mechoulam asked.[24] "The son of somebody who was important, a senator or somebody else [like that], called NIH and asked, 'What do you know about cannabis?' His son had been caught smoking pot and he wanted to know whether his brain was being damaged."[25]

Thankfully, someone remembered that an Israeli professor had applied for a grant to study the plant. Mechoulam had just isolated THC for the first time and discovered its structure. Efron promised financial support for further research, and in return, Mechoulam sent the NIH the entire world supply of synthesized THC, about ten grams. The NIH used Mechoulam's THC sample to conduct many of the original cannabis experiments in the States. In return, "they were very nice and I got a grant, which I've had ever since."[26]

Since then, the NIH and Israeli authorities have given Mechoulam as much marijuana as he wants, free of charge.[27] The steady supply has helped him create a new field of science that has far-reaching implications for treating pain, lack of appetite, nausea, and other medical ailments. "[Raphael] Mechoulam has collaborated with a large number of US and international scientists," says Dr. Nora Volkow, director of the US National Institute on Drug Abuse. "His work has been inspirational to a great number of young and not-so-young scientists."[28]

THE BODY'S INTERNAL HIGH

Humans have been using marijuana for thousands of years.[29] But up until the 1980s, no one knew *why* marijuana gives humans pleasure and reduces pain. The first physical evidence of cannabis use was found in a family tomb from the fourth century CE located about twenty miles outside of Jerusalem. Israeli archeologists discovered the tomb in 1989 near the modern town of Beit Shemesh. The dry earth had kept intact the remains of a fourteen-year-old girl, buried with a fully developed forty-week-old fetus. Israeli scientists analyzed the skeleton and found evidence of marijuana. They concluded that the girl inhaled cannabis smoke during her delivery in order to reduce the pain.[30]

By the time the woman's remains were discovered, a US-based scientist, Allyn Howlett, had discovered the endocannabinoid system, the part of the brain that allows humans to feel pleasure. It also plays a key physiological role in everything from feeding to forming memories.[31] There is even evidence suggesting this system has an effect on our personalities. According to Howlett, her work "would not have been possible" without Mechoulam's research on cannabis prior to her breakthrough,[32] a view that is widely held among scientists.

In 1992, the same year Israel legalized medical marijuana, Mechoulam built on Howlett's research and made another major discovery: the human body releases two compounds when marijuana is consumed, endocannabinoids anandamide and 2-arachidonoyl glycerol.[33] Both chemicals make humans feel high – whether they've heard some exciting news or gone for a ten-mile run. THC mimics these compounds and therefore provides great pleasure.[34]

By studying this part of the brain, Mechoulam says scientists will eventually unlock the key to treating many neurodegenerative psychiatric and oncological disorders, among others.[35] As he puts it: "I believe that the cannabinoids represent a medicinal treasure trove which waits to be discovered."[36]

HEAVEN SCENT

Today, thanks to Mechoulam's research, doctors around the world prescribe marijuana for a variety of disorders including glaucoma, depression, and post-traumatic stress disorder. It's now known that medical cannabis alleviates pain and nausea, and the drug helps patients who have lost their appetites – due to chemotherapy, for instance – eat normally.

Mechoulam's work launched Israel to the top of the field of medical marijuana testing. "Israel is the marijuana research capital of the world," says Dr. Sanjay Gupta, chief medical correspondent for the Health, Medical & Wellness unit at CNN. While the country considers cannabis a dangerous and illegal drug, Israel's Ministry of Health issues thousands of licenses to those who qualify for medical purposes. "I wouldn't give medical cannabis for everything," says Mechoulam. "Israel is going in the right direction by giving approval gradually for different diseases. It's impossible to know if people who say they're in terrible pain [actually are] because it's subjective and can't be measured. I presume there is some abuse."[37]

The risk, he believes, is worth it. But the main obstacle to medical marijuana gaining wider acceptance around the world is doctors themselves. The professor believes the drug is not standard because most physicians are not yet familiar with it. He also believes the vast majority of doctors are uncomfortable with medicine that can be consumed by inhaling its smoke. "The problem is that for many years marijuana was put on the [same] scale as cocaine and morphine," Mechoulam says. "This is not fair. All drugs starting from aspirin to valium [have] side effects. One has to know how to use them."[38]

The vast majority of doctors have been slow to see things Mechoulam's way, even though THC and cannabidiol are potentially wonder drugs. Because marijuana is illegal, there have been very few significant double-blind, placebo-controlled human studies, which are critical for scientific research. "Without those types of studies, marijuana still falls short of the minimum threshold that we expect for our medicines," says Raul Gonzalez, a professor at Florida International University who studies the effects of marijuana on HIV/AIDS patients.[39]

Pharmaceutical companies aren't enthusiastic about doing applied research on the drug, either. The legal ambiguity around cannabis and the difficulty of filing patents on a plant that has existed forever limits their ability to make money.[40] "It is still widely believed that cannabinoids are drugs and they make you crazy, make you mad, that they don't have therapeutic value, and they are addictive," says Manuel Guzman, one of the world's leading scientists on cannabis's effects on cancer cells and professor at the Department of Biochemistry and Molecular Biology at Complutense University in Madrid, Spain. "But that's BS. It is based on ignorance.... Knowledge takes time to get absorbed by society and the clinical community."[41]

Now, a growing number of researchers hope that cannabidiol and THC live up to their potential. "I think CBD is a very promising compound, and it probably has helped a lot of people," says Jahan Marcu, the senior science advisor for Americans for Safe Access, a medical marijuana advocacy group.[42] But others remain skeptical – and will continue to have their doubts until the drug is proven safe and effective, with set dosages and a known list of side effects to help guide doctors and patients.

On that front, there has been considerable progress. At the federal level, cannabis is still considered illegal in the United States, which prevents serious and ongoing research of THC and CBD. But twenty-three states and the District of Columbia have legalized marijuana for some medical uses, and according to polling data, a majority of Americans now favor legalizing weed for recreational purposes.[43] Elsewhere around the world, there is even more momentum. Israel, Canada, and the Netherlands all have medical marijuana programs. Uruguay has legalized pot, and Portugal has decriminalized the drug.

All of this gives reason to be optimistic about the future of medical marijuana research, according to Mechoulam, who is now investigating the effects of the drug on asthma.[44] Some fifty years after he carried eleven pounds of hashish on the bus, the Israeli scientist believes his life's work is slowly changing the minds of his peers. "If a Nobel Prize was given on cannabis research," Dr. Guzman says, "Rafi would be the leading candidate."

CHAPTER 16

Balancing Heaven and Earth

*And God said: "Let the waters swarm with swarms of living crea-
tures, and let fowl fly above the earth in the open firmament of
heaven." And God created the great sea-monsters, and every living
creature that creeps, wherewith the waters swarmed, after its kind,
and every winged fowl after its kind; and God saw that it was good.
And God blessed them, saying: "Be fruitful, and multiply, and fill
the waters in the seas, and let fowl multiply in the earth."*

~ Genesis 1:20–22

Following migrating white storks with a motorized glider
(Eyal Bartov, SPNI)

A FORCE OF TEN TONS

The pilot saw something out of the corner of his eye. Then he heard
a loud explosion, and suddenly the windshield of his $7 million Sky-
hawk fighter jet shattered. It was May 5, 1983, and a bird migrating
south crashed into the plane and hit the ejector handle. The pilot,
Yair Harlev, was propelled, unconscious, into the cold air, where his
automatic parachute blew open. Engulfed in smoke, the Skyhawk

149

kept flying at a speed of almost four hundred miles per hour and crashed into the side of a small mountain.[1] A few minutes later, the aviator woke up near the West Bank city of Hebron, where Israeli Special Forces later found him covered in blood and feathers, with a fractured vertebra in his neck. They brought him to a hospital, where forensic analysts confirmed that a honey buzzard weighing slightly more than two pounds had hit the plane with a force of ten tons.[2] The doctor attending to the young pilot told him that he had come dangerously close to paralysis, or even death.[3]

Harlev wasn't the first pilot to crash because of migrating birds, nor was he the last. Over the past three and a half decades, buzzards, storks, pelicans, and eagles have crashed into Israeli jets and caused hundreds of millions of dollars of losses by cracking their wings and engines, or completely destroying them. In fact, birds have caused more damage to Israeli airplanes than all Arab enemy armies combined.[4]

The reason Israel has this problem: more than a billion birds use its airspace to travel between three continents.[5] In the fall, as the weather gets colder and food supplies shrink, birds start their five- to six-thousand-mile journey from Europe and Western Asia to Africa (the reverse takes place in the spring). The thermals found on Israel's coastal plain and the country's portion of the Great Rift Valley – a thirty-seven-hundred-mile geographic trench that runs from Turkey to Mozambique – are ideal for birds seeking the shortest and most efficient route. These migration patterns create what Yossi Leshem, one of the world's top bird migration experts, calls "a political nightmare, and a bird watcher paradise."[6]

In the early 1980s, with the region's largest air force, Israel had no idea how to solve the challenge. Military leadership was resigned to losing planes and people. That's when Leshem, a leading ornithologist, proposed a novel idea: discover what routes the birds use for migration and avoid them.

BIRD'S-EYE VIEW

Leshem was the right person for the task. Born in 1947 in the Mediterranean city of Haifa, he was fascinated with birds even as a boy. His mother would often take him and his brother on hikes in the Carmel Mountains. It was there that he first learned how to spot and identify different kinds of birds. "My mother couldn't tell the difference between a donkey and a bird," Leshem jokes. "But it is because of her that I fell in love with nature."[7]

Immediately before his military service, Leshem had a powerful experience that shaped the course of his life. In 1963, when he was seventeen years old, he decided to go hiking in the Sde Boker region of the Negev Desert with three friends. They bumped into David Ben-Gurion, who had recently stepped down as prime minister. For two hours, the five men hiked and shared stories. "For me, it was like meeting God," says Leshem. "I never expected to talk to Ben-Gurion so openly."[8] The former prime minister was so taken with the boys that he invited them back to his home, where his wife Pola served them tea and cake. Leshem learned an important lesson from his time with Ben-Gurion: he could share his ideas with powerful people and they would listen.[9]

When he started in the military, Leshem wanted to become an air force pilot. But his poor eyesight kept him from achieving his dream. Or so he thought.[10] After three years in the military, he enrolled at the Hebrew University of Jerusalem and began studying zoology and genetics.[11] But Leshem couldn't stop thinking about birds, and his mother wasn't happy about it. "She was a Jewish mother," he recalls. "She would say to me, 'How can you make a living out of birds?' She wanted me to be a physician or a lawyer."[12]

After he finished school in 1971, he took a job at the Society for the Protection of Nature in Israel, whose primary mission is to protect the country's wildlife and wilderness. Leshem loved the job, loved being outdoors. In the spring of 1972, a colleague invited him on a field mission that tracked long-legged buzzards and their patterns of life. They headed to the Samaritan Mountains, located northwest of Jerusalem, and Leshem soon found himself on a narrow ledge, crouched in a huge bird's nest with three buzzard chicks. As their parents screeched and circled above, Leshem plucked the baby birds out of the nest, placed them in a sack, and whisked them away. The two men weighed and measured the buzzards and tagged them with a small leg band. Leshem then climbed back to the nest and placed the chicks back in it. Before he left, he snapped a few photographs and made a monumental decision: he would spend the rest of his life studying birds and trying to save them. "Birds are important to the world and Israel," he says, "because they are beautiful, they are singing, they are flying. They impact, I think, our soul very much."[13]

SHARING THE SKY

In the early 1980s, Leshem decided to go back to school and pursue a PhD in zoology at Tel Aviv University. He wanted to focus on migrating birds and the dangers they face. No one knew exactly how many birds flew over Israel each year. Leshem and about sixty volunteers started counting. Quickly, however, they realized there were many birds they couldn't tally because the creatures flew too high. Ran Lapid, a colleague and an Israeli Air Force helicopter pilot, suggested Leshem count birds from an aircraft. "Go to the air force and ask them for a plane," he said.[14]

In January 1983, Lapid helped Leshem schedule an appointment with Shlomo Egozi, an Israeli Air Force colonel in charge of flight safety. The three met in Egozi's office in the air force's headquarters in Tel Aviv. Leshem described his research proposal, and the colonel was skeptical. He didn't think it would benefit the military. He was, however, open to exploring a different idea. "Wow, Yossi, you came at the right time," Egozi said.[15] Egozi had just taken over a small top-secret file that contained data on the thousands of birds who had struck planes from 1972 through 1982. "Do you want to see it?"

Leshem nodded, then looked at the statistics and graphs. "I couldn't believe it," he says. "[The air force] felt helpless."[16] There were at least four collisions each year that caused major damage, and the IAF had lost five aircraft over the course of the previous decade. Thirty-three planes had sustained serious damage, and one pilot had died. Over the course of a decade, the Israeli Air Force had lost tens of millions of dollars.

As the colonel explained the problem, Leshem looked at him excitedly.

"What are you doing with this data?" he asked.

The colonel shot him an exasperated look. "What can we do?" he said. "This is part of our life. If you are flying, we are sharing the sky and you [have to learn to live with] colliding."[17]

Leshem was dumfounded. He had never thought about how bird flight patterns impact airplanes, but he immediately realized this was a tremendous research opportunity. From glancing at the data, Leshem saw that birds usually hit planes during migration season. If he was able to better understand their migration patterns, he reasoned, Israel could significantly reduce the number of strikes. He asked Colonel Egozi to fund a project along those lines. "I'm looking for a PhD subject," Leshem said. "Let's join forces. Half and half. You pay, I'll do the study."[18] The colonel wouldn't commit.

Before Leshem left the meeting, however, he predicted that a million honey buzzards would fly over Israel in the spring. The chances were high, he added, that one of them would hit a plane.

WE LOST ANOTHER

On May 5, 1983, not long before midnight, the phone rang at Leshem's house. His wife picked up. It was Colonel Egozi. He told her he needed to speak to her husband. The matter was urgent. Leshem wasn't there; he was at a lecture, but when he returned, he immediately called Egozi back. "You won't believe it, Yossi," the colonel said. "As you predicted, we lost another plane this morning, a Skyhawk, near Hebron."[19] The next day, the air force began funding Leshem's PhD study.

Both Leshem and the air force knew the collisions would continue if they didn't find a solution – and quick. After the Six-Day War, Israel had quadrupled in size, occupying the Sinai Peninsula, a vast desert area southwest of the country. But in 1979, the country signed a peace agreement with Egypt, and pulled out of Sinai in 1982.[20] One of the casualties of the agreement: the air force's training space.

Leshem understood that limiting the air force's ability to fly during migration season was not feasible. But neither was changing the birds' flight patterns. Pilots were going to have to learn how to better share their tiny country with their feathered friends.

A DREAM DEFERRED

Tracking the movement of millions of birds was too much for one person to handle. Leshem needed help – and lots of it. To gather accurate data, he would need multiple ways of tracking the birds, none of which were sufficient on their own. His solution was to enlist the support of Tel Aviv University, the Society for the Protection of Nature in Israel, the air force, and six hundred birdwatchers from seventeen different countries.

In the fall of 1984, Leshem set up twenty-five observation stations in northern Israel – from the Mediterranean Sea to the Jordan River – spaced roughly a mile apart. Each station had one to three birdwatchers, whose mission was to use binoculars and telescopes to count the number of birds and record their flight patterns. Communicating with walkie-talkies, the stations chatted to make sure they didn't count the same bird multiple times. This took place from before sunrise until well after sunset. But birdwatchers couldn't count their targets at night when it was too dark, or when they were too high in the sky during the day.

That same year, Leshem asked representatives from Ben-Gurion Airport's radar station for help. "They told me you couldn't see the birds with radar," recalls Leshem. "But I brought two experts from the Netherlands and Switzerland who showed them how to use the equipment [they already had in place]."[21] Not needing sunlight to track moving objects, radar is able to follow movement day and night from about sixty-five miles away.[22] The only problem: radar can't identify types of birds, register the exact number in a flock, or decipher how high the birds are flying. So the military dedicated four personnel to tracking the birds around the clock six months a year during heavy migration periods.

Leshem finally came around to the view Lapid shared the year before – the only way to understand birds was to fly with them. In late 1984, the Israeli Air Force provided Leshem with a single-engine Cessna that he used to gather data on the speed, location, altitude, and direction of various birds. Twenty years after the air force rejected him, Leshem was finally living his boyhood dream. "Flying with thousands of birds, wing tip to wing tip," he says, "is an incredible experience."[23]

A $1.3 BILLION SOLUTION

Unfortunately, the winged creatures did not feel the same way. The noise from the Cessna's engine scared most of them away. The other problem Leshem encountered was that the plane could not fly slowly enough to stay with a single flock. It would consistently fly ahead, leaving the birds behind.

Undeterred, Leshem tried other types of aircraft. First, he flew a hang glider. But it didn't stay in the air long enough. Next he tried an ultra-light plane, but it was noisy and couldn't handle strong winds. Finally, Leshem hopped in a motorized glider – a hybrid – and it worked perfectly. "No one had ever done this before," recalls Leshem.[24]

Some birds adjusted well, others less so. But flying with the flocks in his glider allowed Leshem to count each bird he saw, and the instrument panel gave him excellent data. The only hitch: flying for many hours left the pilots exhausted, and there were of course no bathroom facilities, so they had to use a special bag. Over the next few months, Leshem spent more than fourteen hundred hours tracking birds using motorized gliders.

In 1987, the IDF provided Leshem with a pilotless drone normally used for military surveillance. Operated remotely, this system was able to follow a flock across Israel, five thousand feet above the ground. The only downside: if the operator lost track of its targets, they were not easy to find again.

Using all of these methods, Leshem was able to produce a very accurate bird migration map. He discovered that there were four times as many birds that migrate over Israel as originally estimated. He was also able to show that birds used one of three flyways as they traveled over the country, and that their routes didn't change significantly. Along the first, birds flew from northeastern Israel through the center of the country, down to Beer Sheva and into northern Sinai. Along the second, birds flew via Israel's portion of the rift valley, through the Judean and Negev Deserts and into the center of Sinai. And along the third route, birds flew from southern Jordan via Eilat and into southern Sinai. The altitude they chose was highly dependent on weather conditions.

Leshem showed that during migration season, the chances of a bird colliding with planes increased exponentially. The solution was clear. Pilots needed to change their behavior, since birds wouldn't. Leshem created two maps detailing bird-heavy zones – one for the fall migration and the other for spring. Each showed when and where to expect birds, and the various types a pilot was likely to encounter. Leshem also included passage times for flocks to cross Israel.

In the mid-1980s, using Leshem's data, maps, and calendars, the air force created a schedule that banned planes from flying in bird-plagued zones during the migration periods. According to former Israeli Air Force commander Avihu Ben-Nun, the IDF plotted out preferred routes and evasive maneuvers that would help pilots avoid the birds and ensure minimal changes to the training program.[25]

The ban has reduced the number of bird strikes by 76 percent – saving the lives of pilots and birds – and an estimated $1.3 billion, according to Major General Ido Nehushtan, the former commander of the Israeli Air Force.[26] Yossi Leshem will be remembered as "an army of one in promoting peace between nature and a very advanced world that neglects the environment," says Nehemia (Chemi) Peres, cofounder of Pitango Venture Capital and former Israeli Air Force pilot (who is also the son of the late former president Shimon Peres).

Each year, air force pilots attend lectures by bird experts who share with them photographs and best practices.[27] Special maps are displayed in every squadron headquarters. "I think we've made the pilots a lot more aware that we share the air," says Leshem.[28]

The professor's work has also had unforeseen global impact. It serves internationally as the "gold standard to help prevent birds from crashing into airplanes," says General Mansour Abu Rashid (Ret.), chairman of the Amman Center for Peace and Development. But in addition, "his vision also rallies together Israelis, Jordanians, and Palestinians in the pursuit of peace."[29]

Israel's past-president Ezer Weizman, a former air force pilot, agrees. "Thanks to [Leshem's work], the number of collisions between fighter aircraft and migrating birds has been dramatically reduced, and the project has become a model for Western air forces."[30]

For once, it seems, Leshem's Jewish mother was wrong.

CHAPTER 17

Resurrecting the Dead

After residing in an old jar for some 2,000 years, a seed from a date palm is nurtured back to life. How amazing! Methuselah is a living window into the past. Into an era when date palm forests flourished in the Middle East, when dates were a vital part of the economy.

~ Dr. Jane Goodall, personal correspondence

Date palm on an ancient Judean coin (Zegomo)

A COMPLETELY MAD IDEA

In the year 72 CE, Jewish rebels under siege committed mass suicide at Masada, choosing death over Roman bondage. Nearly two thousand years later, on November 14, 1963, Yigael Yadin, a former Israeli military strategist, led the first-ever team of researchers and volunteers into the site – the ancient clifftop fortress of the Jewish-Roman king Herod the Great.[1]

Yadin's team didn't know what they would find. But as they dug through the rubble, they saw evidence of widespread destruction:

shattered frescoes, charred beams, gold coins, bronze arrows, and ragged clothing. Later, as Yadin made his way down an improvised wooden stairway into the lower levels of the crumbling palace, some of the diggers called him over. Inside a small bathing pool, they had discovered dark stains resembling blood. And as they continued scouring the area, Yadin's team stumbled across the scattered bones of a young woman, which some have cited as evidence for the mass suicide. The area's dry climate had preserved her long brown braided hair for more than two millennia.[2]

Her hair wasn't the only thing the climate had preserved. At the tip of the mountain, on the thirty-fourth level of their dig, inside an ancient Roman jar, Yadin and his colleagues found several ancient seeds. Scientists later determined they belonged to the Judean date palm, an extinct plant variety that had vanished roughly two thousand years ago.[3]

After the dig, Yadin handed the seeds over to Israel's antiquity authority, which stored them at Bar-Ilan University. For decades, no one gave them much thought. But in 2004, a British-born scientist named Sarah Sallon contacted the university about its seed collection. An expert on botany and ecology, Sallon started the Middle Eastern Medicinal Plant Project ten years earlier to study how plants could potentially heal human diseases. She knew that most archaeological excavations in Israel have botanical collections, and she began to wonder if it was possible to bring some of these ancient seeds back to life to examine their medicinal value.[4]

After speaking to archaeologists around the country, Sallon learned that Ehud Netzer, one of Israel's most renowned archeologists, was the custodian of the seeds found during the Masada excavation. Fortunately for Sallon, her mother knew Netzer's mother, and the Israeli scientist was able to use that family connection to start the conversation.[5]

It didn't go well. At least not at first.

"You're completely mad," Netzer said. "Why would you want to do that?"

"Well, why not?"[6]

Sallon told him she could prove that her hunch was backed by science, and eventually Netzer said he was open to the idea. Over the past few decades, there have been a number of stories suggesting scientists could germinate ancient seeds. Many of these stories, Sallon learned, were myths. But a few of them were true. In 1995, for instance, Jane Shen-Miller of UCLA and a team of international botanists successfully germinated a thirteen-hundred-year-old sacred lotus seed she had recovered in a dry lakebed in Northern China.[7] No one, however, had ever brought an extinct plant back to life.

After six months of research, Sallon presented Netzer with her findings, and he was impressed – so impressed that he arranged for her to collect the seeds from Mordechai Kislev, a professor of botany and archaeobotany at Bar-Ilan. In November 2005, Kislev traveled to Sallon's home in Yemin Moshe, one of Jerusalem's oldest neighborhoods. He arrived bearing several carefully labeled plastic containers. Sallon offered Kislev a cup of tea, and they both sat in her living room and chatted about the seeds. As she looked at them for the first time, she felt a strange sense of excitement creep over her. "I loved that thrill of discovery," she says. "Being the first to hold something in the palm of your hand that hasn't...been held in a human hand for maybe a thousand years."[8]

What had started as a question about Jewish history had transformed into a quest to resurrect a long-dead plant – and change the way human beings understand the meaning of extinction.

A MAD SCIENTIST IN THE LAND OF MILK AND HONEY

Rich in vitamins, minerals, nutrients, and fibers, the fruit of the Judean date palm is considered one of the most important foods in the ancient Mediterranean. Thousands of years ago, historians say date palms forests covered the Holy Land from the Sea of Galilee to the Dead Sea. The trees and their fruit satisfied many of the needs of the people in the area.[9] Some fermented the dates' juice into wine, while others used the trunks of the trees as timber for construction. The biblical verse about Israel being the "land of milk and honey" is actually a reference to dates, not bees.[10] And according to the Book of Leviticus, the Israelites carried branches of the palm tree at the Feast of Tabernacles (Sukkot, a fall harvest holiday).[11]

When the Romans drove the ancient Israelites out of their homeland in the first and second centuries CE, the Jewish people took their trees and seeds with them. But not long after the Jews went into exile, the Judean date palm became extinct. Experts are still not sure why. What they do know, however, is that when the Zionist pioneers returned to the land of Israel in the late nineteenth century, the date palms they brought with them came from Iraq, Morocco, and Egypt (often via California).[12]

Sallon wanted to plant Israel's original date palm across the country. But she wasn't sure how. One of her first moves was to consult Elaine Solowey, one of Israel's foremost experts in sustainable agriculture. It didn't hurt that she was also obsessed with dates.

After Sallon approached her by phone, Solowey's initial response was disbelief. "You want me to do what?" she said.

"Well, look, it's not impossible. It's just a long shot," Sallon replied.

She told Solowey about some of the historical examples of successful reactivation of ancient seeds: Shen-Miller's sprouted lotus seed and seeds Native Americans had stored in gourds that archaeologists discovered and revived after a thousand years. Solowey was convinced. "I do crazy stuff all the time," she says.[13]

Solowey spent about three months coming up with a plan to draw the date seeds out of dormancy. First, she soaked them in warm water to soften their coats. Then she treated them with a hormone-rich, acid concoction, followed by a fertilizer that's full of enzymes and nutrients.[14] Solowey put them in a soil-rich pot and added a drip irrigation system to keep the plant well hydrated. She then "kind of forgot about them."[15] She had no idea if her experiment would work. But for "good luck," on January 19, 2005, she planted the seeds on Tu b'Shevat, the Jewish festival of trees.[16] Historically, this was the day trees emerged from their winter hibernation. About six weeks later, to her astonishment, one of the seeds began to sprout. "I...got wildly excited," Solowey says. "Instead of looking at the thing every three days, I was looking at it every thirty minutes."[17]

The first two leaves were almost white and came out odd-looking, pale and flat. But the third leaf, and every subsequent one, looked like normal date shoots. None of the other seeds ever sprouted, but by June, Solowey knew her date plant was going to make it.[18] "It was like a miracle," she recalls.[19]

MEN ARE RATHER SUPERFLUOUS

When Sallon's and Solowey's peers learned what they were up to, many were skeptical. Some thought they were nuts. Others doubted the seeds were really as old as they claimed. To prove them wrong, the two scientists sent a small piece of a seed for DNA testing in Switzerland. The results showed it was 1990 years old, give or take fifty years. That means the seed she planted dates to between 35 BCE and 65 CE, just before the Roman siege, making it the oldest viable seed ever to germinate.[20]

Solowey kept the tree isolated in her plant nursery for the first two years of its life to protect it from modern diseases. She then moved it outside, where it remains today, protected by a fence and motion detectors.[21] Sallon and Solowey call it Methuselah, the name of the oldest character in the Bible, a man who lived to be 969 years old. Today, the ten-foot-tall tree and its long green leaves have become so popular that it has "actually become a tourist attraction," says Michael Solowey, Elaine's husband.[22]

The only problem: Methuselah is a male date palm, so he will only produce pollen. His female counterparts produce the fruit.

"Men," Sallon says, "are rather superfluous in the date industry."[23] The good news is that Solowey has managed to repeat her success with six more date seeds – as well as other plants found in the area. In the next few years, she should know if she has successfully planted a female date palm for Methuselah to pollinate. "I have six chances," she says, "of getting a girl."[24]

Experts say that Methuselah's sex is actually a good thing, because the male plants produce pollen. Polana Vidyasagar, a date palm specialist and former professor at King Saud University in Riyadh, is very excited about the Judean date palm's rebirth. "[This is the] first time a viable seed has been brought back after two thousand years. It is a novel idea. It opens the gate for other technologies to follow."[25] Professor Vidyasagar even believes there would be interest throughout the Arab world, particularly in the UAE, to take Methuselah's pollen and crossbreed existing species to see which mix produces the best dates.

And if Sallon and Solowey can get a female tree to sprout, they will have another important question to answer – what should the dates be called? "People say, 'You should call them Jesus dates,'" says Solowey. "I don't know about that. And I think if we called them Herod dates, people may not want to eat them."[26]

BIBLICAL MEDICINE

Since reviving the Judean date palm, Sallon and Solowey have used a similar technique on other extinct and endangered plants. Sallon describes a very big team of archaeologists, geneticists, and radiocarbon experts on three continents who are working together to experiment on ancient seeds.[27] The team has managed to bring back the essential oils used by the ancient Israelites and early Christians, including frankincense, balm of Gilead, and myrrh. Biblical figures prized the resin byproduct of these small trees or shrubs for their alluring fragrance and healing qualities. "Incense was made from these plants in the days of the Bible," says Soloway. "But they apparently have characteristics that can make them very useful to modern medicine – especially as anti-inflammatories."[28]

These three plants have historically been very important to Christians and Jews. According to the Book of Matthew, in the first century CE, the three wise men followed a bright star in the eastern sky and walked to Bethlehem. There, they found baby Jesus, fell to their knees, and "presented unto him [the infant] gifts; gold, and frankincense and myrrh."[29] Some academics believe these three plants were the "gold" the magi brought to Mary and Jesus to heal them. These plants were also among the eleven ingredients the high priest used to create the incense for Solomon's Temple, a formula the priests kept secret and handed down orally for generations.[30]

The priests' secrets may be able to help doctors create new forms of medicine. Sallon believes plant genomes from the past can potentially help find cures for deadly diseases. The Five Books of Moses and New Testament, the Quran, Psalms, and Prophets list hundreds of plants, shrubs, and trees located in the region. Inhabitants of the area used many of these native plants for food, rituals, and folk medicine. Over the past two decades, Sallon and her team have studied the works of ancient physicians such as Maimonides, Pliny the Elder, and Abu Ali al-Husayn ibn Abdullah ibn Sina, who relied on plants, many of which are either extinct or endangered, to heal the sick. Today, Sallon and Solowey are studying these plants in an effort to integrate them into conventional medicine and reintroduce species that have become extinct in Israel.

Sallon and Solowey can only guess what medical qualities the Judean date palm may have. Yet DNA testing shows the plant shares only about half of its genetic markers with other types of date palms.[31] It is possible that the Judean date palm's medicinal qualities are specific to its genotype, and therefore lost. Because the Israeli scientists haven't sprouted a female date palm, it's unclear what their discovery might lead to. But experts say that ancient plant-based remedies could have major implications for modern medicine. In

recent decades, some viruses and bacteria have become highly mal-
leable and begun outsmarting steroids and antibiotics. And because
desert plants have a unique chemistry that allows them to survive
harsh climates, some say they could provide doctors with another
way to fight disease. "This," says Rivka Ofir, a cancer, genetics, and
stem cell expert at Ben-Gurion University, "is one of the future
directions for new drugs."[32]

Saving endangered plants from extinction is critical to the future
of humanity. Humans have used plants throughout history to treat
all kinds of illnesses. In fact, over 40 percent of our prescription
medications are derived from plant extracts or synthesized plant
compounds.[33] When plants face extinction, humanity's options for
discovery and scientific advancement are threatened. The Judean
date palm was extinct for hundreds of years and "has emerged from
a time machine," says Dr. Ori Fragman-Sapir, the head scientist of
the Jerusalem Botanical Gardens. "This plant symbolizes the arche-
ological and scientific treasures yet to be found in the land of Israel
that beckon to be found."[34] For his part, former *New York Times*
Jerusalem bureau chief Steven Erlanger says, "Israel is renowned
for its agricultural science and research, particularly about how to
grow things with very little water in desert conditions." He continues, "The Judean date palm is a marvelous example of this kind of
ingenuity and persistence."[35]

Dr. Solowey agrees. "I would like to make sure that our endangered species don't disappear, because it's much easier to save them
now than wring our hands and say, 'Oy, oy, oy, oy; they've gone
extinct,'" she says. "If I can do that for our endangered species, I
will be quite happy."

Sallon would be, too. "Raising the dead is very difficult," she says.
"It's better to preserve them before they become extinct."[36]

CHAPTER 18

Be a Mensch

It is not incumbent on you to complete the task, but nor are you free to desist from it.

~ Ethics of the Fathers 2:21

A little bit of light dispels a lot of darkness.

~ Rabbi Schneur Zalman of Liadi (1745–1812)

The author (*front left*) in Israeli prime minister Menachem Begin's lap, March 1979, the day before the author's family made aliyah and just days after the Egypt-Israel peace accords signing with Egyptian president Anwar Sadat (AP)

MAKING THE WORLD A BETTER PLACE

Several years ago, on a lovely spring evening in Washington, DC, my wife was walking our three kids back from dinner on her own, when Eiden, my oldest, passed a homeless man in ragged clothes, surrounded by plastic bags. "You are a bad man," my then five-year-old said. Shocked, my wife asked him to apologize, which he did – but only half-heartedly.

A short while later, I arrived home to find my children in their pajamas as usual, but the look on my wife's face told me something was wrong. When she explained what had happened, I told Eiden to put his shoes on and a light coat over his PJs.

"Where are we going?" he asked, a bit confused.

"On a mission," I said.

We walked about halfway down the block, when I knelt down and met him at eye level.

"Do you know why you told that man that he was bad?" I asked. "Was it because he smelled? Or because he had torn clothes?"

He didn't know.

We walked another half block and then I stopped again. This time, I sat on the curb and asked Eiden to do the same. Cars whizzed by in the hurrying dusk.

"What are the five rules we have in the house?"

He thought for a second and rattled them off excitedly: "Be a mensch, make the world a better place, try your hardest, never ever give up, and have a good time."

I nodded with approval.

"I know what I said wasn't *menschlich*," Eiden said, admitting he had failed to act like a person of honor and integrity. He suggested we find the man and give him *tzedakah*. This is the Hebrew word loosely translated as "charity," but its actual meaning is "justice."

It was dark by the time we found him. The traffic had died down, and all we could hear was the sound of crickets chirping in the darkness. He was huddled in a corner with two other men in tattered clothes, chatting quietly. The smell of urine wafted through the air. I handed my son a few bucks, and my heart started beating fast. I didn't know these men, and I worried something could go wrong. Were they drunk? Violent? Angry at my son? I pushed those thoughts away. "Gentlemen," I said, stepping forward with Eiden. "Thank you for taking a moment to talk to us. My son has something he wants to tell you."

The men looked at me somewhat confused. Eiden went over to the man he had insulted. He gave him the money. He apologized. He said, "God bless you." And then he reached out his hand to shake.

The man looked back at Eiden, smiled, and shook his hand back. His friends smiled, too. For the next few moments they showered my son with praise, calling him an angel. Then we said goodbye, and Eiden and I began walking back.

We were just a few blocks from home when I once again knelt down to Eiden.

"What just happened here?" I asked.

And with a deep sense of pride, Eidan said: "Baba, I made the world a better place. It feels really good."

WHY I WROTE THIS BOOK

In a book that profiles fifteen wondrous innovators, it feels arrogant to talk about myself. But it's also necessary, so you can understand why I wrote this book and what it means to me.

I was born into a family of Holocaust survivors and raised primarily in New York City. But I also lived in Israel for long stretches of my childhood, through my teenage years, and into adulthood, because of my family's cultural, historic, and religious ties there. For as long as I can remember, Israel's faults and blemishes have been apparent; but so too have its miraculous promise and remarkable achievements.

One of my earliest memories was March 28, 1979, a few months shy of my fourth birthday. Two days earlier, Israeli prime minister Menachem Begin signed the historic peace agreement with Egypt's Anwar Sadat on the White House lawn. My family was invited to the Waldorf-Astoria in New York City to meet Begin; we were making aliyah, and the prime minister had asked to meet with a number of families who were doing so. We entered his spacious suite, and Begin, a grandfatherly man with thick-rimmed glasses, welcomed us to sit down. He handed me a small pita to munch on, and I jumped into his lap. He asked if I could speak any Hebrew, and I told him the only word I knew: *shalom*. Pleased, he gave me a huge hug and told me that living in Israel was important for the future of the country. My sister joined us, and a photographer snapped a few pictures. That conversation, and the ushering in of peace between Egypt and Israel, left a deep impression on me and on the course of my life.

I remember the excitement, joy, and fear of coming to Israel the next day. After landing, we went straight to an absorption center in Tel Aviv, where Jews from every continent were represented. I knew I was an immigrant, but I also felt I had finally come home.

A few years later, my family returned to the United States and eventually I went to college at Binghamton in upstate New York. But for my master's degree I moved back to Jerusalem and attended Hebrew University. From there, I branched out and began to explore the Arab world. I eventually found my way to Egypt, living in Cairo and studying at the American University and al-Azhar University, the preeminent school of Sunni Islam. In 2001, I moved to Washington to work in public policy, focusing on radical Islam, terrorism, and illicit finance. I began my professional career at the Washington Institute for Near East Policy, a prominent think tank, and as is often the case, I began to move back and forth between policy work and government. I was lucky and got to serve at the US Departments of Defense and Treasury.

By the summer of 2014 – when I first began to conceptualize this book – after almost fifteen years in Washington, I had written four books, two of which were heavily influenced by Israel and the Holocaust. My first focused on Hezbollah's al-Manar television and the impact of terrorist-sponsored media. *Beacon of Hatred: Inside Hezbollah's al-Manar Television* (2004) was primarily based on interviews with members of Hezbollah and watching thousands of hours of "psychological warfare against the Zionist enemy." I was horrified. Among other things, Hezbollah officials told me one of the station's aims was to promote what is "called in the West suicide missions."

Al-Manar's programming skillfully combined news, talk shows, and propaganda music videos in order to propagate an ideology of terrorism, hatred, and extremism. At one point, the station aired a twenty-nine-part series based on the infamous anti-Semitic forgery *Protocols of the Elders of Zion*, which claimed that Jews plotted to take over the world. In one particularly vivid scene, a religious Jew takes a Christian child to the basement, slits his throat, and uses his blood to make the ritual Passover matzah.

I couldn't sit still. I decided to organize my first advocacy campaign to try to block al-Manar from satellite providers. I created a coalition of like-minded nonprofit organizations, and convinced government officials in Europe and the United States to designate the station a sponsor of terrorism. We also persuaded fourteen satellite providers around the world to remove al-Manar from its feed and about twenty companies – including Coke, Pepsi, Western Union, and Procter & Gamble – to stop sponsoring the station. Finally, in 2016, the two largest satellite providers in terms of viewership, Saudi Arabia's Arabsat and Egypt's Nilesat, removed al-Manar from their feed as well, effectively shutting down its ability to broadcast their hate-filled message across the globe.

My fourth book, *Iran's Dirty Banking* (2010), was an in-depth exposé of Tehran's financial sector and the international banks it was abusing to move funds around the globe in order to obtain nuclear weapons and engage in crime and terrorism. In researching the book, I discovered Iran's fifty-nine correspondent banking partners around the globe – including Japan's Sumitomo Mitsui, Germany's Deutsche Bank, Holland's ING, and France's Société Générale. I also uncovered Iran's account numbers, SWIFT/BIC codes, and transaction currency. Leveraging my experience at the Treasury Department, I outlined a strategy to stop the Islamic Republic from moving money internationally so long as it tried to develop nuclear weapons.

After the book came out, I held meetings all over the world, trying to convince banks to cut their financial ties to Iran. Some were receptive. Others weren't. But throughout the process, I kept thinking about my grandparents, and about how extended numbers of my family perished during the Holocaust. Had someone published the Nazi regime's banking information in 1936, would the world powers have choked their finances and perhaps saved more lives? I recall one meeting at the German embassy in Washington with one of the country's leading economic and sanctions experts. After explaining the international sanctions in place against Iran, I reminded my German colleagues that they had a special responsibility to Jews across the globe; seventy years ago, their ancestors committed one of the worst atrocities in human history against my people and my immediate family. Now, wittingly or not, they were helping Iran threaten the lives of another six million Jews. I was very quickly shown the door.

Months later, I was deeply pleased to learn that all German banks were ending their relationships with their Iranian counterparts. Most of the European and Asian banks I had named and shamed did the same. I worked closely with members of Congress to pass the Comprehensive Iran Sanctions Accountability and Divestment Act in 2010. This piece of legislation, and the laws that followed, ultimately choked Iran and its banking partners, and arguably helped force Tehran to negotiate a nuclear agreement with the United States and its allies.

After the Iran banking campaign, I felt a deep sense of satisfaction. I wanted to continue writing and speaking, but I wanted to do more than policy work. I had always wanted to start my own business, and a few years later, after my wife and I had our first child, I launched a start-up that focused on banking compliance software and sanctions enforcement. My partners and I raised capital and pitched major financial institutions around the world. The business didn't make it. But I knew I had to keep trying. Eventually I founded IMS, a merchant services company that focuses on helping businesses lower their fee structures and ensure compliance with card brand regulations.

Today, I often joke that the credit card business funds my very expensive Middle East habit. I have continued writing and speaking about Israel and its future, about the country's successes and problems – some of which are of its own making. Yet it is the ideals of a nation – and its attempts to live up to them – that make a nation great.

EXPONENTIAL GROWTH

At many points in its history, Israel has struggled to balance the ideals of its founders and the dangers it faced to maintain its existence. In that context, I have often thought about the legend of how chess was invented and how it relates to the story of the modern State of Israel. It was the third century CE, and the court palace of India's King Shihram was aglow with lights. Sissa ibn Dahir, a high-ranking minister, was nervous. He was about to present Shihram with a new game: chess. Sissa ibn Dahir set out to prove to the king that he needed to treat his citizens well; he hoped he wouldn't lose his head in the process. After playing the checkered board, King Shihram was so pleased that he instructed all Indian temples to carry the game. He also decreed that it was the best way to train generals for war and felt it was a gift to the world. "Name your reward," the king said. Looking pleased, the minister asked Shihram to place one grain of wheat on the first square of the chessboard, two grains on the second square, four on the third, eight on the fourth, doubling the number of grains on each succeeding square one day at a time until all sixty-four squares were accounted for.

It was such a modest request that the king happily complied. "What an idiot," Shihram thought. "That's a tiny reward. I would have given him much more." The king ordered the slaves to bring out the chessboard and the first grain of wheat. This continued for about a month, and on the thirty-second day, the slaves brought out four billion grains of wheat, weighing more than a hundred tons. While Sissa ibn Dahir didn't seem so foolish anymore, the king kept his promise and continued to gift away his grain. Eventually, however, the king understood that he couldn't keep going. The amount of wheat he was providing was too much. If he continued, it would bankrupt his empire.

Futurists often cite this legend to demonstrate the remarkable power of exponential growth. Israel's evolution over the last seventy years is arguably similar, and it is a testament to the country's grit, determination, and chutzpah. Even with all the challenges it has faced, the Jewish state has made amazing strides since 1948, not only in developing its sparse natural resources, but also the innovations that have benefited its people and those around the globe. Entire industries and countries are looking to Israel to help them solve their challenges: Israel has over three hundred research and development centers owned by multinational companies in various fields, including Apple, Amazon, Facebook, Google, Intel, and Microsoft; China, India, and the United States now look to the Jewish state to help solve their emerging water needs; universities around the globe are forging strong partnerships and joint innovation centers with Israel's best and brightest institutions in an effort to work together in fields that include engineering, biology, physics, and chemistry; hospitals, pharmaceutical companies, and agriculture ventures are reaching out to Israel to help them cure the sick and feed the needy. The country is a beacon of hope, and its citizens are ready to help solve local and global challenges.

And as countries look to Israel for guidance on how to create or turbocharge existing cultures of innovation, they should look to Jewish culture to provide this type of insight. Shimon the Righteous, a high priest who lived sometime in the Second Temple period (586 BCE–70 CE) said, "The world stands on three things: Torah, work, and deeds of kindness."[1] In other words, in order to innovate, countries will need to invest in a culture of lifelong learning and high-functioning school systems. For thousands of years, Jews have been called "the people of the book." This part of Israel's culture has been absolutely essential to the country's success.

But a good education system, while necessary, is not sufficient. Former US president Calvin Coolidge was said to have summed up the importance of hard work as follows: "Nothing in this world can take the place of persistence. Talent will not; nothing is more common than unsuccessful men with talent. Genius will not; unrewarded genius is almost a proverb. Education will not; the world is full of educated derelicts. Persistence and determination alone are omnipotent."

And when a culture couples high-powered education, hard work, and acts of charitable giving and volunteering, there is no stopping the infinite power of what humankind can achieve. Using MRI technology, scientists have proven the wisdom of the great Jewish sage Rabbi Hillel, who believed that the basis of the entire Torah is the rule stated in Leviticus 19:18 to "love your fellow as yourself." When one makes a charitable donation, the area of the brain responsible for cravings and pleasure lights up. In other words, doing good actually makes humans happier.[2]

Israel does not have a monopoly on good ideas or proper execution. All countries would benefit from tapping into their own cultures in order to apply their own lessons to the industries and professions they have excelled in for centuries. With this said, the Jewish state's achievements for the benefit of mankind should be celebrated and emulated by the global community.

As Israel enters the second half of the chessboard, I expect its global impact for good to continue into the future. The innovators featured in this book, among others, will continue to forge ahead and do their part to make the country – and the world – a better place.

I am grateful to live at a time when Jews have returned to their historic homeland. David Ben-Gurion once famously said, "In Israel, in order to be a realist you must believe in miracles." Israel is proof positive that miracles do happen. The Jewish state has brought together the children of Israel from the corners of the earth and fulfilled an ancient promise. While the country is relatively new, it is also deeply familiar, combining liberal democratic ideals with the ancient words of Scripture. As I now take my own children to Israel, as my parents did with me, and watch them grapple with the country's complicated reality, it is clear to me that the next chapter of this story will be left to them, and all those who cherish life over death, freedom over tyranny, and prosperity over war. They are what gives me hope.

ACKNOWLEDGMENTS

I have been very lucky to develop a group of colleagues and friends who taught me a lot about innovation, the ecosystem in Israel, and the country's impact on improving the lives of billions of people around the globe. And this book was only possible as a result of the generosity and insight of a lot of people. I had the tremendous pleasure of interviewing well over a hundred people for this book, many of them more than once. These include innovators, CEOS, policy makers, members of the military, NGO executives, engineers, computer programmers, bankers, venture capitalists, think tankers, and others. Every one of them derived tremendous satisfaction from Israel's innovative prowess and their own role in bettering humankind.

Aviv and Einat Ezra were the ultimate champions of this book from the first moment I conceived of it. At every stage along the way, they served as an invaluable resource and provided constant support. They facilitated countless introductions and perhaps above all helped me weather the highs and lows that were part of this project. I am deeply grateful to them for standing by my side.

Jonathan Kessler, AIPAC's director of strategic initiatives, is nothing short of a force of nature in his own right. He has served as a teacher, colleague, and friend. Every few weeks we would meet for lunch at one of Washington, DC's many Chinatown restaurants – and had the great pleasure to travel together in Israel during two separate trips – where he would share his insight and force me to stretch my mind farther and emotionally dig deeper to get to the essence of what ultimately became this book.

No one was more generous with his time and connections than Stein Mitchell's managing partner, Jonathan Missner. Through hundreds of emails, text messages, and phone calls, he helped open doors to some of the most interesting people on several continents.

Ross Schneiderman served as my chief editor and intellectual companion on this journey. He did his best to teach me the art of storytelling, ask the next question, and search for interesting facts just waiting to be uncovered.

It is the innovators themselves who were a constant source of inspiration. As I was conducting the interviews, I literally felt my genetic composition changing – I felt that I was learning to see the world through new and fresh eyes. I cherish the time I spent with Yossi Vardi at his home in Tel Aviv, the Kinnernet gatherings in Nazareth, and in the Hamptons. Eli Beer and Dov Maisel not only allowed me to interview them multiple times at the United Hatzalah command center (among other places), but also went to great lengths to inspire my children about the importance of saving lives and what it means to be a mensch. Alpha Omega's Imad and Reem Younis – and their wonderful children – opened their home and their heart to my family, and I am grateful for their gift of friendship. Yossi Leshem (aka the bird man) and the founder of ReWalk, Amit Goffer, both epitomized the importance of never, ever giving up. And to Bernard Bar-Natan, a landsman.

Oded Distel, the indefatigable director of Israel NewTech and Eco Systems for Israel's Ministry of Economy and Industry, went above and beyond to connect me to the relevant people in the Israeli ecosystem and deepened my appreciation for the sacrifice it takes to get government initiatives off the ground. Saul and Wendy Singer, along with Dan Senor, could not have been more gracious and supportive – and their work, both on *Start-Up Nation* and the organization that followed, Start-Up Nation Central, have served as a constant source of inspiration. I met Rabbi Irwin Kula at the very beginning of my *Thou Shalt Innovate* journey. I often felt his presence, and gentle encouragement to dream as big as possible.

Red Dot Capital's managing partner and former Israeli 8200 military intelligence officer Yaniv Stern was one of the very first people I talked to about the ideas in this book. I vividly remember looking out over big sky country in Albuquerque, New Mexico, as I told him about all the Israeli innovations I realized were making the world better. Through hundreds of conversations, WhatsApp messages, and cups of black Arabic coffee in Washington, DC, New York, and Tel Aviv, Yaniv's enthusiasm and sense of humor kept me going.

I would not have survived the publishing world's rollercoaster ride without Georgetown law professor Brad Snyder. Brad and I would often meet in the mornings in our children's schoolyard after drop-off; over many family meals, picnics, and trick-or-treat adventures, I would update him on where things stood on the manuscript, the people I was interviewing, and the various items on my to-do list. Above all, I am grateful for his gift of friendship and wonderful disposition, to say nothing of his no-nonsense attitude.

Carolyn Starman Hessel of the Jewish Book Council took me under her wing and helped me find my way as I tried to find the right literary agent and publisher. She would call me on a regular basis, check in, and find out when I was going to be in New York so we could get together. Literary agent Deborah Harris also played a critical role in helping me navigate the publishing world. She could not have been more genuine or generous, and her insight was critical to this book seeing the light of day. It was Deborah who ultimately steered me to my publisher.

I could not have asked for a better relationship than the one I have with Gefen Publishing House. I vividly remember my first call with Gefen's owner, Ilan Greenfield, in which I described the book, the featured innovators, and the underlying premise of *Thou Shalt Innovate*. We agreed to meet the following day at his office near Jerusalem's Central Bus Station – he immediately grasped what I was trying to achieve. He wanted to publish the book as quickly as possible, and personally do whatever he could to ensure the book's message became part of the mainstream. Gefen's project manager,

Emily Wind, did a wonderful job shepherding the process along. And Kezia Raffel Pride's keen eye and strong editing skills were a pleasure to work with. I am also extremely grateful to Lisa Mendelow and Dan Kohan, who together designed my stunning book cover.

There were a number of people who read the manuscript at various stages and whose input was invaluable: I am extraordinarily grateful to Ilan Berman, vice president of the American Foreign Policy Council, where I serve as a senior fellow. Ilan has been a supporter and friend for many years and has always had my back. Other helpful readers included Gabe Murphy of the Allen Institute for Brain Research, an excellent friend and smart scientist; Professor Aaron Tapper of the University of San Francisco, who did his best to share the worldview of today's college students and the liberal mindset as it relates to Israel; Associate Professor Marlene Kazir of Broward College, whose insight was spot on; US Navy captain (Ret.) Matthew Sharpe, who offered some critical additions and whose friendship has been a gift over many years; and Judy Heiblum, who made an important contribution to the structure of the manuscript.

I had some wonderful research assistants who helped me launch this project. I could not have asked for a better researcher and colleague than Adam Basciano, who worked tirelessly to make this book a reality. I am also thankful for the contributions of Kayla Wold, Alexandra Zimmern, and Laura Adkins.

A hearty thanks to Yaakov Katz, the editor in chief of the *Jerusalem Post* and author of *The Weapon Wizards: How Israel Became a High-Tech Military* (St. Martin's Press, 2017), whom I would meet and speak to with some frequency, often at Baqa's Kalu Café, so he could give me a download on the ins and outs of navigating the Israeli system – and spice up my day with his sense of humor. Similarly, Seth M. Siegel, author of *Let There Be Water* (St. Martin's Press, 2015), went above and beyond. I first told Seth I was writing this book at a quiet meeting behind the scenes at one of AIPAC's policy conferences. He shared his playbook on how he succeeded with his own book and encouraged me to follow his lead. His inventiveness served as a real motivator for me and gave me a sense for what was possible.

Rabbi David Rosen, my neighbor in Jerusalem, was always open to sharing his insight, Rolodex, and cookies on what might be described as the most beautiful and timeless view from his balcony. I always walked away recharged after our interviews and Shabbat dinners with his family.

A special thanks to Stephen Schneider, AIPAC's director of international affairs, who went to great lengths to open up his international network. He has also been a wonderful promoter of the book's message.

Over numerous trips to Israel, there were four individuals who consistently opened their homes and hearts, giving me love and support as I kept a punishing schedule, driving all over the country: Shlomit Shushan, whose beautiful *bustan* has wonderful trees and tropical fruit from all over the world; Irit Lerner, whose home in the north was nothing short of a wonderful refuge; Avi Lichter, whose family has been extraordinarily generous and whose compound overlooks what could easily be confused with Tuscany; and my sister Simone Pinsky – I couldn't have asked for a more caring and wonderful sibling.

I interviewed a number of people from the West Bank and throughout the Arab world who requested anonymity – I have of course respected their wishes, since speaking positively about Israel could potentially put them and/or their family members in harm's way. I hope that in the years to come, innovation will serve as one of the bridges to peaceful reconciliation between Israel and its neighbors.

My sincerest thanks to the following individuals for some special conversations and helpful introductions: Brian Abrahams, former Midwest regional director for AIPAC; Yosef Abramowitz, CEO of Energiya Global Capital; Yoav Adler, head of innovation and cyber-technology at Israel's Ministry of Foreign Affairs; Sarah Bard,

Hillary Clinton's presidential campaign's Jewish outreach director; Rob Bassin, AIPAC's political director; Peter Berkowitz, senior fellow at the Hoover Institution; Orna Berry, Israel's former chief scientist and now vice president of Dell EMC; Josh Block, CEO and president of the Israel Project; Zack Bodner, CEO of the Palo Alto JCC; Jordana Cutler, head of policy and communications for Facebook's Israel office; Doug Feith, senior fellow and director of the Center for National Security Strategies at the Hudson Institute, and his wife Pamela Auerbach; Ari Feinstein, founder of World Check; Marvin Feuer, AIPAC's director of policy and government affairs; Emma Freedman; Chris Gile of Amazon; Susie Gilfix, Pivotal's associate general counsel; Joanna Gordon, former head of the Information Technology Industry at the World Economic Forum; Jonathan Calt Harris, former AIPAC assistant director for policy and government affairs; Amy Hawthorne, deputy director for research at Project on Middle-East Democracy (POMED); Malcolm Hoenlein, executive vice chairman of the Conference of Presidents of Major American Jewish Organizations; Gidi Grinstein, founder of Reut Institute; Gulzar Hussein; Anat Katz, head of trade mission for the Israeli embassy to the United States; Netta Korin, senior advisor to Israel's deputy minister for public diplomacy, Michael Oren; Ken Kwartler, former senior in-house trademark counsel to Nike; Anne Mandelbaum and her husband Michael Mandelbaum, professor emeritus at Johns Hopkins School of Advanced International Studies; Adam Milstein, philanthropist, businessman, and founder of the Israeli American Council; Ahmed Qureshi, president and COO at BILT; Jessica Rine; Asaf Romirowsky, executive director, Scholars for Peace in the Middle East; Lee Rosenberg, venture investor and past president of AIPAC; Dennis Ross, former US Special Middle East Coordinator; David Rotbard, founder of MicroOffice; Amit Shafrir, seasoned entrepreneur and CEO; Jonathan Schanzer, vice president of research at the Foundation for Defense of Democracies; Rivkah Slonim, the education director at the Chabad Center for Jewish Student Life at Binghamton University; Guy Spigelman, CEO of PresenTense Israel; Nir Tzuk, social entrepreneur; David Victor, president of the American Educational Institute and past president of AIPAC; Robert Worth, former *New York Times* Beirut bureau chief; Avi Yaron, founder, Visionsense; above all, I thank each of them deeply for going the extra mile.

Larry Glick, my partner at IMS, has been a godsend. His mentorship, support, and gift of friendship have been priceless. He understood my passion for writing this book and was supportive from start to finish.

And finally, I could not have written *Thou Shalt Innovate* without the encouragement of my family and in-laws, but above all my wife, Eleana. Over the past three years I have spoken incessantly to Eleana and my three children, Eiden, Oren, and Yaniv, about the innovations that have come out of Israel that are shaping humanity. They have been my biggest supporters and source of inspiration.

As I think about all the wonderful friends, colleagues, and family members from all over the world who supported this project, how could I not believe that each of us has the power to use our ingenuity to repair the world?

Avi Jorisch
Washington, DC
January 2018

Israel's Fifty Greatest Contributions to the World

1948 – SELF-DEFENSE MARTIAL ART. Imre Lichtenfeld invents Krav Maga, meaning hand-to-hand combat. This self-defense system combines aikido, judo, boxing, and wrestling.

1955 – SOLAR WATER COLLECTOR. Dr. Harry Zvi Tabor develops the black stripping that gathers solar energy and connects it to a contraption to collect heated water. This new type of solar heater, also known as the *dud shemesh*, yields more hot water and produces more electricity than a turbine.

1955 – AWARENESS THROUGH MOVEMENT. Moshe Feldenkrais designs a holistic program called the Feldenkrais method for better posture.

1958 – CREATING THE LANGUAGE OF DANCE. Noa Eshkol and Abraham Wachman create a revolutionary notation system to document movement in a way that can be universally understood and replicable. With a language for movement, experts can record dance, physical therapy, and animal behavior.

1961 – GEOTHERMAL TURBINE. Dr. Harry Zvi Tabor and Dr. Lucien Yehuda Bronicki create a solar-powered turbine that uses an alternative liquid to move an electric generator – even when the sun's rays aren't strong. Bronicki and his wife Dita apply this innovation to geothermal energy with great success through their global company Ormat.

1963 – CHEMICAL STRUCTURE OF MARIJUANA. Raphael Mechoulam discovers the chemical structure of the active compounds in marijuana, including cannabidiol (CBD) and tetrahydrocannabinol (THC), which is later used to treat seizures, among other disorders.

1965 – MODERN DRIP IRRIGATION. Simcha Blass and Kibbutz Hatzerim sign a contract to start Netafim and mass-produce the world's first modern drip irrigator, which helps farmers, cooperatives, and governments conserve more water.

1967 – DRUG FOR MULTIPLE SCLEROSIS. Michael Sela, Ruth Arnon, and Dvora Teitelbaum begin experimenting with synthetic substances to reduce the symptoms associated with MS. Almost thirty years later, the FDA approves Copaxone, the drug the three developed along with Teva Pharmaceuticals.

1973 – IMPENETRABLE DOOR AND LOCK. Avraham Bachri and Moshe Dolev invent the Rav Bariach geometric door lock, the cylinders of which connect throughout the doorframe. Four years later, the duo create Pladelet, a steel security door that incorporates their lock.

1976 – NATURAL MOSQUITO REPELLANT. Dr. Yoel Margalith discovers *Bacillus thuringiensis israelensis* (Bti), a microbial agent that is lethal to most mosquitos and black flies. This natural agent is cheaper than pesticides and just as effective. It also doesn't harm the environment.

1976 – LINKING LIBRARIES AND BOOKS. A team of Hebrew University librarians, systems analysts, and computer programmers launch an effort to create the world's first automated library system, known as Aleph.

1979 – SUPER COMPUTER CHIP. Intel Haifa produces the first PC microprocessor, the Intel 8088.

1979 – DRUG FOR MULTIPLE SCLEROSIS. Michel Revel discovers a novel way to treat multiple sclerosis by experimenting on foreskin. He develops Rebif, one of the leading drugs to treat MS.

1980 – CHERRY TOMATOES. Chaim Rabinovitch and Nahum Keidar genetically modify a tomato into a miniature version called the cherry tomato.

1983 – AN ARMY OF PESTILENCE. Mario Moshe Levi and Yaakov Nakash launch Bio-Bee Biological Systems, which cultivates bees, wasps, and mites for pest control and natural pollination, while making sure that these insects don't take over the environment and cause harmful side effects.

1985 – GRAIN BAGS. Dr. Shlomo Navarro develops the Grain Cocoon, a large, hermetically sealed bag for rice, grain, spices, and legumes that doesn't require pesticides.

1987 – PREVENTING BIRD AND AIRCRAFT COLLISIONS. Using radar, motorized gliders, drones, and a network of bird watchers, Yossi Leshem creates a precise map of the one billion birds that fly over Israel each year. His research reduces the collision rate between birds and planes by 76 percent, savings almost a billion dollars.

1989 – FLASH DRIVE. Dr. Dov Moran creates the world's first flash drive, called DiskOnKey. This device is smaller, faster, and has significantly more storage capacity than a floppy disk or CD.

1990 – BETTER BANDAGE. Bernard Bar-Natan develops the Emergency Bandage, a unique life-saving product that instantly controls massive bleeding and prevents infections in trauma situations.

1991 – BABY BREATHING MONITOR. Utilizing a sensor pad under a crib, Haim Shtalryd builds the first modern baby breathing monitor.

1993 – INTERNET FIREWALL. Gil Shwed, Shlomo Kramer, and Marius Nacht create the first firewall to protect corporate and personal data online.

1993 – GPS FOR BRAIN SURGERIES. Imad and Reem Younis launch Alpha Omega, the largest Arab high-tech company in Israel. It has created the industry standard for devices that act as a GPS inside the brain for deep brain stimulation procedures used to treat essential tremor, Parkinson's, and other neurological disorders.

1995 – DRUG FOR OVARIAN CANCER. Yechezkel Barenholz and Dr. Alberto Gabizon develop the first FDA-approved nanodrug, Doxil. Given by infusion, Doxil can extend life by 25 to 33 percent over the next best treatment for ovarian cancer.

1996 – INSTANT CHAT. Yair Goldfinger, Sefi Vigiser, Amnon Amir, Arik Vardi, and Yossi Vardi launch Mirabilis, a company that created ICQ (pronounced "I Seek You"), the first online instant messaging program.

1996 – DRUG FOR PARKINSON'S. Moussa Youdim publishes a paper claiming the compound Rasagiline can play a role in fighting Parkinson's disease. Three years later, Teva Pharmaceuticals develops Azilect and begins marketing it in the United States and Europe.

1997 – ECOLOGICALLY FRIENDLY FISH FARMS. Jaap van Rijn files his second patent for a unique zero-discharge system to recycle wastewater from fish farms. By using specially developed bacteria and biological filters, van Rijn figures out how to reproduce fish anywhere using extremely limited amounts of water, and without harming the environment.

1998 – PILLCAM. Dr. Gavriel Iddan creates an ingestible camera and radio transmitter that can travel through the gastrointestinal tract to take photos of your insides. PillCam provides doctors with an effective tool for less invasive screening, diagnosis, and treatment of gastrointestinal-related diseases.

1998 – FIGHTING GUM DISEASE: The US Food and Drug Administration approves for sale the PerioChip, the first biodegradable delivery system for reducing adult periodontitis. Created by Michael Friedman, Michael Sela, Doron Steinberg, and Aubrey Soskolny, the PerioChip is inserted directly into the periodontal pockets in the gums.

1999 – MOBILEYE. Amnon Shashua and Ziv Aviram invent Mobileye, a system to prevent accidents by warning drivers of a dangerous situation. The device sends out an audio sound if a vehicle ahead gets too close or if the driver veers out of his lane in an unsafe manner.

2001 – ROBOTIC BACK SURGERY. Moshe Shoham and Eli Zehavi, the founders of Mazor Robotics, create a guidance system that transforms spinal procedures into more of a science. Mazor's revolutionary technology allows doctors to take a CT image before surgery and create a three-dimensional blueprint of the spine. This gives medical personnel the ability to plan the operation with a high degree of precision.

2004 – HOSPITAL SMART BEDS. Dr. Danny Lange, Yossi Gross, Dr. Guy Shinar, and Avner Halperin create a sensor plate that turns a hospital mattress into a smart bed. This iPad-sized device monitors a patient's heartbeat, respiratory rate, sleep stages, and movement, then wirelessly transmits them to a smartphone application.

2004 – EXOSKELETON WALKING DEVICE. Dr. Amit Goffer creates ReWalk, an exoskeleton that allows paraplegics to walk again.

2005 – REVIVING EXTINCT PLANTS. Using ancient seeds found in Masada in the early 1960s, Dr. Sarah Sallon and Dr. Elaine Solowey find a way to resurrect something that vanished roughly two thousand years ago: the Judean date palm, one of the ancient Mediterranean's most important plants.

2006 – DRUG FOR DEMENTIA. Marta Weinstock-Rosin, Michael Chorev, and Dr. Zeev Ta-Shma develop Exelon, the first drug approved for treating mild to moderate dementia associated with Parkinson's disease.

2006 – FIRST RESPONDER GEO-LOCATOR AND AMBUCYCLE. Eli Beer starts a group of volunteer EMTs called United Hatzalah, all of whom have a standardized app on their smartphones that acts as a dispatch, immediately notifying the five closest people to a victim. These EMTs often travel by way of ambucycles – refitted motorcycles that act as mini-ambulances and are nimble enough to weave through traffic.

2007 – NANO BIBLE. Uri Sivan and Dr. Ohad Zohar use a focused ion laser beam to complete in ninety minutes what would normally take years to finish: a complete version of the Hebrew Bible consisting of 1,200,000 letters. The only difference is this version is nano-sized.

2007 – HELPING THE BLIND SEE. Dr. Amir Amedi devises a method called EyeMusic, which allows the blind to use their other senses to recognize everyday items, including colors. Users wear special glasses with a camera that scans the environment and translates items into a specific musical code.

2008 – WAZE. Uri Levine, Ehud Shabtai, and Amir Shinar start Waze, the world's most widely used app for navigating traffic. The system utilizes real-time updates and road conditions, and helps drivers reduce their commute time and consumption of gasoline.

2008 – PREVENTING WATER LEAKS. Amir Peleg launches a software platform that marries big data and the cloud to monitor water networks. His system, Takadu, gives cities, municipalities, and countries the capability to check their water infrastructure and detect leaks and burst pipes, saving millions of gallons of water.

2008 – REVOLUTIONARY TOILET. Oded Shoseyov and Oded Halperin create the AshPoopie, a toilet that doesn't require water or electricity and leaves no waste.

2009 – CURBING AIDS. To reduce the number of people who contract HIV, Oren Fuerst, Ido Kilemnick, and Shaul Shohat create Prepex, a nonsurgical circumcision device that requires no anesthesia, is completely safe, bloodless, and virtually painless.

2010 – INTERNAL WATER WHEELS. Danny Peleg creates Hydrospin, a small rotating wheel that turns within a water pipe in order to generate an electrical current, a perpetual source of clean energy.

2010 – THE HARDY POTATO. David Levy develops a potato strain that can grow in hot, dry climates, where water is scarce.

2010 – BIODEGRADABLE FOOD PACKAGING. Daphna Nissenbaum and Tal Neuman create TIPA, biodegradable food packaging that has the same mechanical properties as regular plastic.

2011 – IRON DOME MISSILE SYSTEM. Brigadier General Danny Gold and Chanoch Levine successfully down a Hamas rocket from Gaza using the revolutionary Iron Dome targeting system. Using advanced radar and software, this device predicts a rocket's trajectory and shoots it out of the sky.

2011 – HANDS-FREE SMARTPHONE. Oded Ben-Dov and Giora Livne develop the Sesame Phone, the world's first smartphone for people who have limited use of their hands.

2011 – EFFICIENT BIOGAS MACHINE. Yair Teller and Oshik Efrati create HomeBioGas, the first highly efficient, easy-to-assemble machine that takes pet excrement, alongside organic kitchen and garden waste, and turns it into renewable gas.

2012 – CARRYING THE INJURED. Elie Isaacson and Itzhak Oppenheim create a practical injured personnel carrier to replace the fireman's carry. Similar in function to a backpack, it provides the ability to carry or evacuate an incapacitated person hands free.

2015 – SNIFFING OUT CANCER. Hossam Haick develops NA-Nose, a breathalyzer test for lung cancer, using technology that's capable of detecting compounds not normally recognized by the human olfactory system.

2016 – STABLE AND BIOABSORBABLE BANDAGE. Israel's Core Scientific Creations goes to market with a bandage called Wound Clot that is able to absorb large quantities of blood before dissolving the bandage into the human body.

HONORABLE MENTION

2014 – TIKKUN OLAM MAKERS (TOM). The first Make-a-thon prototyping and design competition is held in Nazareth, creating a first-of-a-kind platform that brings together thinkers, engineers, designers, and project managers to solve unmet social challenges in disadvantaged communities. These technology marathons – now held all over the world – build custom-made models and prototypes for people with disabilities. Solutions are uploaded online and available for free use.

NOTES

Preface – Let There Be Light

1 G.K. Chesterton, *What I Saw in America* (New York, 1922), 12.

Chapter 1 – Israel's DNA

1 Avi Yaron, author's interview, Nazareth, April 16, 2016.
2 Ibid.
3 Ibid.
4 Ibid.
5 Reem Younis, author's interview, Washington, DC, September 13, 2016.
6 Jill Jacobs, "The History of Tikkun Olam," *Zeek*, June 2007, www.zeek.net/706tohu /index.php?page=2e?.
7 Rabbi David Rosen, author's interview, Jerusalem, July 21, 2016.
8 Yossi Vardi, author's interview, Hamptons, NY, July 3, 2017.
9 "Declaration of the Establishment of the State of Israel," May 14, 1948, www.mfa.gov .il/mfa/foreignpolicy/peace/guide/pages/declaration%20of%20establishment %20of%20state%20of%20israel.aspxot.
10 Theodor Herzl, "Excerpts from *The Jewish State*," February 1896, www.jewishvirtual library.org/jsource/Zionism/herzlex.htmltxz.
11 Theodor Herzl, "Quotes on Judaism and Israel," *Jewish Virtual Library*, www .jewishvirtuallibrary.org/jsource/Quote/herzlq.htmltl.
12 "Tikkun Olam," Israel Ministry of Education [in Hebrew], http://meyda.education .gov.il/files/Tarbut/PirsumeAgaf/KitveEt/kitaHBenGoryon.pdf. See also "Herzl's Better Society," Israel Ministry of Education [in Hebrew], http://cms.education .gov.il/NR/rdonlyres/7D90F636-B63F-443C-84A0-CF6C9C9C6FC6/148474 /hahevra_hametukenet.pdf. And see Charles Ward, "Protestant Work Ethic That Took Root in Faith Is Now Ingrained in Our Culture," *Houston Chronicle*, September 1, 2007, www.chron.com/life/houston-belief/article/Protestant-work-ethic-that -took-root-in-faith-is-1834963.php-.

Chapter 2 – Jews Cannot Remain Indifferent

1 Jake Wallis, "Saving Their Sworn Enemy," *Daily Mail*, December 8, 2015, www.dailym ail.co.uk/news/article-3315347/Watch-heart-pounding-moment-Israeli-comman dos-save-Islamic-militants-Syrian-warzone-risking-lives-sworn-enemies.htmlok.
2 "IDF Medical Units Treat Wounded Syrians," *The Tower*, August 9, 2016, www.thetow er.org/3759-watch-idf-medical-units-treat-wounded-syrians/.
3 Eugene Kandel, author's email exchange, December 28, 2016.
4 Batsheva Sobelman, "One Country That Won't Be Taking Syrian Refugees: Israel,"

Los Angeles Times, September 6, 2015, www.latimes.com/world/middleeast/la-fg-syrian-refugees-israel-20150906-story.htmlo.

5 Golda Meir, *My Life* (New York: G.P. Putnam's Sons, 1975), 317–37. See also D. Ben-Gurion, "Trends in State Education" [in Hebrew], lecture at Nineteenth National Pedagogical Conference of the Teacher's Union, October 17, 1954, *Hahinukh* 27 (1954): 3–8, quoted in Ronald W. Zweig, *David Ben-Gurion: Politics and Leadership in Israel* (Oxford, UK: Routledge, 1991), 272n61.

6 Meir, *My Life*, 319–20.

7 Ibid., 317–18.

8 Ehud Avriel, "Some Minute Circumstances," *Jerusalem Quarterly* (winter 1980): 28, quoted in Aliza Belman Inbal and Shachar Zahavi, *The Rise and Fall of Israel's Bilateral Aid Budget, 1958–2008* (Tel Aviv: Tel Aviv University Hartog School for Government and Policy with the Pears Foundation, 2009), 27.

9 Meir, *My Life*, 18.

10 Inbal and Zahavi, *The Rise and Fall of Israel's Bilateral Aid Budget, 1958–2008*, 16.

11 Ibid., 9.

12 Ibid., 19.

13 Ibid., 9.

14 Meir, *My Life*, 333.

15 Ibid., 337.

16 Ibid.

17 Ibid., 336. This trip took place in 1964.

18 Joel Peters, *Israel and Africa: The Problematic Friendship* (London: British Academic Press, 1992), 15, quoted in Inbal and Zahavi, *The Rise and Fall of Israel's Bilateral Aid Budget, 1958–2008*, 27.

19 Meir, *My Life*, 318.

20 Mordechai E. Kreinin, *Israel and Africa: A Study in Technical Cooperation* (New York: Frederick A. Praeger, 1964), 11, quoted in Inbal and Zahavi, *The Rise and Fall of Israel's Bilateral Aid Budget, 1958–2008*, 30.

21 Ibid., 9, 19.

22 Meir, *My Life*, 325.

23 But MASHAV did continue to train Africans if their expenses were covered. And about fifty Israelis continued to train on the continent under the auspices of the UN and other multilateral organizations. See Inbal and Zahavi, *The Rise and Fall of Israel's Bilateral Aid Budget, 1958–2008*, 41.

24 Judy Siegel-Itzkovich, "Is This Where Charity Ends?" *Jerusalem Post*, October 24, 2004.

25 "Map of IDF Delegations around the World," *IDF Blog*, www.idfblog.com/blog/2013/11/27/idfwithoutborders-map-idf-aid-delegations-around-world/. And for a detailed map of IDF aid missions around the world, please google #IDFWithoutBorders.

26 Avi Mayer, "Another Side of Israel: The Impact of Tikkun Olam," Jewish Policy Center, spring 2013, www.jewishpolicycenter.org/2013/02/28/israel-tikkun-olam/o.

27 Dov Maisel, author's phone interview, September 1, 2016.

28 Ruth Eglash, "A Light among the Nations," *Jerusalem Post*, May 7, 2008.

29 Dr. Dan Engelhard, author's phone interview, November 10, 2016. See also Eglash, "A Light among the Nations."

30 "A Drop of Hope in a Sea of Despair," CSPAN, January 13, 2014, www.c-span.org/video/ ?c4480721/ariel-bar-aipacab.

31 Viva Sarah Press, "WHO Ranks IDF Field Hospital as World's Best," Israel21c, November 14, 2016, https://www.israel21c.org/who-ranks-idf-field-hospital-as-worlds -best/-.

32 "Bill Clinton Hails Israel Relief Mission to Haiti," *Haaretz*, January 28, 2010, http:// www.haaretz.com/news/bill-clinton-hails-israel-relief-mission-to-haiti-1.262274-t.

33 As of November 2016. Judah Ari Gross, "UN Ranks IDF Emergency Medical Team as 'No. 1 in the World,'" *Times of Israel*, November 13, 2016, http://www.timesofisrael .com/un-ranks-idf-emergency-medical-team-as-no-1-in-the-world/t-.

34 Judah Ari Gross, "Masters of Disaster, IDF Field Hospital May Be Recognized as World's Best," *Times of Israel*, October 18, 2016, www.timesofisrael.com/masters -of-disaster-idf-field-hospital-may-be-recognized-as-worlds-bestrd.

35 "Israeli Humanitarian Relief: MASHAV-Israel's Agency for International Development Cooperation," Israel Ministry of Foreign Affairs, http://mfa.gov.il/MFA /ForeignPolicy/Aid/Pages/Israeli%20Humanitarian%20Relief-%20MASHAV%20 -%20the%20Israel%20F.aspx#countries. See also "Israel's Agency for International Development Cooperation," Embassy of Israel in China, http://embassies.gov.il /beijing-en/mashav/Pages/MASHAV.aspx/.

36 CSPAN, "A Drop of Hope in a Sea of Despair."

Chapter 3 – The Uber of Ambulances

1 Eli Beer, author's interview, Washington, DC, March 20, 2016.

2 TEDMED, "The Fastest Ambulance? A Motorcycle," April 2013, www.ted.com/talks /eli_beer_the_fastest_ambulance_a_motorcycle?language=en. See also Allison Josephs, "The Orthodox Man Who Saved a Life with His Yarmulke," Jew in the City, May 29, 2014, http://jewinthecity.com/2014/05/the-orthodox-man-who-saved-a -life-with-his-yarmulke; "Behind Israel's Fast Response to Medical Emergencies," *San Diego Jewish World*, April 6, 2014, www.sdjewishworld.com/2014/04/06/be hind-israels-fast-response-medical-emergencies; "Bus Bomb Toll: Six Dead, 19 Injured," Jewish Telegraphic Agency, June 5, 1978, www.jta.org/1978/06/05/arch ive/bus-bomb-toll-six-dead-19-injured; "Scattered Saviors," *Economist*, January 28, 2012, www.economist.com/node/21543488844.

3 TEDMED, "The Fastest Ambulance?" See also United Hatzalah, "Ambucycle Zooms into AIPAC 2015 Conference," March 1, 2015, www.youtube.com/watch?v=iYAolB 9lZfU; Josephs, "The Orthodox Man."

4 United Hatzalah, "Ambucycle Zooms." See also Josephs, "The Orthodox Man."

5 "Behind Israel's Fast Response to Medical Emergencies," *San Diego Jewish World*.

6 Eli Beer, author's interview, Washington, DC, March 20, 2016.

7 TEDMED, "The Fastest Ambulance?"

8 Greer Fay Cashman, "Rivlin Salutes First Responders as the 'Light in the Darkness,'" *Jerusalem Post*, December 8, 2015, www.jpost.com/Israel-News/Rivlin-salutes-first-responders-as-the-light-in-the-darkness-436641e.

9 "Six Minutes to Save a Life," *Harvard Health Publications*, January 2004, www.health .harvard.edu/press_releases/heart_attack_advicedt.

10 TEDMED, "The Fastest Ambulance?"

11 United Hatzalah, "Ambucycle Zooms." See also Josephs, "The Orthodox Man."

12 TEDMED, "The Fastest Ambulance?" See also Josephs, "The Orthodox Man."

13 United Hatzalah, "Ambucycle Zooms."

14 TEDMED, "The Fastest Ambulance?" See also United Hatzalah, "Ambucycle Zooms."

15 United Hatzalah, "Ambucycle Zooms."

16 Judy Siegel-Itzkovich, "Capital's Light Rail Survives First Simulated Terror Attack," *Jerusalem Post*, July 26, 2012.

17 Eli Beer, author's phone interview, May 31, 2016.

18 "Ministry of Health: United Hatzalah Authorized to Train Ambulance Drivers," United Hatzalah, https://israelrescue.org/detail.php?nid=176&m=p.

19 Judy Siegel-Itzkovich, "Ambucycle Zooms into AIPAC Conference," *Jerusalem Post*, March 3, 2015, www.jpost.com/Diaspora/Ambucycle-zooms-into-AIPAC -conference-392729. See also Judy Siegel-Itzkovich, "Opening Their Eyes," *Jerusalem Post*, December 20, 2015, www.jpost.com/Business-and-Innovation/Health-and -Science/Opening-their-eyes-437828; TEDMED, "The Fastest Ambulance?"

20 TEDMED, "The Fastest Ambulance?"

21 Eitan Arom and Erica Schachne, "Just an Ambucycle Ride Away," *Jerusalem Post*, January 2, 2015.

22 Dov Maisel, author's phone interview, June 1, 2016.

23 Peter Bloom, author's phone interview, May 23, 2016.

24 Dov Maisel, author's phone interview, June 1, 2016.

25 Siegel-Itzkovich, "Opening Their Eyes." See also Keren Ghitis, *Jerusalem SOS*, 2010, www.gaaal.com/films/jerusalem-sos. The "GPS" system is called the Life-Compass system, which was developed with NowForce. NowForce is an Israeli-headquartered company that was founded in 2008 (see the company website, www.nowforce.com).

26 Arom and Schachne, "Just an Ambucycle Ride Away."

27 Roland Huguenin, "Courage under Fire," *Magazine of the International Red Cross and Red Crescent Movement*, http://www.redcross.int/EN/mag/magazine2000 _4/Palestina.html; A. Harpaz, "United Hatzalah: Thirty Arab Volunteers from East Jerusalem Join the Organization with the Encouragement of the Organization's Senior Executives," *Actuality* [in Hebrew], October 24, 2009, www.actuality.co.il /articles/art.asp?ID=3684&SID=7&CID=14&MID=14. And for their part, the Palestinian Red Crescent Society have asked MDA to operate in the West Bank or

East Jerusalem. Tovah Lazaroff, "Int'l Red Cross Slams MDA for Operating in East Jerusalem, West Bank," *Jerusalem Post*, July 5, 2013, www.jpost.com/Diplomacy-and -Politics/Intl-Red-Cross-slams-MDA-for-operating-in-e-Jlem-West-Bank-318827.

28 See also Sam Sokol, "Fighting Together to Save Lives," *Jerusalem Post*, December 12, 2012.

29 Ghitis, *Jerusalem SOS*.

30 Muhammad Asli, author's phone interview, May 25, 2016.

31 Abigail Klein Leichman, "Peace Prize for Jewish and Muslim Leaders of United Hatzalah," Israel21c, July 24, 2014, www.israel21c.org/peace-prize-for-jewish-and -muslim-leaders-of-united-hatzalah/. See also Sokol, "Fighting Together"; Greer Fay Cashman, "United Hatzalah Leaders Receive Prize for Peace in the Mid East," *Jerusalem Post*, June 25, 2013, www.jpost.com/National-News/United-Hatzalah-le aders-receive-prize-for-peace-in-the-Mid-East-317610Eta.

32 Leichman, "Peace Prize." See also Sokol, "Fighting Together."

33 Muhammad Asli, author's phone interview, May 25, 2016.

34 Ibid.

35 TEDMED, "The Fastest Ambulance?"

36 Muhammad Asli, author's phone interview, May 25, 2016.

37 Siegel-Itzkovich, "Opening Their Eyes."

38 Muhammad Asli, author's phone interview, May 25, 2016.

39 United Hatzalah, "Eli Beer and Murad Alian Win Victor Goldberg Prize for Peace," July 2, 2013, www.youtube.com/watch?v=oj_oCDKTWlk. See also United Hatzalah, "IBA News in Arabic from Jerusalem," June 27, 2013, www.youtube.com/watch?v=4 MmN8QZn2WQ&feature=youtu.beuu.

40 Dov Maisel, author's phone interview, June 1, 2016. See also Dov Maisel, author's email exchange, January 3, 2017.

41 Judy Siegel-Itzkovich, "30 E. J'Lem Arabs Become Hatzalah Emergency Medics," *Jerusalem Post*, October 16, 2009.

42 TEDMED, "The Fastest Ambulance?"

43 Judy Siegel-Itzkovich, "Before the Ambulance Comes," *Jerusalem Post*, September 13, 2009.

44 TEDMED, "The Fastest Ambulance?"

45 United Hatzalah, "Eli Beer and Murad Alian Win Victor Goldberg Prize for Peace."

46 Mark Gerson, author's interview, New York, October 27, 2016.

47 Siegel-Itzkovich, "Ambucycle Zooms." See also Siegel-Itzkovich, "Opening Their Eyes"; "Eli Beer," Schwab Foundation for Social Entrepreneurship, www .schwabfound.org/content/eli-beere-.

48 Alan Dershowitz, author's email exchange, November 19, 2016.

49 "When Seconds Count," United Hatzalah, www.israelrescue.org/faqs.phpp.

50 Siegel-Itzkovich, "Before the Ambulance Comes."

51 There are only two places that have made serious headway in replicating the Israeli model: Jersey City, New Jersey, and Panama City, Panama. Other chapters that are

starting to duplicate the Israeli model include Australia, Argentina, Brazil, Bangladesh, Dubai, Ethiopia, Ghana, India, Lithuania, Mexico, Rwanda, United Kingdom, and Ukraine. Sometimes these organizations are called United Rescue. Dov Maisel, author's phone interview, June 1, 2016. See also Eli Beer, author's interview, Washington, DC, March 20, 2016; Siegel-Itzkovich, "Ambucycle Zooms"; Greer Fay Cashman, "The Ties That Bind," *Jerusalem Post*, May 30, 2014; United Hatzalah, "United Hatzalah's Partnership in Dubai," *Youtube*, July 19, 2015, www.youtube.com /watch?v=yJRmeya5SLw); United Hatzalah, "A Great Moment from Eli Beer's Visit with Panama's United Hatzalah Crew," *Youtube*, December 8, 2015, www.youtube .com/watch?v=57U7zuuV_lc_u.

52 Eli Beer, author's phone interview, May 31, 2016.

53 TEDMED, "The Fastest Ambulance?"

Chapter 4 – One Drop at a Time

1 "Inventors: Simcha Blass," Netafim.com, www.netafimlegacy.com/people. See also "CEOs: Uri Werber," Netafim.com, www.netafimlegacy.com/people; Sharon Udasin, "A Drip Revolution around the World," *Jerusalem Post*, April 22, 2015, www.jpost.com/Israel-News/A-drip-revolution-around-the-world-398660.

2 Naty Barak, author's interview, Kibbutz Hatzerim, July 5, 2015.

3 "Inventors: Simcha Blass," Netafim.com.

4 Alastair Bland, "Hiding in the Shallows," *Comstock's*, September 15, 2015, www .comstocksmag.com/longreads/hiding-shallowswa.

5 David Tidhar, *Encyclopedia of the Founders and Builders of Israel* [in Hebrew], vol. 7 (1956), 2945, www.tidhar.tourolib.org/tidhar/view/7/29459.

6 Ibid.

7 Maureen Gilmer, "Dry Land Thrives with Drip Irrigation: Systems Traced to Discovery in Arid Israel in 1960s," *Dayton Daily News*, May 7, 2015. See also Uri Drori, "Danny Retter: Co-Founder," https://vimeo.com/channels/netafim/420673787.

8 Alon Tal, *Pollution in a Promised Land: An Environmental History of Israel* (Berkeley: University of California Press, 2002), p. 228

9 Seth M. Siegel, *Let There Be Water* (New York: St. Martin's Press, 2015), 56.

10 Siegel, *Let There Be Water*, 58.

11 Gilmer, "Dry Land Thrives."

12 Yael Freund Avraham, "A Drop of Respect: Who Really Invented Drip Irrigation?" *Makor Rishon* [in Hebrew], June 7, 2015, www.nrg.co.il/online/1/ART2/698 /679.html..

13 Dr. V. Praveen Rao, "History of Irrigation," Netafim Legacy, www.netafimlegacy.com /exhibitions?history-of-irrigation. See also "The History of Drip Irrigation," Drip Depot, www.dripdepot.com/a/529cbef775eb51467e8c14000.

14 According to Netafim, drip irrigation is 30 percent more efficient than flooding; the combination of drip irrigation and fertigation (i.e., fertilization and irrigation

together) increases productivity up to 200 percent. Netafim, "7 Facts about Drip," January 25, 2015, www.youtube.com/watch?v=1R_1rjgVezEe.

15 Udasin, "A Drip Revolution."

16 "CEOs: Uri Werber," Netafim.com, www.netafimlegacy.com/people. See also "Simcha Blass," Netafim.com, www.netafimlegacy.com/peoplel.

17 "CEOs: Uri Werber," Netafim.com; Naty Barak, author's interview, Kibbutz Hatzerim, July 5, 2015.

18 Siegel, *Let There Be Water*, 60.

19 "CEOs: Uri Werber," Netafim.com.

20 Naty Barak, author's interview, Kibbutz Hatzerim, July 5, 2015.

21 Netafim, "The Evolving Story of Netafim and Drip Irrigation," May 27, 2012, www.youtube.com/watch?v=QAGlTooquR4R.

22 "Timeline: 1966," Netafim Legacy, www.netafimlegacy.com/timeline.

23 "Timeline: 1967," Netafim Legacy.

24 David Shamah, "What Israeli Drips Did for the World," *Jerusalem Post*, August 20, 2013, www.timesofisrael.com/what-israeli-drips-did-for-the-world.

25 "Founders: Oded Winkler," Netafim.com, www.netafimlegacy.com/people.

26 He filed the patent December 22, 1966, and it was issued on January 7, 1969. See USPTO patent number 3420064.

27 "CEOs: Avinoam ("Abie") Ron," Netafim.com, www.netafimlegacy.com/people.

28 Siegel, *Let There Be Water*, 62.

29 "CEOs: Uri Werber," Netafim.com.

30 Siegel, *Let There Be Water*, 63.

31 Diana Bkhor Nir, "Flowing," *Calcalist* [in Hebrew], March 19, 2015, http://tx.techn ion.ac.il/~presstech/newsletter/mehudar.pdfhr.

32 Bkhor Nir, "Flowing."

33 Ibid.

34 Udasin, "A Drip Revolution."

35 "Inventors: Rafi Mehoudar," Netafim.com.

36 Udasin, "A Drip Revolution."

37 According to the Food and Agricultural Organization (FAO) of the United Nations, the world population will increase from 6.9 billion people today to 9.1 billion in 2050. "The State of the World's Land and Water Resources," Food and Agriculture Organization of the United Nations, 2011, www.fao.org/docrep/017/i1688e/i1688e.pdf..

38 Lain Stewart, "How Can Our Blue Planet Be Running out of Fresh Water," BBC, www.bbc.co.uk/guides/z3qdd2p2.

39 In 2017, USAID's Famine Early Warning System Network, an initiative that tracks acute food insecurity around the world, revised its estimate of the maximum number of people requiring food aid from 70 million people to 81 million people. The new estimate is 20 percent higher than food assistance needed in 2016, and 70 percent higher than food assistance needed in 2015. This alarming increase in numbers comes despite the $2.2 billion the global community has committed to emergency

food security assistance to date. "Already Unprecedented Food Assistance Needs Grow Further; Risk of Famine Persists," Famine Early Warning Systems Network, June 21, 2017, www.fews.net/global/alert/june-20170e.

40 Seth M. Siegel, author's email exchange, October 29, 2016.

41 Arin Kerstein, "The Impact of Drip Irrigation: 'More Crop per Drop,'" *Borgen Magazine*, July 20, 2015, www.borgenmagazine.com/impact-drip-irrigation-crop-per -drop. See also Associated Press, "Farms Waste Much of World's Water," March 19, 2006, www.wired.com/2006/03/farms-waste-much-of-worlds-water; Netafim, "Netafim Corporate Image Video," December 19, 2012, www.youtube.com/watch ?v=IGHFdsDVLDgDs.

42 Oded Distel, author's email exchange, November 16, 2016.

43 Naty Barak, author's interview, Kibbutz Hatzerim, July 5, 2015.

44 David Shamah, "Israel's Drip Irrigation Pioneer Says His Tech Feeds a Billion People," *Times of Israel*, April 21, 2015, www.timesofisrael.com/israels-drip-irrigation-pione er-our-tech-feeds-a-billion-people-e.

Chapter 5 – Real Iron Men

1 Aharon Lapidot, "The Gray Matter behind the Iron Dome," *Israel Hayom*, February 23, 2012, www.israelhayom.com/site/newsletter_article.php?id=6509. See also Charles Levinson and Adam Entous, "Israel's Iron Dome Defense Battled to Get off Ground," *Wall Street Journal*, November 26, 2012, https://www.wsj.com/articles /SB10001424127887324712504578136931078468210. Gold headed the Ministry of Defense's Administration for the Development of Weapons and Technological Infrastructure.

2 Lapidot, "The Gray Matter."

3 Levinson and Entous, "Israel's Iron Dome Defense." See also Bill Robertson, "Israel's Iconic Iron Dome: General Danny Gold, Father," *Huffington Post*, December 4, 2015, www.huffingtonpost.com/billrobinson/israels-iron-dome-by-gene_b_8411436 .html6_.

4 Abigail Klein Leichman, "The Maverick Thinker behind Iron Dome," Israel21c, August 3, 2014, https://www.israel21c.org/the-maverick-thinker-behind-iron-dome/h.

5 Uzi Rubin, "Hezbollah's Rocket Campaign against Northern Israel: A Preliminary Report," *Jerusalem Center for Public Affairs* 6, no. 10 (August 31, 2006), www.jcpa.org/brief/brief006–10.htm..

6 Chanoch Levine, author's interview, Washington, DC, May 27, 2016.

7 Ibid.

8 Ibid.

9 "Middle East Crisis: Facts and Figures," BBC, August 31, 2006, http://news.bbc.co.uk /2/hi/middle_east/5257128.stm85.

10 "Recovery and Reconstruction Facts," Presidency of the Council of Ministers – Higher Relief Council, https://web.archive.org/web/20071227165718/ http://www .lebanonundersiege.gov.lb/english/F/Main/index.aspn?.

11 Chanoch Levine, author's interview, Washington, DC, May 27, 2016.

12 Ibid. Other companies proposed creating laser systems, among other things.

13 Levinson and Entous, "Israel's Iron Dome Defense."

14 Chanoch Levine, author's email exchange, June 27, 2016.

15 Lapidot, "The Gray Matter."

16 Ibid. See also Stewart Ain, "Iron Dome Ready for Future," *Jewish Week*, February 9, 2015, www.thejewishweek.com/features/jw-qa/iron-dome-ready-futuref.

17 "Dedication, Zionism, and a Few Pieces from Toys R Us: An Interview with the Team That Oversees the Iron Dome, All the Members of Which Are Graduates of the Technion, and the Secret of the Project's Success," *Hayadan* [in Hebrew], July 9, 2014, www.hayadan.org.il/interview-iron-dome-rp09071417.

18 Chanoch Levine, author's interview, Washington, DC, May 27, 2016.

19 Ibid.

20 *Hayadan*, "Dedication, Zionism, and a Few Pieces from Toys R Us."

21 Because "Colonel Chico" is still in the military, Mr. Levine preferred to keep his last name anonymous. Chanoch Levine, author's interview, Washington, DC, May 27, 2016.

22 Yael Livnat, "One Year after the First Iron Dome Interception: Success, Thanks to the Warriors" [in Hebrew], Israel Defense Forces, April 5, 2012, accessed September 3, 2016.

23 *Hayadan*, "Dedication, Zionism, and a Few Pieces from Toys R Us."

24 Levinson and Entous, "Israel's Iron Dome Defense."

25 Ibid.

26 Chanoch Levine, author's interview, Washington, DC, May 27, 2016.

27 Chanoch Levine, author's email exchange, June 27, 2016.

28 Chanoch Levine, author's interview, Washington, DC, May 27, 2016.

29 Ibid.

30 Ibid.

31 "Brig. Gen. (Res.) Dr. Danny Gold went against Defense Ministry directive 20.02 when he decided in August 2005 to develop the anti-missile defense system Iron Dome, to set a timetable for this development and ordered a 'telescopic acceleration' of the project," accused Lindenstrauss. "[These steps], which are not under the authority of the Administration for the Development of Weapons and Technological Infrastructure... were, in this instance, under the authority of the IDF chief of general staff, the defense minister and the government of Israel." See Lapidot, "The Gray Matter."

32 Ben Hartman, "Iron Dome Doesn't Answer Threats," *Jerusalem Post*, May 9, 2010, www.jpost.com/Israel/Iron-Dome-doesnt-answer-threatsr.

33 Chanoch Levine, author's interview, Washington, DC, May 27, 2016. See also Yuval Azulai, "Eight Facts about Iron Dome," *Globes* (Israel), October 7, 2014, www.globes .co.il/en/article-everything-you-wanted-to-know-about-iron-dome-1000953706. Many have compared the Raytheon Patriot missile system – used extensively in

the First Gulf War to counter Saddam Hussein's Scud missiles – to the Iron Dome. But while the two share the same mission, they have key differences. First, a single Patriot missile reportedly costs more than $2 million, and the Tamir missile costs about $75 thousand.

34 Reuters, "Obama Seeks $205 Million for Israel Rocket Shield," May 14, 2010, http:// www.reuters.com/article/us-israel-usa-irondome/obama-seeks-205-million-for -israel-rocket-shield-idUSTRE64C5JO20100513. In total, US investment in Iron Dome production since fiscal year 2011 has been over $1 billion. See "Department of Defense Appropriations Bill, 2015," United States Senate, July 17, 2014, www.gpo .gov/fdsys/pkg/CRPT-113srpt211/html/CRPT-113srpt211.htm11.

35 Aviv Ezra, author's email exchange, July 5, 2016.

36 Leichman, "The Maverick Thinker." See also Lapidot, "The Gray Matter."

37 Within three days of the original hit, Israel had managed to knock eight more Hamas rockets out of the sky. Lapidot, "The Gray Matter." See also Lazar Berman, "Israel's Iron Dome: Why America Is Investing Hundreds of Millions of Dollars," American Enterprise Institute, September 24, 2012, http://www.aei.org/publication/israels- iron-dome-why-america-is-investing-hundreds-of-millions-of-dollars/; Anshel Pfeffer and Yanir Yagna, "Iron Dome Successfully Intercepts Gaza Rocket for the First Time," *Haaretz*, April 7, 2011, www.haaretz.com/israel-news/iron-dome- successfully-intercepts-gaza-rocket-for-first-time-1.354696.

38 Yair Ramati, author's phone interview, March 2, 2016.

39 Dusco25, "Iron Dome Intercepts Rockets from Gaza during Wedding 11–14–2012," November 15, 2015, www.youtube.com/watch?v=2M-BQtp4WwwW.

40 Michael Oren, author's phone interview, January 8, 2017.

41 Dennis Ross, author's interview, Washington, DC, January 6, 2017.

42 Ain, "Iron Dome Ready for Future."

43 "Iron Dome Developers Named as Israel Defense Prize Recipients," Israel Defense Forces, June 25, 2012, www.idf.il/1283–16384-en/Dover.aspx..

44 Leichman, "The Maverick Thinker."

45 Ibid.

Chapter 6 – Modern-Day Joseph

1 Shlomo Navarro, author's email exchange, December 24–26, 2015.

2 Laurence Simon, author's phone interview, October 29, 2015.

3 "Montreal Protocol on Substances That Deplete the Ozone Layer," United Nations Environment Programme, January 1, 1989, http://ozone.unep.org/en/treaties-and- decisions/montreal-protocol-substances-deplete-ozone-layer. See also Laurence Simon, author's phone interview, October 29, 2015.

4 Caspar van Vark, "No More Rotten Crops: Six Smart Inventions to Prevent Har- vest Loss," *Guardian* (UK), October 27, 2014, www.theguardian.com/global -development-professionals-network/2014/oct/27/farming-post-harvest-loss -solutions-developing-worldoi.

5 Shlomo Navarro, author's email exchange, December 24–26, 2015. See also Shlomo Navarro, author's interview, Rehovot, June 25, 2015.

6 Laurence Simon, author's phone interview, October 29, 2015.

7 "2015 World Hunger and Poverty Facts and Statistics," World Hunger Education Service, www.worldhunger.org/articles/Learn/world%20hunger%20facts%202002 .htm2%.

8 "Save Food: Global Initiative on Food Loss and Waste Reduction," Food and Agriculture Organization of the United Nations, www.fao.org/save-food/resources /keyfindings/en/i.

9 "E! 3747 IPM-RICE," Eureka Network, March 16, 2011, www.eurekanetwork.org /content/e-3747-ipm-ricei.

10 Because he was an Israeli government employee, Navarro could only legally receive a small, symbolic amount of stock and a consulting role within the company. Simon meanwhile became chairman of the board, and the Volcani Center (the Agricultural Research Organization) received all the royalties from the company's patents.

11 "GrainPro: About the Company," GrainPro.com, www.grainpro.com/index.php /layout/company/profile. A geo map detailing the specific locations can be found at "GrainPro: Global Cocoon Locations," http://gpmap.grainpro.com/gpimap /index.phppe.

12 "Israeli Agro Expert Offers Farmers Bug-Free Solutions," Xinhua News Agency, November 29, 2011, www.soyatech.com/news_story.php?id=262172.

13 Martin Gummert, author's phone interview, November 17, 2015.

14 Shlomo Navarro, author's phone interview, December 16–17, 2015. See also Shlomo Navarro, Seventieth Birthday Book, 2010, unpublished manuscript.

15 Shlomo Navarro, author's phone interview, December 16–17, 2015. See also Navarro, Seventieth Birthday Book.

16 Navarro, Seventieth Birthday Book.

17 Shlomo Navarro, LinkedIn page, retrieved March 8, 2016.

18 Navarro, Seventieth Birthday Book.

19 Shlomo Navarro, author's email exchange December 16–17, 2015. See also Navarro, Seventieth Birthday Book.

20 Laurence Simon, author's phone interview, October 29, 2015.

21 "Studies on the effect of alterations in pressure and composition of atmospheric gases on the tropical warehouse moth, Ephestia cautella (Wlk.), as a model for stored-product insect pests," PhD thesis submitted to the Senate of Hebrew University, Jerusalem (1974).

22 Shlomo Navarro, author's phone interview, December 16–17, 2015.

23 Ibid.

24 Ibid.

25 Ibid.

26 For twenty years, these trenches held thirty to sixty thousand tons of grain, which the country sold on the market depending on supply, demand, and rainfall. But

starting in 2000, Israel decided to no longer store any strategic grain reserves – the US made a similar decision in 2008. The vast majority of Israel's domestic cereals consumption, about 1.5 million tons annually, is imported from abroad. Once the cereal industry was privatized in Israel, and in an effort to streamline business, excess grain was no longer stored for long periods of time to cut cost – only what is necessary for the market is bought and immediately stored. It is also worth noting that Australia, Argentina, Brazil, Cyprus, Jordan, Turkey, and the United States have all successfully utilized Israeli bunker technology. Frederick Kaufman, "How to Fight a Food Crisis," *Los Angeles Times*, September 21, 2012, http://articles.latimes.com/2012/sep/21/opinion/la-oe-kaufman-food-hunger-drought-20120921. See also Francisco Cayol, "Argentine Bunker Silo Dry Storage Grain," January 23, 2011, www.youtube.com/watch?v=6muQXBL hRJ8); P. Villers, S. Navarro, and T. de Bruin, "New Applications of Hermetic Storage for Grain Storage and Transport," GrainPro, June 2010, grainpro.com /gpi/images/PDF/Commodity/NewApplicationsOfHermeticStorage4Grain Storage_Compressed_PU2044PV0310–3C.pdf; "Bunker Storage Technology," Food Technology Information Center, http://ftic.co.il/Bunker%20Storage-en.php; Shlomo Navarro, author's phone interview, December 16–17, 2015.

27 Laurence Simon, author's phone interview, October 29, 2015. See also Laurence Simon, author's phone interview, December 16, 2015.

28 Shlomo Navarro, author's phone interview, December 16–17, 2015.

29 Laurence Simon, author's phone interview, October 29, 2015. See also Laurence Simon, author's phone interview, December 16, 2015.

30 Bella English, "For Phil Villers, Helping Feed the World Is in the Bag," *Boston Globe*, December 17, 2013, www.bostonglobe.com/lifestyle/2013/12/17/concord-based -company-aims-help-alleviate-world-hunger/aIGEHu8DbD3nI2yViuiABP/sto ry.html. And according to Tom de Bruin, the CEO of GrainPro's wholly owned subsidiary in the Philippines, the company is now focusing on three segments of the market. The first is storage. Government agencies, particularly in Africa, are buying the cocoons to stave off potential famine, ensure food security, and prevent significant price fluctuations. The company is also focusing on coffee and cocoa bean storage using a smaller product, called the SuperGrain bag, which can hold up to 150 pounds. This product is attractive to private farmers who don't have a need for or want to spend money on large cocoons. The third segment is the organic market.

31 "GrainPro: Order Form," GrainPro.com, http://shop.grainpro.com.

32 Maria Otília Carvalho, author's phone interview, January 7, 2016.

33 And Gummert, the IRRI researcher, says another hurdle is that the bag system takes much more time and effort than storing grain in silos, which is the preferred method in developed countries. Martin Gummert, author's phone interview, November 17, 2015. See also Laurence Simon, author's phone interview, October 29, 2015.

34 Stephen Daniels, "US Organic Food Market to Grow 14% from 2013–2018," *Food*

Navigator, January 3, 2014, www.foodnavigator-usa.com/Markets/US-organic-food
-market-to-grow-14-from-2013-18.

35 Shlomo Navarro, author's email exchange, December 24–26, 2015. See also Laurence
Simon, author's phone interviews, October 29, 2015, and December 16, 2015.

36 Shlomo Navarro, author's phone interview, December 16–17, 2015.

37 It is clear that large parts of the developing world and an increasing number of farmers
are relying on hermetic storage technology. In Rwanda, for example, post-harvest
losses of maize and rice fell in 2013 from 32 percent to 9.2 percent and 25 percent to
15.2 percent, respectively. "Post Harvest Handeling and Storage Task Force," Rwandan Ministry of Agriculture and Animal Resources, www.minagri.gov.rw/index
.php?id=571. In Rwanda's Kabarore district, famers gained a 40 percent increase
in profit because they were able to store grain for at least four months. As more
farmers adopt this technology, their post-harvest losses will be reduced and net
profits will increase. See "Hermetic Storage a Viable Option," *New Agriculturist,*
January 2008, www.new-ag.info/en/developments/devItem.php?a=349a..

38 Gadi Loebenstein, author's phone interview, December 7, 2016.

Chapter 7 – The Fourth Day

1 "Solar Energy Water Heating System Monitoring," Adventech.com, September 2013,
http://www2.advantech.com/EDM/e1bd89e4-c89a-2497-db18-0e7c3915cf5e/ap
pstory02ga.html?utm_source=eCampaign&utm_medium=E_mail&utm_campa
ign=Advantech%20September%202013%20iAutomation%20Link%20(GA%20Ver
sio)_1-0&CampId=a7133440cd&UID=rt2.

2 "A Thriving Green Economy," *Ynet* [in Hebrew], December 15, 2015, http://www.yn
et.co.il/articles/0,7340,L-4739893,00.html09-.

3 Harry Zvi Tabor, "Answers to a Journalist's Questions," Zvi Tabor Private Collection, January 1996.

4 Harry Zvi Tabor, *Selected Reprints of Papers by Harry Zvi Tabor, Solar Energy Pioneer* (Rehovot: Balaban Publishers and International Solar Energy Society, 1999),
ix.

5 He served in this position from 1945 to 1948. See "Sambursky, Samuel," Jewish Virtual Library, https://www.jewishvirtuallibrary.org/jsource
/judaica/ejud_0002_0017_0_17390.html0_.

6 Ehud Zion Waldoks, "Bright Ideas," *Jerusalem Post,* October 1, 2008, http://www.jp
ost.com/Features/Bright-idease-g.

7 Waldoks, "Bright Ideas."

8 *Ynet,* "A Thriving Green Economy."

9 Harry Zvi Tabor, "Answers to a Journalist's Questions," Zvi Tabor Private Collection, January 1996. See also Abigail Klein Leichman, "A Lifetime in Solar Energy,"
Israel21c, May 5, 2009, http://www.israel21c.org/a-lifetime-in-solar-energy/r.

10 Waldoks, "Bright Ideas."

11 Paul Sánchez Keighley, "96-Year-Old Solar Energy Genius Harry Zvi Tabor Talks

to NoCamels about Pioneering Solar Power," NoCamels, August 13, 2006, http://nocamels.com/2013/08/96-year-old-solar-energy-genius-harry-zvi-tabor-talks-to-nocamels-about-pioneering-solar-power/. See also "A Center of Exactness Has Been Established in the Israeli Physics Lab," *Mishmar* [in Hebrew], January 4, 1953, http://goo.gl/jLc83w3.

12 *Ynet*, "A Thriving Green Economy."

13 Leichman, "A Lifetime in Solar Energy." See also John Perlin, *Let It Shine: The 6000 Year Story of Solar Energy* (2013), http://john-perlin.com/let-it-shine.htmlhi.

14 Perlin, *Let It Shine.*

15 John Perlin, "Solar Thermal," California Solar Center, http://californiasolarcenter.org/history-solarthermal//a.

16 "A Brief History of the American Solar Water Heating Industry," Contractors Institute.com, http://www.contractorsinstitute.com/downloads/Solar/Contractors' %20Domestic%20Hot%20Water%20Educational%20PDF's/History%20of %20SDHW.pdf. See also http://www.google.com/patents/US45138485.

17 John Perlin, "Solar Thermal."

18 Cutler J. Cleveland, *Concise Encyclopedia of the History of Energy* (San Diego: Elsevier, 2009), 270.

19 Waldoks, "Bright Ideas."

20 Ibid.

21 Leichman, "A Lifetime in Solar Energy."

22 "Weizmann Prize Winners for 1956," *Davar* [in Hebrew], July 20, 1956, http://goo.gl/XzQiBq.

23 "Black Brings Light," *Davar* [in Hebrew], July 26, 1961, http://goo.gl/fwIZqc.

24 Harry Zvi Tabor, author's interview, Jerusalem, July 16, 2015.

25 "Why Do Users of the *Dud Shemesh* Get Special Electric Meters?" *Ma'ariv* [in Hebrew], January 1, 1960, http://goo.gl/8HWWEJ.

26 *Ynet*, "A Thriving Green Economy."

27 "The Opposition to Installing the *Dud Shemesh* in the Workers Housing Union's Apartments," *Davar* [in Hebrew], May 27, 1971, http://goo.gl/VPCs6I.

28 *Ynet*, "A Thriving Green Economy."

29 Rhonda Winter, "Israel's Special Relationship with the Solar Water Heater," Reuters, March 18, 2011, www.reuters.com/article/idUS311612153620110318S.

30 Amit Shafrir, author's email exchange, January 11, 2017.

31 Dr. Yaniv Ronen, "The Possibility of Installing the *Dud Shemesh* in Tall Buildings above Nine Floors" [in Hebrew], The Knesset's Research and Information Center, November 29, 2012, 2, http://www.knesset.gov.il/mmm/data/pdf/m03028.pdf8.

32 Abraham Kribus, author's phone interview, June 27, 2016.

33 *Ynet*, "A Thriving Green Economy."

34 Waldoks, "Bright Ideas." See also Merav Ankori, "Solar Power unto the Nations," *Globes*, October 28, 2007.

35 Tabor, *Selected Reprints*, iii.

36 Abraham Kribus, author's phone interview, June 27, 2016.

37 Sharon Udasin, "Zvi Tabor, Solar Pioneer, Dies at 98," *Jerusalem Post*, December 17, 2015, http://www.jpost.com/Israel-News/Zvi-Tabor-solar-pioneer-dies-at -98–4375639e.

38 Ibid.

39 Shimon Peres, Facebook, December 15, 2015.

Chapter 8 – *The Lame Shall Walk*

1 Ari Libsker, "An Invention with Legs" (Hebrew), *Calcalist* (Israel), August 5, 2010, www.calcalist.co.il/local/articles/0,7340,L-3413629,00.htmlo.

2 Ibid.

3 Ibid. See also Issie Lapowsky, "This Computerized Exoskeleton Could Help Millions of People Walk Again," *Wired*, July 22, 2014, www.wired.com/2014/07/rewalkle.

4 Libsker, "An Invention with Legs."

5 Amit Goffer, author's interview, ReWalk Office, Yokneam, June 5, 2015.

6 Lapowsky, "This Computerized Exoskeleton."

7 Libsker, "An Invention with Legs."

8 Goffer, author's interview, June 5, 2015.

9 Christina Symanski, "Shitty Day," *Life; Paralyzed*, March 8, 2011, http://lifepara lyzed.blogspot.com/2011/03/shitty-day.html-i..

10 Libsker, "An Invention with Legs."

11 Lapowsky, "This Computerized Exoskeleton."

12 Goffer, author's interview, June 5, 2015.

13 Ibid. See also Libsker, "An Invention with Legs."

14 Goffer, author's interview, June 5, 2015.

15 Ibid.

16 Dr. Bonita Sawatzky, "Wheeling in a New Millennium: The History of the Wheelchair and the Driving Force of the Wheelchair Design of Today," www.wheelc hairnet.org/wcn_wcu/slidelectures/sawatzky/wc_history.htmlhye.

17 Interestingly, Dean Kamen went on to create the Segway. See Bill Sobel, "Segway Inventor Dean Kamen: Science Isn't a Spectator Sport," *CMS Wire*, January 6, 2015, www.cmswire.com/cms/customer-experience/segway-inventor-dean-kamen-science-isnt-a-spectator-sport-027638.php-a-.

18 Lauri Wantanbe, "Independence Technology Discontinues the iBOT," *Mobility Management*, February 1, 2009, https://mobilitymgmt.com/Articles/2009/02 /01/Independence-Technology-Discontinues-the-iBOT.aspxB-n.

19 Goffer earned his BA from the Technion, his MS from Tel Aviv University, and his PhD from Drexel University.

20 Adam Robinson, "The History of Robotics in Manufacturing," *Cerasis*, October 6, 2014, http://cerasis.com/2014/10/06/robotics-in-manufacturing/r.

21 Goffer, author's interview, June 5, 2015.

22 Libsker, "An Invention with Legs."

23 Goffer, author's interview, June 5, 2015.

24 Ibid.

25 Ibid.

26 Ibid.

27 Ibid.

28 Dr. Ann Spungen, author's phone interview, November 10, 2015.

29 Ibid.

30 Ibid.

31 Ibid.

32 Nilufer Atik, "Claire Lomas' Inspiring Story: My Life Has Been Amazing since I Was Paralyzed," *Mirror* (UK), May 10, 2013, www.mirror.co.uk/news/real-life-sto ries/claire-lomas-inspiring-story-life-1879107. See also Bianca London, "Paralyzed Marathon Heroine Claire Lomas: 'Things Go Wrong in Life but You Have to Fight Back," *Daily Mail* (UK), May 16, 2013, www.dailymail.co.uk/femail/article-23254 63/Paralysed-Marathon-heroine-Claire-Lomas-Things-wrong-life-fight-make-lu ck.html; "Fundraiser Claire Lomas to Set on Her Next Big Challenge from Nottingham Trent University," Nottingham Trent University, April 22, 2013, www.ntu .ac.uk/apps/news/137066–8/Fundraiser_Claire_Lomas_to_set_off_on_her_ne xt_big_challenge_from_Nottingha.aspxm_e.

33 "'Bionic' Claire Lomas Trained for London Marathon in East Yorkshire," *Hull Daily Mail* (UK), May 10, 2012, www.hulldailymail.co.uk/Bionic-Claire-Lomas-trained -London-Marathon-East/story-16040411-detail/story.html/1.

34 Ibid.

35 Chris Wickham, "'Bionic Woman' Claire Lomas Is First Woman to Take Robotic Suit Home," *Independent* (UK), September 4, 2012, www.independent.co.uk/news /science/bionic-woman-claire-lomas-is-first-woman-to-take-robotic-suit-home -8104838.html.

36 *Hull Daily Mail*, "'Bionic' Claire Lomas."

37 "IPO Preview," Seeking Alpha, September 12, 2014, http://seekingalpha.com/article /2489765-ipo-preview-rewalk-roboticso.

38 Wickham, "'Bionic Woman' Claire Lomas."

39 Ted Greenwald, "Ekso's Exoskeletons Let Paraplegics Walk, Will Anyone Actually Wear One?" *Fast Company*, March 19, 2012, www.fastcompany.com/1822791/eksos -exoskeletons-let-paraplegics-walk-will-anyone-actually-wear-onewt.

40 Dr. Ann Spungen, author's phone interview, November 10, 2015.

41 Dr. Arun Jayaraman, author's phone interview, October 15, 2015.

42 Adario Strange, "FDA Approved First Robotic Exoskeleton for Paralyzed Users," June 30, 2014, http://mashable.com/2014/06/30/fda-approves-robotic-exoskeleton-p aralyzed-ReWalk/#FUfHo81qRgqIHWy.

43 Shane McGlaun, "ReWalk Robotic Exoskeletons Let Paraplegics Walk Again," Technabob, May 3, 2012, http://technabob.com/blog/2012/05/03/ReWalk-robotic -exoskeletonsl.

44 Dr. Zev Rymer, author's phone interview, October 4, 2015.

45 "What Is Rewalk?" Einstein Health Care Network, https://382.thankyou4caring.org/page.aspx?pid=374=?.

46 A. Esquenazi, M. Talaty, A. Packel, and M. Saulino, "The ReWalk Powered Exoskeleton to Restore Ambulatory Function to Individuals with Thoracic-Level Motor-Complete Spinal Cord Injury," National Center for Biotechnology Information, November 2012, https://www.ncbi.nlm.nih.gov/pubmed/230857035/.

47 Einstein Health Care Network, "What Is Rewalk?"

48 Hiawatha Bray, "ReWalk Exoskeleton Puts the Disabled Back on Their Feet," *Boston Globe*, July 7, 2014, www.bostonglobe.com/business/2014/07/06/putting-disabled-back-their-feet/8gFcM33JyTuL92J2kReDeI/story.htmls2.

49 Dr. Arun Jayaraman, author's phone interview, October 15, 2015.

50 Danny Deutch, "The Israeli Innovation That Has Changed the Lives of the Disabled" [in Hebrew], Arutz 2 (Israel), March 15, 2013, http://www.mako.co.il/news-israel/health/Article-3e947df9a7f6d31004.htmo7.

51 Ibid.

52 Ibid.

53 The 700 Club, "Made in Israel – Medicine," September 5, 2013, www.youtube.com/watch?time_continue=482&v=20Zfk8uQXakf&.

54 Deutch, "The Israeli Innovation."

55 David Shamah, "ReWalk's Benefits Go beyond Ambulation, Company Says," *Times of Israel*, May 20, 2015, www.timesofisrael.com/ReWalks-benefits-go-beyond-ambulation-company-says-0.

56 Jennifer L. Schenker, "Driven to Success: Amit Goffer's Quest to Hold His Head High," Informilo, September 7, 2015, www.informilo.com/2015/09/driven-to-success-amit-goffers-quest-to-hold-his-head-highhs.

Chapter 9 – GPS for the Brain

1 "Evergreen Is Changing Lives with Expert Deep Brain Stimulation Programming," Macmillan, May 26, 2010, http://macmillan.articlealley.com/dbs-programming-deep-brain-stimulation-programming-1568730.html3.

2 "Clinical Programs," University of California San Francisco, http://neurosurgery.ucsf.edu/index.php/movement_disorders_parkinsons.html#how_surgery_mo.

3 TAUVOD, "Alpha Omega – The Journey," December 4, 2011, www.youtube.com/watch?v=hTauLLZnUTQTZu.

4 The US Food and Drug Administration approved DBS as a treatment for essential tremor in 1997, Parkinson's in 2002, dystonia in 2003, and OCD in 2009.

5 Hagai Bergman, author's phone interview, January 1, 2016.

6 Vittorio A. Sironi, "Origin and Evolution of Deep Brain Stimulation," *Front Integrated Neuroscience* 5, no. 42 (2011), www.ncbi.nlm.nih.gov/pmc/articles/PMC315783 17Mea.

7 Imad Younis, author's interview, Nazareth, June 23, 2015. See also Tani Goldstein,

"Arab High-Tech Blooming in Galilee," *Ynet*, April 21, 2011, www.ynetnews.com/ar
ticles/0,7340,L-4057013,00.html35..

8 Reem Younis, author's interview, Washington, DC, February 29, 2016.

9 Imad Younis, author's interview, Nazareth, June 23, 2015.

10 Reem Younis, author's interview, Washington, DC, February 29, 2016. See also Avi-
gayil Kadesh, "Unique Neuroscience Tools Developed in Nazareth," Israel Ministry of Foreign Affairs, January 12, 2014, http://mfa.gov.il/MFA/InnovativeIsrael
/ScienceTech/Pages/Neuroscience-tool-company-12-January-20140112–5841.aspx.
See also Drake Bennett, "What It's Like to Be an Arab Entrepreneur in a Divided
Israel," Bloomberg, November 26, 2014, www.bloomberg.com/bw/articles/2014
–11–26/what-its-like-to-run-an-arab-tech-startup-in-israel#pp.

11 TAUVOD, "Alpha Omega – The Journey."

12 Imad Younis, author's interview, Nazareth, June 23, 2015.

13 Hagai Bergman, author's phone interview, January 1, 2016.

14 Ibid.

15 Imad Younis, author's interview, Nazareth, June 23, 2015. See also Reem Younis,
author's interview, Latrun, July 17, 2015; Bennett, "What It's Like." Orthodox Christians celebrate Christmas Day on or near January 7, following the Julian calendar,
which predates the commonly observed Gregorian calendar.

16 Hagai Bergman, author's phone interview, January 1, 2016.

17 H. Bergman, T. Wichmann, and M.R. DeLong, "Reversal of Experimental Parkinsonism by Lesions of the Subthalamic Nucleus," *Science* 249 (1990): 1436–1438,
https://www.ncbi.nlm.nih.gov/pubmed/24026382.

18 Israel, "Alpha Omega: The Largest Arab Israeli Hi Tech Company," October 29, 2013,
www.youtube.com/watch?v=fAvWODm3uaEa.

19 Reem Younis, author's interview, Washington, DC, February 29, 2016. See also TAU-
VOD, "Alpha Omega – The Journey."

20 Hagai Bergman, author's phone interview, January 1, 2016.

21 Alim-Louis Benabid, author's phone interview, January 12, 2016. See also "History of
Deep Brain Stimulation," The Parkinson's Appeal, http://www.parkinsonsappeal
.com/dbs/dbshistory.htmlty.

22 Alim-Louis Benabid, author's phone interview, January 12, 2016.

23 Reem Younis, author's interview, Washington, DC. See also TAUVOD, "Alpha Omega –
The Journey."

24 Abigail Klein Leichman, "GPS for Brain Surgeons," Israel21c, January 7, 2013, www
.israel21c.org/health/gps-for-brain-surgeonse-.

25 Orr Hirschauge, "Israeli Tech Needs to Be More Inclusive, Says Yossi Vardi," *Wall
Street Journal*, September 11, 2014, http://blogs.wsj.com/digits/2014/09/11/israeli-
tech-needs-to-be-more-inclusive-says-yossi-vardi/y.

26 Ken Shuttleworth, "Biblical Nazareth Goes High-Tech Thanks to Arab Push," *USA
Today*, February 20, 2015, www.usatoday.com/story/tech/2015/02/18/nazareth-
tech-sector/224595032.

27 "The Unit," *Forbes*, February 8, 2007, www.forbes.com/2007/02/07/israel-military -unit-ventures-biz-cx_gk_0208israel.htmls.

28 Organizations include the Technion; the Israeli Employment Service; the ORT Braude College of Engineering; Tsofen, a nonprofit that integrates Israel's Arab citizens into the high-tech industry; the New Israel Fund; Breaking the Impasse (BTI), whose members are prominent Palestinian and Israeli businesspeople and civil society committed to a peaceful resolution of the Israeli-Palestinian conflict through a two-state solution; and Kav Mashve, which encourages Arab high school students to study engineering and helps Arab college graduates to find employment in high-tech companies. Reem Younis, author's interview, Latrun, July 17, 2015.

29 Judith Sudilovsky, "Arabs Make Gains in Joining Israel's High-Growth, High-Tech Industries," Catholic News Service, January 7, 2013.

30 Goldstein, "Arab High-Tech Blooming."

31 Ibid.

32 President Reuven Rivlin, author's email exchange, January 1, 2017.

33 "Alpha Omega: The Largest Arab Israeli Hi Tech Company," October 29, 2013, www.youtube.com/watch?v=fAvWODm3uaEa.

34 Ibid.

35 Goldstein, "Arab High-Tech Blooming."

36 Leichman, "GPS for Brain Surgeons."

37 Ibid.

38 Israel Brain Technologies, "A Spotlight on the Israeli NeuroTech Industry," November 7, 2013, www.youtube.com/watch?v=mo5qvZftpsw. See also Conexx, "2011 Professional Seminar: Imad Younis, CEO Alpha Omega," 2011, https://vimeo.com /282117242.

39 Goldstein, "Arab High-Tech Blooming."

40 Hagai Bergman, author's phone interview, January 1, 2016.

41 Imad Younis, author's interview, Nazareth, June 23, 2015.

42 Hagai Bergman, author's phone interview, January 1, 2016.

43 TAUVOD, "Alpha Omega – The Journey."

Chapter 10 – Golden Firewall

 1 "Rocket Kitten: A Campaign with 9 Lives," *Check Point Blog*, November 9, 2015, https:// blog.checkpoint.com/wp-content/uploads/2015/11/rocket-kitten-report.pdf. See also David Sanger and Nicole Perlroth, "Iranian Hackers Attack State Department via Social Media Accounts," *New York Times*, November 24, 2015, https://www.ny times.com/2015/11/25/world/middleeast/iran-hackers-cyberespionage-state-depa rtment-social-media.html-ee-.

 2 "Rocket Kitten: A Campaign with 9 Lives." See also David Shamah, "Bumbling Iran Hackers Target Israelis, Saudis . . . Badly, Report Shows," *Times of Israel*, November 10, 2015, www.timesofisrael.com/bumbling-iran-hackers-target-israelis-saudis-bad ly-report-shows/; "Iran Said to Hack Former Israeli Army Chief-of-Staff, Access

His Entire Computer," *Times of Israel*, February 9, 2016, www.timesofisrael.com /iran-said-to-hack-former-israeli-army-chief-of-staff-access-his-entire-computer; "Israeli Generals Said among 1,600 Global Targets of Iran Cyber-Attack," *Times of Israel*, January 28, 2016, www.timesofisrael.com/israeli-generals-said-among-1600 -global-targets-of-iran-cyber-attack; Reuters, "Iran 'Rocket Kitten' Cyber Group Hit in European Raids after Targeting Israeli Scientists," November 9, 2015, www .jpost.com/Middle-East/Iran/Iran-Rocket-Kitten-cyber-group-hit-in-European-r aids-after-targeting-Israeli-scientists-432485e-rr.

3 Treadstone 71, "Wool3NH4T – Rocket Kitten – Raw Videos," January 16, 2016, https:// cybershafarat.com/2016/01/16/woolenhat/. See also Jeff Bardin, "What It's Like to Be a Hacker in Iran," *Business Insider*, February 23, 2016, www.businessinsider .com/what-its-like-to-be-a-hacker-in-iran-2016-2.

4 "Hi-Tech: Gil Shwed," *Ynet* [in Hebrew], www.ynet.co.il/Ext/App/Ency/Items/Cd aAppEncyEconomyPerson/0,8925,L-3836,00.html/,.

5 "Checking in with Check Point's Gil Shwed," Israel21c, June 3, 2003, www.israel21c .org/checking-in-with-check-points-gil-shwed-.

6 Ibid.

7 *Ynet*, "Hi-Tech: Gil Shwed." See also Rupert Steiner, "Army Fired an Enthusiasm to Wage War on Hackers," *Sunday Times* (London), July 13, 1997.

8 Israel21c, "Checking in with Check Point's Gil Shwed." See also "A Fortune in Fire-walls," *Forbes*, March 18, 2002, www.forbes.com/forbes/2002/0318/102.htmlh.

9 Steiner, "Army Fired an Enthusiasm." See also Donna Howell, "Check Point Copes with Competition," *Investor's Business Daily*, May 13, 2002.

10 Steiner, "Army Fired an Enthusiasm."

11 *Forbes*, "A Fortune in Firewalls."

12 Currently Orbotech.

13 Steiner, "Army Fired an Enthusiasm."

14 *Forbes*, "A Fortune in Firewalls."

15 "Number 73: Marius Nacht," *Forbes Israel* [in Hebrew], April 14, 2014, www.forbes .co.il/news/new.aspx?0r9VQ=IEEJ=?.

16 Hagai Golan, "I Work for the Interest and the Challenge," *Globes* (Israel), June 6, 2013.

17 Reinhardt Krause, "Check Point's Gil Shwed: He Joined Interest and Opportunity to Fill a Computer Niche," *Investor's Business Daily*, September 12, 2000.

18 Ibid. See also Israel21c, "Checking in with Check Point's Gil Shwed."

19 David Neiger, "Getting to the Point on Security Software," *The Age* (Australia), October 21, 2003.

20 "Computer Niche," *Investor's Business Daily*, September 12, 2000.

21 *Forbes*, "A Fortune in Firewalls."

22 IP addresses allow computers (or other digital devices) to communicate through the internet. Similar to a mailing address when sending a letter, an IP addresses pinpoints the exact location of billions of digital devices that are connected to the internet in order to differentiate one from the other.

23 Howell, "Check Point Copes."

24 Stacy Perman, *Spies, Inc.: Business Innovation from Israel's Masters of Espionage* (Upper Saddle River, NJ: Pearson, 2005), 174.

25 Steiner, "Army Fired an Enthusiasm." See also *Forbes*, "A Fortune in Firewalls."

26 Avi Machlis, "Firm Building a 'Firewall' against Competitors," *Financial Post*, March 7, 1998.

27 Steiner, "Army Fired an Enthusiasm."

28 Ibid.

29 Israel21c, "Checking in with Check Point's Gil Shwed."

30 Neiger, "Getting to the Point."

31 *Forbes*, "A Fortune in Firewalls."

32 Ibid.

33 Perman, *Spies, Inc.*, 175.

34 Israel21c, "Checking in with Check Point's Gil Shwed."

35 "Check Point FireWall-1 Continues to Garner Top Industry Honors," PR *Newswire*, April 25, 1997, www.prnewswire.com/news-releases/check-point-firewall-1-conti nues-to-garner-top-industry-honors-75333602.html. See also Avi Machlis, "Firm Building a 'Firewall.'"

36 Perman, *Spies, Inc.*, 176.

37 Ibid.

38 Jared Sandberg, "Even '60 Minutes' Couldn't Turn Computer Crime into High Drama," Associated Press News Archive, February 24, 1995, www.apnewsarchive .com/1995/Even-60-Minutes-Couldn-t-Turn-Computer-Crime-Into-High-Drama /id-fd7547b1c7a6cf738de5ad02bfaf44315b.

39 "These Cybercrime Statistics Will Make You Think Twice about your Password: Where's the CSI Cyber Team When You Need Them?" CBS, March 3, 2015, www .cbs.com/shows/csi-cyber/news/1003888/these-cybercrime-statistics-will-make -you-think-twice-about-your-password-where-s-the-csi-cyber-team-when-you -need-them-es.

40 Jose Pagliery, "Half of American Adults Hacked this Year," CNN *Tech*, May 28, 2014, http://money.cnn.com/2014/05/28/technology/security/hack-data-breach-k.

41 Elizabeth Weise, "43% of Companies Had a Data Breach This Past Year," *USA Today*, September 24, 2014, www.usatoday.com/story/tech/2014/09/24/data-breach -companies-60/16106197/n.

42 "Net Losses: Estimating the Global Cost of Cybercrime," McAfee, June 2014, http:// www.mcafee.com/us/resources/reports/rp-economic-impact-cybercrime2.pdfmc.

43 Yoav Adler, author's phone interview, April 18, 2016.

44 "Customer Stories," Check Point, checkpoint.com/testimonials.

45 The market value of a company's outstanding shares is calculated by taking the stock price and multiplying it by the total number of shares outstanding. See Shiri Habib-Valdhorn, "Check Point Launches Malware Protection Solution," *Globes* (Israel), March 10, 2015. See also Neal Ungerleider, "How Check Point Became the Fortune

500's Cybersecurity Favorite," *Fast Company*, June 4, 2013, www.fastcompany.com /3012414/the-code-war/how-check-point-became-the-fortune-500s-cybersecurity -favorite; "Customer Stories," Check Point, www.checkpoint.com/testimonialsl.

46 Perman, *Spies, Inc.*, 172.

47 Orna Berry, author's phone interview, December 22, 2016.

48 David Rosenberg, "BRM Bets Big on the Internet," *Jerusalem Post*, March 5, 2000.

49 Steiner, "Army Fired an Enthusiasm."

Chapter 11 – Swallow the Camera

1 Avishai Ovadia, "The Long and Winding Road," *Globes* (Hebrew), August 7, 2003, www.globes.co.il/news/article.aspx?did=7128167.

2 Endoscopy is a general term for any type of scope. Enteroscopy is endoscopy of the small bowel. Colonoscopy is of the colon, and gastroscopy is imaging of the esophagus and stomach.

3 Charles W.L. Hill, Melissa A. Schilling, and Gareth R. Jones, *Strategic Management: An Integrated Approach* (Boston: Cengage Learning, 2016), 75–83. See also Ovadia, "The Long and Winding Road."

4 Colm McCaffrey, Olivier Chevalerias, Clan O'Mathuna, and Karen Twomey, "Swallowable-Capsule Technology," IEEE *Pervasive Computing* 7, no. 1 (January–March 2008).

5 Rachel Sarah, "New Israeli Export an Easy Pill for Patients to Swallow," *Jewish News of Northern California*, November 4, 2005, www.jweekly.com/article/full/27605 /new-israeli-export-an-easy-pill-for-patients-to-swallow/. See also "Going Live to the Small Intestine," *Hayadan* [in Hebrew], July 6, 2000, www.hayadan.org.il /given-imagings-breakthrough-technology060700170.

6 The procedure also lowers the chances of incurring a life-threatening allergic reaction to sedatives or perforation of the intestine, which occur in rare instances during colonoscopy. Deborah Kotz, "Swallowable Imaging Capsules Not Widely Used," *Boston Globe*, August 19, 2013, www.bostonglobe.com/lifestyle/health-wellness /2013/08/18/swallowable-imaging-capsule-keeps-improving-but-still-not-routine -here-why/jVhJGvrS25uo14saRdi8EK/story.htmlR/.

7 Gavriel J. Iddan and Paul Swain, "History and Development of Capsule Endoscopy," *Gastrointestinal Endoscopy Clinics of North America* 14 (2004), www.giendo .theclinics.com/article/S1052–5157(03)00145–4/abstract.

8 Donna Rosenthal, *The Israelis: Ordinary People in an Extraordinary Land* (New York: Free Press, 2003), 84–87.

9 "Inventor Makes New Strides in Medical Diagnostics Technology," European Patent Office, 2011, www.epo.org/learning-events/european-inventor/finalists/2011/iddan /impact.htmlca.

10 Ibid.

11 Iddan and Swain, "History and Development of Capsule Endoscopy." See also Miri Eder, "Live from the Small Intestine," *Ma'ariv* [in Hebrew], May 6, 2012,

www.nrg.co.il/online/archive/ART/224/085.html. In this article Gavriel Meron has described Iddan's position as "senior scientist at Rafael...who contributed greatly to Israel's national security."

12 Hill, Schilling, and Jones, *Strategic Management*, 75–83.

13 Rosenthal, *The Israelis*, 84–87

14 Ibid.

15 Hill, Schilling, and Jones, *Strategic Management*, 75–83. See also Rosenthal, *The Israelis*, 84–87; *Hayadan*, "Going Live to the Small Intestine."

16 Hill, Schilling, and Jones, *Strategic Management*, 75–83.

17 Ovadia, "The Long and Winding Road."

18 *Hayadan*, "Going Live to the Small Intestine."

19 Ovadia, "The Long and Winding Road." See also Avishai Ovadia, "Taro and Given Imaging Set to Raise a Quarter of a Billion Dollars on the Nasdaq This Week," *Globes* [in Hebrew], September 30, 2001, www.globes.co.il/news/article.aspx?did =524787. See also *Hayadan*, "Going Live to the Small Intestine." "Given" is an acronym, according to Meron: GI is gastrointestinal, the *v* stands for video, and *en* for endoscopy. See "Gavriel Meron – Given Imaging," TWST, September 13, 2002.

20 Hill, Schilling, and Jones, *Strategic Management*, 75–83.

21 Rosenthal, *The Israelis*, 84–87. See also "Camera-in-a-Pill Gives a Closer Look," Israel21c, November 1, 2001, www.israel21c.org/camera-in-a-pill-gives-a-closer -look/-.

22 Ovadia, "The Long and Winding Road." See also Netta Ya'akovi, "Given Imaging Is Planning Another Giant Public Offering – Mostly Selling Shares of Interested Parties," *The Marker* [in Hebrew], January 28, 2001, www.themarker.com/wallstreet /1.9561996.

23 Rosenthal, *The Israelis*, 84–87.

24 Ibid.

25 Joseph Walker, "New Ways to Screen for Colon Cancer," *Wall Street Journal*, June 8, 2014, www.wsj.com/articles/new-ways-to-screen-for-colon-cancer-14020631240.

26 Eric Goldberg, author's phone interview, December 29, 2016.

27 Patients wear a sensor belt around the waist that records approximately fifty to sixty thousand images, which are sent directly to the attending physician. See Robin Eisner, "An Ingestible 'Missile' Helps Target Disease," *Forward*, November 14, 2003, http://forward.com/articles/7098/an-ingestible-missile-helps-target-disease/. See also Yoram Gabizon, "Given Imaging – 22 Million Insured within 10 Months," *Haaretz* [in Hebrew], July 3, 2002, www.haaretz.co.il/misc/1.806844. Most individuals feel no sensation whatsoever as the PillCam travels through the GI tract. Some patients have insisted on getting X-rays to prove that the device has actually left their bodies through the stool, which usually occurs before the end of its ten-hour battery life. See Linda Bren, "Incredible Journey through the Digestive System," *U.S. Food and Drug Administration Consumer Magazine*, March–April 2005,

http://permanent.access.gpo.gov/lps1609/www.fda.gov/fdac/features/2005/205
_pillcam.htmll.

28 Eder, "Live from the Small Intestine."

29 Doctors and hospitals spend $17,500 on each workstation needed for the procedure
and $5,450 for a recorder. See Eisner, "An Ingestible 'Missile.'" See also "Colonos-
copy," *Consumer Health Reports*, 2012, http://consumerhealthchoices.org/wp
-content/uploads/2012/10/Colonoscopy-HCBB.pdf; Lily Hay Newman, "You
Might Be Able to Avoid Colonoscopies Now That the PillCam Is FDA Approved,"
Slate, February 6, 2014, www.slate.com/blogs/future_tense/2014/02/06/fda
_approval_for_pillcam_could_mean_swallowing_a_pill_instead_of_having
.html; Ovadia, "The Long and Winding Road."

30 *Hayadan*, "Going Live to the Small Intestine."

31 Jeanne Whalen, "Tiny Cameras to See in the Intestines," *Wall Street Journal*, February
29, 2016, www.wsj.com/articles/tiny-cameras-to-see-in-the-intestines-14567761455i.

32 "Inventor Makes New Strides in Medical Diagnostics Technology," European Patent Office. See also David Shamah, "Pillcam's Inventor Regrets Sale of 'Biblical'
Tech Firm to Foreign Firm," *Times of Israel*, April 23, 2015, www.timesofisrael.com
/pillcams-inventor-regrets-sale-of-biblical-tech-to-foreign-firm/n.

33 Kevin Flanders, "A Focus on Innovation – PillCam Colon Offers Some Unique Perspective on the Future," *Health Care News*, February 2015, http://healthcarenews
.com/a-focus-on-innovation-pillcam-colon-offers-some-unique-perspective-on
-the-future/e.

34 In 2014, Ireland-based Covington, a medical device company, bought Given Imaging
for approximately $860,000. A year later, US-based Medtronic purchased Coving-
ton for $49.9 billion. Given Imaging now has the resources and the salesforce to
dominate and transform the gastrointestinal market, which is expected to reach
$3.83 billion in 2020. See "3.8 Billion Smart Pills," *Business Wire*, February 12, 2016,
www.businesswire.com/news/home/20160212005740/en/3.8-Billion-Smart-Pills-
Capsule-Endoscopy-Drug. Iddan now increasingly looks to the future and the
great innovations he expects to continue coming out of Israel in the fields of brain
research, nanotechnology, biotechnology, and others. He predicts that Israelis
will continue to innovate and change the world for the better: "New methods of
treatment will yield solutions that we could never have envisioned before," he says.
See also Shamah, "Pillcam's Inventor Regrets Sale"; Mor Shimoni, "Inspirers: Who
Are the Researchers Lighting the Torch This Year?" *Walla* [in Hebrew], March 8,
2015, http://healthy.walla.co.il/item/28360340.

Chapter 12 – Eye on the Spine

1 Mazor Robotics, "Standing Taller with Renaissance," May 3, 2013, https://www.you-
tube.com/watch?v=4GWjcfOd9WU.

2 Avi Shauli, "Another Bonanza? The Innovator behind the Mazor Robot, Worth
Today 1.3 Billion Shekels, Tells BizPortal about His Next Innovation," Bizportal

[in Hebrew], October 16, 2013, www.bizportal.co.il/capitalmarket/news/article /37088600e.

3 Atiya Zar, "Professor Moshe Shoham, Who Heads the Technion Robotics Lab, Believes That Everyone in the Future Will Have a Personal Robot," *Arutz Sheva*, July 15, 2010, www.inn.co.il/Besheva/Article.aspx/96909.

4 Ibid.

5 "Moshe Shoham," Technion – Israel Institute of Technology, https://meeng.techn ion.ac.il/members/moshe-shoham/h-0.

6 Moshe Shoham, author's phone interview, May 11, 2016. See also Zar, "Professor Moshe Shoham."

7 Moshe Shoham, author's phone interview, May 11, 2016. See also Technion, "Moshe Shoham."

8 Shauli, "Another Bonanza?"

9 "Report from Israel: SpineAssist Is First Miniature Robotic to Receive FDA OK," *Medical Device Daily*, June 11, 2004.

10 Eli Zehavi, author's phone interview, May 25, 2016.

11 Moshe Shoham, author's phone interview, May 11, 2016.

12 Eli Zehavi, author's phone interview, May 25, 2016.

13 DenX merged with Australian financial group's Helm Corp. in July 2002, making it the first Israeli company to be listed on an Australian stock market. Neal Sandler, "Israeli Startup Finds Funding Down Under," *Daily Deal*, July 26, 2002.

14 "Report from Israel: SpineAssist Is First Miniature Robotic to Receive FDA OK." See also Eli Shimoni, "Mazor's Robot for Back Surgery Raises 10 Million Dollars," *Ynet* [in Hebrew], May 4, 2005, www.ynet.co.il/articles/0,7340,L-3081277,00.html.

15 "Mazor: Section 7 – Summary of Safety and Effectiveness," U.S. Food and Drug Administration, January 7, 2004.

16 Moshe Shoham, author's phone interview, May 11, 2016.

17 Judy Siegel-Itzkovich, "Robots Back Breakthrough Surgery," *Jerusalem Post*, March 6, 2011, www.jpost.com/Health-and-Science/Robots-back-breakthrough-surgeryu.

18 Charlie Patton, "Woman Gets Back Relief with Unique Surgery: Robot Has Key Role to Help Surgeon in Two-Part Procedure," *Florida Times-Union*, February 16, 2014.

19 Hagi Amit, "Meet Mazor's Medical Robot That Multiplied Its Worth by Six Times in a Year," *The Marker* [in Hebrew], June 13, 2013, www.themarker.com/markerweek /1.204602880.

20 Ibid.

21 Ibid. See also Moshe Shoham, author's phone interview, May 11, 2016.

22 "Mazor Robotics: An Interesting Company to Put on Your Watch List," Seeking Alpha, December 19, 2014, http://seekingalpha.com/article/2768765-mazor-robotics-an -interesting-company-to-put-on-your-watch-listwo.

23 The Mazor system costs $830,000 in the United States and $700,000 in Europe – which by industry standards is considered a reasonable price in comparison to other robotic devices that assist with surgery – and utilizes the Emerald, a $1500

non-reusable disposable robotic implant, named after one of the breastplate jewels worn by the High Priest in the Jerusalem Temple about two thousand years ago. Mazor also makes money by selling annual service agreements at approximately 10 percent of the fixed equipment cost beginning the second year after installation of the system. See Amit, "Meet Mazor's Medical Robot." See also Seeking Alpha, "Mazor Robotics"; Tali Tzipori, "Mazor Robotics Worth 7 Times More in a Year; How Did the Company Do It?" *Globes* [in Hebrew], July 4, 2013, www.globes.co.il/news/article.aspx?did=1000859350; Siegel-Itzkovich, "Robots Back Breakthrough Surgery."

24 Hillel Koren, "Mazor Sees FDA Nod for SpineAssist Brain Surgery Use," *Globes* (Israel), July 28, 2010, www.globes.co.il/en/article-10005777617.

25 Siegel-Itzkovich, "Robots Back Breakthrough Surgery."

26 Zar, "Professor Moshe Shoham."

27 Mazor Robotics, "Standing Taller with Renaissance," May 3, 2013, https://www.youtube.com/watch?v=4GWjcfOd9WU9c.

Chapter 13 – A Better Band-Aid

1 Jana Winter, "Suspected Arizona Gunman Reportedly Planned Shooting in Advance," Fox News Channel, January 9, 2011, www.foxnews.com/politics/2011/01/09/fbi-director-robert-mueller-takes-lead-arizona-shooting-investigation.html. See also "Arizona Safeway Shootings Fast Facts," CNN, December 10, 2015, www.cnn.com/2013/06/10/us/arizona-safeway-shootings-fast-facts/-sh.

2 Daniel Hernandez, *They Call Me a Hero: A Memoir of My Youth* (New York: Simon and Schuster, 2013), 11, www.advocate.com/commentary/2013/02/05/book-excerpt-daniel-hernandez-recalls-shooting-gabby-giffordsil.

3 Ron Kampeas, "Israeli Bandage May Have Saved Giffords' Life after Shooting," *Jewish News of Northern California*, February 17, 2011, www.jweekly.com/includes/print/60886/article/israeli-bandage-may-have-saved-giffords-life-after-shooting/i.

4 Bernard Bar-Natan, author's email exchange, June 29, 2016.

5 Bernard Bar-Natan, author's phone interview, May 24, 2016.

6 Bernard Bar-Natan, author's interview, Givatayim, July 10, 2015.

7 Ibid.

8 Ibid. See also David Horovitz, "The Guy with the Bandage," *Jerusalem Post*, April 29, 2011, www.jpost.com/Opinion/Columnists/Editors-Notes-The-guy-with-the-bandageh.

9 Bernard Bar-Natan, author's interview, Givatayim, July 10, 2015.

10 Bernard Bar-Natan, author's phone interview, May 24, 2016.

11 Bernard Bar-Natan, author's interview, Givatayim, July 10, 2015.

12 If the company is successful, the grant is considered a loan to be paid back over time. If the company fails, the start-up capital does not need to be returned, and the government assumes the loss. In neither case does the Israeli government own a piece of the company.

13 Bernard Bar-Natan, author's interview, Givatayim, July 10, 2015.

14 Ahmed Heib, author's phone interview, January 29, 2016.

15 Bernard Bar-Natan, author's phone interview, May 24, 2016.

16 Ahmed Heib, author's phone interview, January 29, 2016.

17 Bernard Bar-Natan, author's phone interview, May 24, 2016.

18 Roee Madai, author's interview, First Care Factory, Rosh Ha'Ayin, July 14, 2015.

19 Ahmed Heib, author's phone interview, January 29, 2016.

20 Areej Kabishi, author's phone interview, February 1, 2015.

21 Horovitz, "The Guy with the Bandage."

22 Bernard Bar-Natan, author's interview, Givatayim, July 10, 2015.

23 Nicky Blackburn, "Israeli Innovative Bandages Saving American Lives in Iraq," Israel21c, January 9, 2005, www.israel21c.org/israeli-innovative-bandages-saving-american-lives-in-iraq/-e.

24 Horovitz, "The Guy with the Bandage."

25 Ibid.

26 Bernard Bar-Natan, author's interview, Givatayim, July 10, 2015.

Chapter 14 – Working for Tips

1 Michel Revel, author's interview, Jerusalem, August 14, 2016. See also Kathryn Berman, "Hidden Children in France during the Holocaust," The International School for Holocaust Studies, http://www.yadvashem.org/yv/en/education/newsletter/24/hidden_children.asp; "About the OSE," *The Children of Chabannes*, http://childrenofchabannes.org/about-the-ose. Children included future writer and Nobel laureate Elie Wiesel and future chief rabbi of Israel Rav Israel Lau.

2 Michel Revel, author's interview, Jerusalem, August 14, 2016.

3 Siegel-Itzkovich, "Unraveling the Mysteries."

4 Ibid. See also "Multiple Sclerosis: Using Hamster Cells to Fight Multiple Sclerosis," *Merck*, January 17, 2015, www.magazine.emerck/darmstadt_germany/innovation/Michel_Revel/multiple_sclerosis.html; Michel Revel, author's interview, Ness Ziona, June 30, 2015.

5 Thomas Tan, "Dr. Michel Revel Elected to ISICR Honorary Membership," *International Society for Interferon and Cytokine Research* 10, no. 2 (April 2003): 1–4, http://cytokinesociety.org/wp-content/uploads/2016/11/Newsletter10.2.pdf..

6 *Merck*, "Multiple Sclerosis."

7 Rick Doust, "No 'Magic Bullet' out of Interferon, but Work in Labs Showing Promise," *Globe and Mail* (Canada), February 16, 1984.

8 "Rebif and Its Connection to Israel," Multiple Sclerosis Society of Israel [in Hebrew], http://mssociety.org.il/2015021717. See also "Happy Birthday to the Medication," Weizmann Institute [in Hebrew], June 4, 2007, http://stwww.weizmann.ac.il/g-junior/weizmann-paper/47/13.html3.

9 Michel Revel, author's interview, Ness Ziona, June 30, 2015. See also Michel Revel, author's interview, Jerusalem, August 14, 2016.

10 Michel Revel, author's interview, Ness Ziona, June 30, 2015.

11 Michel Revel, author's interview, Jerusalem, August 14, 2016.

12 Multiple Sclerosis Society of Israel, "Rebif and Its Connection to Israel." See also Weizmann Institute, "Happy Birthday to the Medication."

13 Harold Schmeck Jr., "Interferon Makes Inroads against Some Infections, Including Colds," *New York Times,* June 1, 1982.

14 Revel specifically conducted his research on interferon beta.

15 Michel Revel, author's interview, Jerusalem, August 14, 2016.

16 Jessica Steinberg, "Disease Be Not Proud," *Jerusalem Post,* February 27, 2004.

17 Ibid. See also Multiple Sclerosis Society of Israel, "Rebif and Its Connection to Israel."

18 *Merck,* "Multiple Sclerosis."

19 Ibid.

20 Michel Revel, author's interview, Jerusalem, August 14, 2016.

21 Michel Revel, author's interview, Ness Ziona, June 30, 2015.

22 *Merck,* "Multiple Sclerosis."

23 Menachem Rubinstein, author's phone interview, July 4, 2016.

24 Lawrence Jacobs, Judith A. O'Malley, and Arnold Freeman, "Intrathecal Interferon in the Treatment of Multiple Sclerosis: Patient Follow-Up," *Archives of Neurology* 42, no. 9 (1985): 841–47, http://archneur.jamanetwork.com/article.aspx?articleid=5844978i.

25 Ann Pietrangelo and Valencia Higuera, "Multiple Sclerosis by the Numbers: Facts, Statistics, and You," Healthline, March 24, 2015, www.healthline.com/health/multiple-sclerosis/facts-statistics-infographicai.

26 In addition to MS, Revel's team discovered that interferon beta-1a is also effective against papillomavirus genital warts (which can lead to cervical cancer) and against recurrent herpes. Siegel-Itzkovich, "Unraveling the Mysteries."

27 Menachem Rubinstein, author's phone interview, July 4, 2016.

28 Michel Revel, author's interview, Ness Ziona, June 30, 2015.

29 Ibid. See also Carly Helfand, "Rebif," *Fierce Pharma,* www.fiercepharma.com/special-report/rebif; "Kadimastem to Receive Sponsored Research Agreement with National Multiple Sclerosis Society Fast Forward Program," *India Pharma News,* September 29, 2015.

30 Michel Revel, author's interview, Ness Ziona, June 30, 2015.

31 Dr. Bernhard Kirschbaum, author's email exchange, November 19, 2016.

32 Alex Philippidis, "Top 10 Multiple Sclerosis Drugs," *Genetic Engineering & Biotechnology News,* February 18, 2014, http://www.genengnews.com/the-lists/top-10-multiple-sclerosis-drugs/77900039?page=19.

33 Steinberg, "Disease Be Not Proud."

34 Weizmann Institute of Science, "Treatment of Multiple Sclerosis," November 24, 2010, www.youtube.com/watch?v=WHvTh510XBMB.

35 Dr. Tamir Ben-Hur, author's phone interview, December 12, 2016.

Chapter 15 – A Higher Calling

1 Raphael Mechoulam, author's email exchange, May 28, 2016. See also Judy Siegel-Itzkovich, "The World Is Going to Pot," *Jerusalem Post*, May 18, 2014, www.jpost.com/Health-and-Science/The-world-is-going-to-pot-352563; Assaf Uni, "Meet the Man Who Discovered Weed's Secret Ingredient," *Vocativ*, December 18, 2014, www.vocativ.com/culture/science/raphael-mechoulam-thc-marijunana/; Fundación CANNA, "The Scientist Documentary," July 23, 2015, www.youtube.com/watch?v=qwfC5ye2UBkBy.

2 "The Scientist – The Life and Work of Raphael Mechoulam," *EuropaWire*, July 31, 2015, www.projectcbd.org/article/scientist-life-and-work-raphael-mechoulamhl.

3 Anisa Rawhani, "Pioneering Pot Prof Still Studying at 85," *Kingston Whig-Standard*, June 29, 2015.

4 "Cannabis," World Health Organization, www.who.int/substance_abuse/facts/cannabis/en/. There are over one million US patients and approximately twenty thousand in Israel. "Number of Legal Medical Marijuana Patients," ProCon, March 1, 2016, http://medicalmarijuana.procon.org/view.resource.php?resourceID=005889. See also Asaf Finkelstein, "The Grass Is Always Greener," *Jerusalem Post*, December 11, 2015.

5 Dr. Nora Volkow, author's email exchange, May 31, 2016.

6 "Conversation with Raphael Mechoulam," *Addiction* 102, no. 6 (June 2007): 887–93.

7 "Weizmann Institute of Science," Academic Ranking of World Universities, www.shanghairanking.com/World-University-Rankings/Weizmann-Institute-of-Science.htmle.

8 David Jay Brown, "An Interview with Dr. Raphael Mechoulam," Mavericks of the Mind, http://mavericksofthemind.com/dr-raphael-mechoulamah.

9 *Addiction*, "Conversation with Raphael Mechoulam."

10 Mechoulam determined that cannabidiol is only one of about five dozen active "cannabinoids." Cannabis has more than 480 natural compounds, sixty-six of which have now been classified as cannabinoids. Abigail Klein Leichman, "The Israeli Pharmacologist Who Kick-Started Marijuana Research," Israel21c, May 14, 2012, www.israel21c.org/the-israeli-pharmacologist-who-kick-started-marijuana-researcheu.

11 Siegel-Itzkovich, "The World Is Going to Pot."

12 Ibid.

13 Rawhani, "Pioneering Pot Prof."

14 The Biological Research Institute specializes in biology, medical chemistry, and environmental science, with much of its work a closely guarded secret.

15 *Addiction*, "Conversation with Raphael Mechoulam." See also Noga Tarnopolsky, "At 82, He's the World's Most Eminent Pot Scientist," *Eureka Times Standard*, August 27, 2013, http://www.times-standard.com/article/ZZ/20130827/NEWS/1308289628.

16 Hampton Sides, "Science Seeks to Unlock Marijuana's Secrets," *National Geographic*, June 2015, http://ngm.nationalgeographic.com/2015/06/marijuana/sides-text.

17 Raphael Mechoulam, author's email exchange, May 28, 2016.

18 Fundación CANNA, "The Scientist Documentary."

19 Raphael Mechoulam, author's email exchange, May 28, 2016.

20 Siegel-Itzkovich, "The World Is Going to Pot."

21 Fundación CANNA, "The Scientist Documentary."

22 Uni, "Meet the Man."

23 *Addiction*, "Conversation with Raphael Mechoulam."

24 Nico Escondido, "The Man Who Discovered THC," *High Times*, May 31, 2011.

25 Sam Sokol, "The Marijuana Maven," *Jerusalem Post*, April 6, 2012.

26 Adam Van Heerden, "Professor Raphael Mechoulam, the Father of Marijuana Research, Talks to NoCamels about His Studies and Breaking the Law in the Name of Science," NoCamels, *September 24, 2013*, http://nocamels.com/2013/09/profes sor-raphael-mechoulam-the-father-of-marijuana-research-talks-to-nocamels-abo ut-his-studies-and-breaking-the-law-in-the-name-of-science.

27 Anthony Wile, "Dr. Raphael Mechoulam: The Promise of Cannabis," *Daily Bell*, October 19, 2014, www.thedailybell.com/exclusive-interviews/35732/Anthony-Wile-Dr-Raphael-Mechoulam-The-Promise-of-Cannabis.

28 Dr. Nora Volkow, author's email exchange, May 31, 2016.

29 While it is challenging to pinpoint the exact origin of medical cannabis, there is evidence that suggests humans have been consuming it as far back as 4000 BCE in China. Its first documented use is found in the Ebers Papyrus, the oldest and most important medical papyrus of ancient Egypt, which dates to the sixteenth century BCE. And cannabis is mentioned in ancient Assyrian, Greek, and Roman texts. "Long-Dead Teenager Tells Tale of Pot-Smoking in Era of 300 AD," *Vancouver Sun*, May 20, 1993. See also Alyson Martin and Nushin Rashidian, "Martin and Rashidian: Little Green Pill," *National Post* (Canada), April 3, 2014, http://nationalpost.com/opinion/martin-rashidian-little-green-pill.

30 *Vancouver Sun*, "Long-Dead Teenager Tells Tale."

31 Dr. Howlett was the primary investigator and worked alongside her graduate student William Devane to discover the system. Dr. Allyn Howlett, author's phone interview, June 2, 2016. See also Martin A. Lee, "The Discovery of the Endocannabinoid System," O'Shaughnessy's Online, 2010, www.beyondthc.com/wp-content/uploads/2012/07/eCBSystemLee.pdfe.

32 Dr. Allyn Howlett, author's phone interview, June 2, 2016.

33 Anandamide is released by the brain, and 2-arachidonoyl glycerol is released by the peripheral organs. Siegel-Itzkovich, "The World Is Going to Pot."

34 Tarnopolsky, "At 82."

35 Siegel-Itzkovich, "The World Is Going to Pot."

36 Klein Leichman, "The Israeli Pharmacologist."

37 Siegel-Itzkovich, "The World Is Going to Pot." Mechoulam stresses that medical marijuana and recreational use of the drug are two different issues entirely. The professor does not advocate for the approval of recreational cannabis, calling it "very dangerous." See ibid.

38 Sokol, "Marijuana Maven."

39 Lizzie Wade, "Researchers Are Finally Studying the Other Chemical in Pot," *Wired*, June 4, 2015.

40 Uni, "Meet the Man." See also Sokol, "Marijuana Maven."

41 Dr. Manuel Guzman, author's phone interview, June 1, 2016.

42 Wade, "Researchers Are Finally Studying."

43 Gallup, "In U.S., 58% Back Legal Marijuana Use," October 21, 2015, www.gallup.com /poll/186260/back-legal-marijuana.aspxj..

44 Shoshanna Solomon, "Can Cannabis Treat Asthma? Jerusalem Experts to Find Out," *Times of Israel*, October 24, 2017, https://www.timesofisrael.com/jerusalem-cannabis-guru-to-study-effect-of-weed-on-asthma/.

Chapter 16 – Balancing Heaven and Earth

1 Yossi Leshem and Ofir Bahat, *Flying with the Birds* (Tel Aviv: Yediot Ahronoth/ Chemed Books, 1999), 111.

2 Yossi Leshem, author's phone interview, July 31, 2016. See also Thomas Friedman, "Israel and the Birds Vie for Precious Air Space," *New York Times*, September 17, 1985, www.nytimes.com/1985/09/17/science/israel-and-the-birds-vie-for-precious -air-space.html?pagewanted=allp-.

3 Yossi Leshem, author's phone interview, July 31, 2016.

4 Ibid. See also Friedman, "Israel and the Birds Vie."

5 Ben Jacobson, "It's for the Birds," *Jerusalem Post*, January 18, 2008. Israel's neighbors, including Syria, Lebanon, Jordan, and Egypt, all face similar challenges.

6 Yossi Leshem, author's phone interview, July 31, 2016.

7 Ibid.

8 Ibid.

9 Carole Garbuny Vogul and Yossi Leshem, *The Man Who Flies with Birds* (Minneapolis: Kar Ben Press, 2009), 7.

10 Yossi Leshem, author's phone interview, July 31, 2016.

11 Ibid.

12 Ibid.

13 Israel21c, "The Man Who Taught Me to Fly," September 26, 2013, www.youtube.com /watch?v=k2WvIDgCHlAlg.

14 Yossi Leshem, author's phone interview, July 31, 2016.

15 Ibid.

16 Judy Siegel-Itzkovich, "Birds on His Brain," *Jerusalem Post*, November 6, 2005, www.jpost.com/Health-and-Sci-Tech/Science-And-Environment/Birds-on-his-braini.

17 Yossi Leshem, author's phone interview, July 31, 2016.

18 Ibid.

19 Ibid.

20 David K. Shipler, "Israel Completes Pullout, Leaving Sinai to Egypt," *New York Times*,

April 26, 1982, www.nytimes.com/1982/04/26/world/israeli-completes-pullout
-leaving-sinai-to-egypt.html?pagewanted=allgy.

21 Yossi Leshem, author's phone interview, July 31, 2016.

22 Ibid.

23 Yossi Leshem, author's interview, New York, October 28, 2016.

24 Yossi Leshem, author's phone interview, July 31, 2016.

25 The Fisher Institute for Air and Space Strategic Studies, "Avihu Ben-Nun Tells
about the Bird Problem" [in Hebrew], https://www.youtube.com/watch?v=
pokdBNGaSywSB.

26 Leshem and Bahat, *Flying with the Birds*, 13. See also Sharon Udasin, "Israel Bird
Expert Wins 25,000 Euro German Prize," *Jerusalem Post*, November 14, 2012.

27 Leshem and Bahat, *Flying with the Birds*, 188.

28 Doug Struck, "Birder Sows Goodwill in Mideast," *Washington Post*, April 9, 1998,
www.washingtonpost.com/archive/politics/1998/04/09/birder-sows-goodwill
-in-mideast/a72fe666–966f–4766–86a2–0827d64cca44/a.

29 Mansour Abu Rashid, author's phone interview, December 13, 2016.

30 Leshem and Bahat, *Flying with the Birds*, 11.

Chapter 17 – Resurrecting the Dead

1 Neil Asher Silberman, *A Prophet from amongst You: The Life of Yigael Yadin; Soldier,
Scholar, and Mythmaker of Modern Israel* (New York: ACLS Humanities, 2013), 1–2.

2 Ibid.

3 Steven Erlanger, "After 2000 Years, a Seed from Ancient Judea Sprouts," *New York
Times*, June 12, 2005, www.nytimes.com/2005/06/12/world/middleeast/after-
2000-years-a-seed-from-ancient-judea-sprouts.html?_r=1u.

4 Sarah Sallon, author's phone interview, December 9, 2015.

5 Ibid.

6 Ibid.

7 Jane Shen-Miller, Mary Beth Mudgett, J. William Schopf, Steven Clarke, and Rainer
Berger, "Exceptional Seed Longevity and Robust Growth: Ancient Sacred Lotus
from China," *American Journal of Botany* 82, no. 11 (November 1995): 1367–80,
www.botany.org/ajb/82–11–1995–1367.pdf3.

8 Sarah Sallon, author's phone interview, December 9, 2015.

9 Erlanger, "After 2000 Years, a Seed." See also Dr. Jane Goodall, author's email exchange,
February 5, 2017.

10 Erlanger, "After 2000 Years, a Seed."

11 Leviticus 23:40.

12 Erlanger, "After 2000 Years, a Seed."

13 Elaine Solowey, author's phone interview, January 21, 2016.

14 Sarah Sallon, Elaine Solowey, Yuval Cohen, Raia Korchinsky, Markus Egli, Ivan
Woodhatch, Orit Simchoni, and Mordechai Kislev, "Supporting Online Material
for Germination, Genetics, and Growth of an Ancient Date Seed," *Science AAAS*,

June 13, 2008, https://www.sciencemag.org/content/320/5882/1464/suppl/DC1. See also Elaine Solowey, author's interview, Jerusalem, June 25, 2015.

15 Steven Erlanger, "After 2000 Years, a Seed."

16 Ofer Ilany, "2,000-Year-Old Date Seed Grows in the Arava," *Haaretz*, February 15, 2007, www.haaretz.com/print-edition/news/2–000-year-old-date-seed-grows-in-the -arava-1.213054. See also Hana Levi Julian, "Date Tree Sprouts from 2000-Year-Old Seed Found on Masada," *Arutz Sheva*, June 13, 2008, www.israelnationalnews.com /News/News.aspx/126484#.VVDlxtJVikoVV.

17 Elaine Solowey, author's interview, Jerusalem, June 25, 2015.

18 Ibid.

19 Ilany, "2,000-Year-Old Date Seed."

20 Elaine Solowey, author's interview, Jerusalem, June 25, 2015. See also Sarah Sallon, author's phone interview, December 9, 2015. In 2012 Russian scientists reportedly managed to grow a thirty-two-thousand-year-old seed buried in Siberia that had apparently been buried by an ice-age squirrel. They did so by extracting the embryo and successfully germinating the plants in vitro. But the Judean date palm remains the oldest mature seed that has grown into a viable plant.

21 Elaine Solowey, author's interview, Jerusalem, June 25, 2015.

22 Ibid.

23 Steven Erlanger, "After 2000 Years, a Seed."

24 Elaine Solowey, author's interview, Jerusalem, June 25, 2015.

25 Polana Vidyasagar, author's phone interview, December 21, 2015.

26 Elaine Solowey, author's interview, Jerusalem, June 25, 2015.

27 Sarah Sallon, author's phone interview, December 9, 2015.

28 Ofer Ilany, "2,000-Year-Old Date Seed."

29 Matthew 2:11, King James Version.

30 Matthew Kalman, "After 1,500 Years, Frankincense Returns to the Holy Land in Time for Christmas," *Times of Israel*, December 23, 2012, http://blogs.timesofisrael.com /after-1500-years-frankincense-returns-to-the-holy-land/yt.

31 Randolph E. Schmid, "Tree from 2,000-Year-Old Seed Is Doing Well," June 12, 2008, www.freerepublic.com/focus/f-news/2030302/postss2.

32 Kalman, "After 1,500 Years, Frankincense Returns."

33 "Plant Medicines," PBS, www-tc.pbs.org/wgbh/nova/julian/media/lrk-disp -plantmedicines.pdfnn.

34 Dr. Ori Fragman-Sapir, author's phone interview, December 2, 2016.

35 Steven Erlanger, author's phone interview, December 19, 2016.

36 Schmid, "Tree from 2,000-Year-Old Seed."

Chapter 18 – Be a Mensch

1 Ethics of the Fathers 1:2.

2 Brady Josephson, "Want to Be Happier? Give More. Give Better," *Huffington Post*, November 11, 2014, https://www.huffingtonpost.com/brady-josephson/want-to-be-happier-give-m_b_6175358.html5.

BIBLIOGRAPHY

BOOKS

Cleveland, Cutler J. *Concise Encyclopedia of the History of Energy.* San Diego: Elsevier, 2009.

Garbuny Vogul, Carole, and Yossi Leshem. *The Man Who Flies with Birds.* Minneapolis: Kar Ben Press, 2009.

Hernandez, Daniel. *They Call Me a Hero: A Memoir of My Youth.* New York: Simon and Schuster, 2013. www.advocate.com/commentary/2013/02/05 /book-excerpt-daniel-hernandez-recalls-shooting-gabby-giffords.

Hill, Charles W.L., Melissa A. Schilling, and Gareth R. Jones. *Strategic Management: An Integrated Approach.* Boston: Cengage Learning, 2016.

Inbal, Aliza Belman, and Shachar Zahavi. *The Rise and Fall of Israel's Bilateral Aid Budget, 1958–2008.* Tel Aviv: Tel Aviv University Hartog School for Government and Policy with the Pears Foundation, 2009.

Kreinin, Mordechai E. *Israel and Africa: A Study in Technical Cooperation.* New York: Frederick A. Praeger, 1964.

Leshem, Yossi, and Ofir Bahat. *Flying with the Birds.* Tel Aviv: Yediot Ahronoth/Chemed Books, 1999.

Meir, Golda. *My Life.* New York: G.P. Putnam's Sons, 1975.

Perlin, John. *Let It Shine: The 6000 Year Story of Solar Energy.* Self-published, 2013. http://john-perlin.com/let-it-shine.html.

Perman, Stacy. *Spies, Inc.: Business Innovation from Israel's Masters of Espionage.* Upper Saddle River, NJ: Pearson, 2005.

Peters, Joel. *Israel and Africa: The Problematic Friendship.* London: British Academic Press, 1992.

Rosenthal, Donna. *The Israelis: Ordinary People in an Extraordinary Land.* New York: Free Press, 2003.

Siegel, Seth M. *Let There Be Water.* New York: St. Martin's Press, 2015.

Silberman, Neil Asher. *A Prophet from amongst You: The Life of Yigael Yadin; Soldier, Scholar, and Mythmaker of Modern Israel.* New York: ACLS Humanities, 2013.

Tabor, Harry Zvi. *Selected Reprints of Papers by Harry Zvi Tabor, Solar Energy*

Pioneer. Rehovot: Balaban Publishers and International Solar Energy Society, 1999.

Tal, Alon. *Pollution in a Promised Land: An Environmental History of Israel*. Berkeley: University of California Press, 2002.

ARTICLES

Addiction. "Conversation with Raphael Mechoulam." 102, no. 6 (June 2007): 887–93.

Ain, Stewart. "Iron Dome Ready for Future." *Jewish Week*, February 9, 2015. www.thejewishweek.com/features/jw-qa/iron-dome-ready-future.

Amit, Hagi. "Meet Mazor's Medical Robot That Multiplied Its Worth by Six Times in a Year." *The Marker* [in Hebrew], June 13, 2013. www.themarker.com/markerweek/1.2046028.

Ankori, Merav. "Solar Power unto the Nations." *Globes*, October 28, 2007.

Arom, Eitan, and Erica Schachne. "Just an Ambucycle Ride Away." *Jerusalem Post*, January 2, 2015.

Associated Press. "Farms Waste Much of World's Water." March 19, 2006. www.wired.com/2006/03/farms-waste-much-of-worlds-water.

Atik, Nilufer. "Claire Lomas' Inspiring Story: My Life Has Been Amazing since I Was Paralyzed." *Mirror* (UK), May 10, 2013. www.mirror.co.uk/news/real-life-stories/claire-lomas-inspiring-story-life-1879107.

Avraham, Yael Freund. "A Drop of Respect: Who Really Invented Drip Irrigation?" *Makor Rishon* [in Hebrew], June 7, 2015. www.nrg.co.il/online/1/ART2/698/679.html.

Azulai, Yuval. "Eight Facts about Iron Dome." *Globes* (Israel), October 7, 2014. www.globes.co.il/en/article-everything-you-wanted-to-know-about-iron-dome-1000953706.

Bardin, Jeff. "What It's Like to Be a Hacker in Iran." *Business Insider*, February 23, 2016. www.businessinsider.com/what-its-like-to-be-a-hacker-in-iran-2016-2.

BBC. "Middle East Crisis: Facts and Figures." August 31, 2006. http://news.bbc.co.uk/2/hi/middle_east/5257128.stm.

Bennett, Drake. "What It's Like to Be an Arab Entrepreneur in a Divided Israel," Bloomberg, November 26, 2014. Available online (www.bloomberg.com/bw/articles/2014–11–26/what-its-like-to-run-an-arab-tech-startup-in-israel#p).

Bergman, H., T. Wichmann, and M.R. DeLong. "Reversal of Experimental Parkinsonism by Lesions of the Subthalamic Nucleus." *Science* 249 (1990): 1436–1438. https://www.ncbi.nlm.nih.gov/pubmed/2402638.

Bkhor Nir, Diana. "Flowing." *Calcalist* [in Hebrew], March 19, 2015. http://tx.technion.ac.il/~presstech/newsletter/mehudar.pdf.

Blackburn, Nicky. "Israeli Innovative Bandages Saving American Lives in Iraq." Israel21c, January 9, 2005. www.israel21c.org/israeli-innovative-bandages-saving-american-lives-in-iraq/.

Bland, Alastair. "Hiding in the Shallows." *Comstock's*, September 15, 2015. www.comstocksmag.com/longreads/hiding-shallows.

Bray, Hiawatha. "ReWalk Exoskeleton Puts the Disabled Back on Their Feet." *Boston Globe*, July 7, 2014. www.bostonglobe.com/business/2014/07/06/putting-disabled-back-their-feet/8gFcM33JyTuL92J2kReDeI/story.html.

Bren, Linda. "Incredible Journey through the Digestive System." *U.S. Food and Drug Administration Consumer Magazine*, March–April 2005. http://permanent.access.gpo.gov/lps1609/www.fda.gov/fdac/features/2005/205_pillcam.html.

Brown, David Jay. "An Interview with Dr. Raphael Mechoulam." Mavericks of the Mind. http://mavericksofthemind.com/dr-raphael-mechoulam.

Business Wire. "3.8 Billion Smart Pills." February 12, 2016. www.businesswire.com/news/home/20160212005740/en/3.8-Billion-Smart-Pills-Capsule-Endoscopy-Drug.

Cashman, Greer Fay. "Rivlin Salutes First Responders as the 'Light in the Darkness.'" *Jerusalem Post*, December 8, 2015. www.jpost.com/Israel-News/Rivlin-salutes-first-responders-as-the-light-in-the-darkness-436641.

———. "The Ties That Bind." *Jerusalem Post*, May 30, 2014.

———. "United Hatzalah Leaders Receive Prize for Peace in the Mid East." *Jerusalem Post*, June 25, 2013. www.jpost.com/National-News/United-Hatzalah-leaders-receive-prize-for-peace-in-the-Mid-East-317610.

CBS. "These Cybercrime Statistics Will Make You Think Twice about your Password: Where's the CSI Cyber Team When You Need Them?" March 3, 2015. www.cbs.com/shows/csi-cyber/news/1003888/these-cybercrime-statistics-will-make-you-think-twice-about-your-password-where-s-the-csi-cyber-team-when-you-need-them-.

CNN. "Arizona Safeway Shootings Fast Facts." December 10, 2015. www.cnn.com/2013/06/10/us/arizona-safeway-shootings-fast-facts/.

Consumer Health Reports. "Colonoscopy." 2012. http://consumerhealthchoices
.org/wp-content/uploads/2012/10/Colonoscopy-HCBB.pdf.

CSPAN. "A Drop of Hope in a Sea of Despair." January 13, 2014. www.c-span
.org/video/?c4480721/ariel-bar-aipac.

Davar. "Black Brings Light" [in Hebrew]. July 26, 1961. http://goo.gl/fwIZqc.

————. "The Opposition to Installing the *Dud Shemesh* in the Workers
Housing Union's Apartments" [in Hebrew]. May 27, 1971. http://goo.gl
/VPCs6I.

————. "Weizmann Prize Winners for 1956" [in Hebrew]. July 20, 1956.
http://goo.gl/XzQiBq.

Doust, Rick. "No 'Magic Bullet' out of Interferon, but Work in Labs Showing
Promise." *Globe and Mail* (Canada), February 16, 1984.

Economist. "Scattered Saviors." January 28, 2012. www.economist.com/node
/21543488.

Eder, Miri. "Live from the Small Intestine." *Ma'ariv* [in Hebrew], June 5, 2012.
www.nrg.co.il/online/archive/ART/224/085.html.

Eglash, Ruth. "A Light among the Nations." *Jerusalem Post,* May 7, 2008.

Eisner, Robin. "An Ingestible 'Missile' Helps Target Disease." *Forward,*
November 14, 2003. http://forward.com/articles/7098/an-ingestible
-missile-helps-target-disease/.

English, Bella. "For Phil Villers, Helping Feed the World Is in the Bag." *Boston
Globe,* December 17, 2013. www.bostonglobe.com/lifestyle/2013/12/17
/concord-based-company-aims-help-alleviate-world-hunger/aIGEHu8
DbD3nI2yViuiABP/story.html.

Erlanger, Steven. "After 2000 Years, a Seed from Ancient Judea Sprouts."
New York Times, June 12, 2005. www.nytimes.com/2005/06/12/world
/middleeast/after-2000-years-a-seed-from-ancient-judea-sprouts.html
?_r=1.

Escondido, Nico. "The Man Who Discovered THC." *High Times,* May 31, 2011.

EuropaWire. "The Scientist – The Life and Work of Raphael Mechoulam."
July 31, 2015. www.projectcbd.org/article/scientist-life-and-work-raphael
-mechoulam.

Finkelstein, Asaf. "The Grass Is Always Greener." *Jerusalem Post,* December
11, 2015.

Flanders, Kevin. "A Focus on Innovation – PillCam Colon Offers Some
Unique Perspective on the Future." *Health Care News,* February 2015.

http://healthcarenews.com/a-focus-on-innovation-pillcam-colon-offers
-some-unique-perspective-on-the-future/.

Forbes. "A Fortune in Firewalls." March 18, 2002, www.forbes.com/forbes
/2002/0318/102.html.

———. "The Unit." February 8, 2007. www.forbes.com/2007/02/07/israel
-military-unit-ventures-biz-cx_gk_0208israel.html.

Forbes Israel. "Number 73: Marius Nacht" [in Hebrew]. April 14, 2014. www
.forbes.co.il/news/new.aspx?or9VQ=IEEJ.

Friedman, Thomas. "Israel and the Birds Vie for Precious Air Space." *New
York Times,* September 17, 1985. www.nytimes.com/1985/09/17/science
/israel-and-the-birds-vie-for-precious-air-space.html?pagewanted=all.

Gabizon, Yoram. "Given Imaging – 22 Million Insured within 10 Months."
Haaretz [in Hebrew], July 3, 2002. www.haaretz.co.il/misc/1.806844.

Gallup. "In U.S., 58% Back Legal Marijuana Use." October 21, 2015. www.gallup
.com/poll/186260/back-legal-marijuana.aspx.

Gilmer, Maureen. "Dry Land Thrives with Drip Irrigation: Systems Traced
to Discovery in Arid Israel in 1960s." *Dayton Daily News,* May 7, 2015.

Golan, Hagai. "I Work for the Interest and the Challenge." *Globes* (Israel).
June 6, 2013.

Goldstein, Tani. "Arab High-Tech Blooming in Galilee." *Ynet,* April 21, 2011.
www.ynetnews.com/articles/0,7340,L-4057013,00.html.

Greenwald, Ted. "Ekso's Exoskeletons Let Paraplegics Walk, Will Anyone
Actually Wear One?" *Fast Company,* March 19, 2012. www.fastcompany
.com/1822791/eksos-exoskeletons-let-paraplegics-walk-will-anyone-ac
tually-wear-one.

Gross, Judah Ari. "Masters of Disaster, IDF Field Hospital May Be Recognized
as World's Best." *Times of Israel,* October 18, 2016. www.timesofisrael.com
/masters-of-disaster-idf-field-hospital-may-be-recognized-as-worlds-best.

———. "UN Ranks IDF Emergency Medical Team as 'No. 1 in the World.'"
Times of Israel, November 13, 2016. http://www.timesofisrael.com/un-ra
nks-idf-emergency-medical-team-as-no-1-in-the-world/.

Haaretz. "Bill Clinton Hails Israel Relief Mission to Haiti." January 28, 2010.
http://www.haaretz.com/news/bill-clinton-hails-israel-relief-mission
-to-haiti-1.262274.

Habib-Valdhorn, Shiri. "Check Point Launches Malware Protection Solution."
Globes (Israel), March 10, 2015.

Harpaz, A. "United Hatzalah: Thirty Arab Volunteers from East Jerusalem Join the Organization with the Encouragement of the Organization's Senior Executives." *Actuality* [in Hebrew], October 24, 2009. www.actuality.co.il/articles/art.asp?ID=3684&SID=7&CID=14&MID=14.

Hartman, Ben. "Iron Dome Doesn't Answer Threats." *Jerusalem Post*, May 9, 2010. www.jpost.com/Israel/Iron-Dome-doesnt-answer-threats.

Hayadan. "Dedication, Zionism, and a Few Pieces from Toys R Us: An Interview with the Team That Oversees the Iron Dome, All the Members of Which Are Graduates of the Technion, and the Secret of the Project's Success" [in Hebrew]. July 9, 2014. www.hayadan.org.il/interview-iron-dome-rp0907141.

———. "Going Live to the Small Intestine" [in Hebrew]. July 6, 2000. www.hayadan.org.il/given-imagings-breakthrough-technology0607001.

Helfand, Carly. "Rebif." *Fierce Pharma*, www.fiercepharma.com/special-report/rebif.

Hirschauge, Orr. "Israeli Tech Needs to Be More Inclusive, Says Yossi Vardi." *Wall Street Journal*, September 11, 2014. http://blogs.wsj.com/digits/2014/09/11/israeli-tech-needs-to-be-more-inclusive-says-yossi-vardi/.

Horovitz, David. "The Guy with the Bandage." *Jerusalem Post*, April 29, 2011. www.jpost.com/Opinion/Columnists/Editors-Notes-The-guy-with-the-bandage.

Howell, Donna. "Check Point Copes with Competition." *Investor's Business Daily*, May 13, 2002.

Huguenin, Roland. "Courage under Fire." *Magazine of the International Red Cross and Red Crescent Movement*, http://www.redcross.int/EN/mag/magazine2000_4/Palestina.html.

Hull Daily Mail. "'Bionic' Claire Lomas Trained for London Marathon in East Yorkshire." May 10, 2012. www.hulldailymail.co.uk/Bionic-Claire-Lomas-trained-London-Marathon-East/story-16040411-detail/story.html.

Iddan, Gavriel J., and Paul Swain. "History and Development of Capsule Endoscopy." *Gastrointestinal Endoscopy Clinics of North America* 14 (2004). www.giendo.theclinics.com/article/S1052–5157(03)00145–4/abstract.

Ilany, Ofer. "2,000-Year-Old Date Seed Grows in the Arava." *Haaretz*, February 15, 2007. www.haaretz.com/print-edition/news/2–000-year-old-date-seed-grows-in-the-arava-1.213054.

India Pharma News. "Kadimastem to Receive Sponsored Research Agree-

ment with National Multiple Sclerosis Society Fast Forward Program."
September 29, 2015.

Investor's Business Daily. "Computer Niche." September 12, 2000.

Israel21c. "Camera-in-a-Pill Gives a Closer Look." November 1, 2001. www
.israel21c.org/camera-in-a-pill-gives-a-closer-look/.

———. "Checking in with Check Point's Gil Shwed." June 3, 2003. www
.israel21c.org/checking-in-with-check-points-gil-shwed.

Jacobs, Jill. "The History of Tikkun Olam." *Zeek,* June 2007. www.zeek.net
/706tohu/index.php?page=2.

Jacobs, Lawrence, Judith A. O'Malley, and Arnold Freeman. "Intrathecal Interferon in the Treatment of Multiple Sclerosis: Patient Follow-Up." *Archives
of Neurology* 42, no. 9 (1985): 841–47. http://archneur.jamanetwork.com
/article.aspx?articleid=584497.

Jacobson, Ben. "It's for the Birds." *Jerusalem Post,* January 18, 2008.

Jewish Telegraphic Agency. "Bus Bomb Toll: Six Dead, 19 Injured." June 5, 1978.
www.jta.org/1978/06/05/archive/bus-bomb-toll-six-dead-19-injured.

Josephs, Allison. "The Orthodox Man Who Saved a Life with His Yarmulke."
Jew in the City, May 29, 2014. http://jewinthecity.com/2014/05/the-or
thodox-man-who-saved-a-life-with-his-yarmulke.

Josephson, Brady. "Want to Be Happier? Give More. Give Better." *Huffington Post,* November 11, 2014. https://www.huffingtonpost.com/brady
-josephson/want-to-be-happier-give-m_b_6175358.html.

Kalman, Matthew. "After 1,500 Years, Frankincense Returns to the Holy
Land in Time for Christmas." *Times of Israel,* December 23, 2012. http://
blogs.timesofisrael.com/after-1500-years-frankincense-returns-to-the
-holy-land/.

Kampeas, Ron. "Israeli Bandage May Have Saved Giffords' Life after Shooting." *Jewish News of Northern California,* February 17, 2011. www.jweekly
.com/includes/print/60886/article/israeli-bandage-may-have-saved
-giffords-life-after-shooting/.

Kaufman, Frederick. "How to Fight a Food Crisis." *Los Angeles Times,* September 21, 2012. http://articles.latimes.com/2012/sep/21/opinion/la-oe
-kaufman-food-hunger-drought-20120921.

Keighley, Paul Sánchez. "96-Year-Old Solar Energy Genius Harry Zvi Tabor
Talks to NoCamels about Pioneering Solar Power." NoCamels, August

13, 2006. http://nocamels.com/2013/08/96-year-old-solar-energy-geni us-harry-zvi-tabor-talks-to-nocamels-about-pioneering-solar-power/.

Kerstein, Arin. "The Impact of Drip Irrigation: 'More Crop per Drop.'" *Borgen Magazine*, July 20, 2015. www.borgenmagazine.com/impact-drip -irrigation-crop-per-drop.

Klein Leichman, Abigail. "GPS for Brain Surgeons." Israel21c, January 7, 2013, www.israel21c.org/health/gps-for-brain-surgeons.

———. "A Lifetime in Solar Energy." Israel21c, May 5, 2009. http://www .israel21c.org/a-lifetime-in-solar-energy/.

———. "The Israeli Pharmacologist Who Kick-Started Marijuana Research." Israel21c, May 14, 2012. www.israel21c.org/the-israeli-pharmacologist-who -kick-started-marijuana-research.

———. "The Maverick Thinker behind Iron Dome." Israel21c, August 3, 2014. https://www.israel21c.org/the-maverick-thinker-behind-iron-dome/.

———. "Peace Prize for Jewish and Muslim Leaders of United Hatzalah." Israel21c, July 24, 2014. www.israel21c.org/peace-prize-for-jewish-and-m uslim-leaders-of-united-hatzalah/.

Koren, Hillel. "Mazor Sees FDA Nod for SpineAssist Brain Surgery Use." *Globes* (Israel), July 28, 2010. www.globes.co.il/en/article-1000577761.

Kotz, Deborah. "Swallowable Imaging Capsules Not Widely Used." *Boston Globe*, August 19, 2013, www.bostonglobe.com/lifestyle/health-wellness /2013/08/18/swallowable-imaging-capsule-keeps-improving-but-still-not -routine-here-why/jVhJGvrS25u014saRdi8EK/story.html.

Krause, Reinhardt. "Check Point's Gil Shwed: He Joined Interest and Opportunity to Fill a Computer Niche." *Investor's Business Daily*, September 12, 2000.

Lapidot, Aharon. "The Gray Matter behind the Iron Dome." *Israel Hayom*, February 23, 2012. www.israelhayom.com/site/newsletter_article.php ?id=6509.

Lapowsky, Issie. "This Computerized Exoskeleton Could Help Millions of People Walk Again." *Wired*, July 22, 2014. www.wired.com/2014/07 /rewalk.

Lazaroff, Tovah. "Int'l Red Cross Slams MDA for Operating in East Jerusalem, West Bank." *Jerusalem Post*, July 5, 2013. www.jpost.com/Diplomacy -and-Politics/Intl-Red-Cross-slams-MDA-for-operating-in-e-Jlem-West -Bank-318827.

Lee, Martin A. "The Discovery of the Endocannabinoid System." O'Shaughnessy's Online, 2010. www.beyondthc.com/wp-content/uploads/2012/07/eCBSystemLee.pdf.

Levi Julian, Hana. "Date Tree Sprouts from 2000-Year-Old Seed Found on Masada." *Arutz Sheva*, June 13, 2008. www.israelnationalnews.com/News/News.aspx/126484#.VVDlxtJViko.

Levinson, Charles, and Adam Entous. "Israel's Iron Dome Defense Battled to Get off Ground." *Wall Street Journal*, November 26, 2012. https://www.wsj.com/articles/SB10001424127887324712504578136931078468210.

Libsker, Ari. "An Invention with Legs" [in Hebrew]. *Calcalist* (Israel), August 5, 2010. www.calcalist.co.il/local/articles/0,7340,L-3413629,00.html.

London, Bianca. "Paralyzed Marathon Heroine Claire Lomas: 'Things Go Wrong in Life but You Have to Fight Back." *Daily Mail* (UK), May 16, 2013. www.dailymail.co.uk/femail/article-2325463/Paralysed-Marathon-heroine-Claire-Lomas-Things-wrong-life-fight-make-luck.html.

Ma'ariv. "Why Do Users of the *Dud Shemesh* Get Special Electric Meters?" [in Hebrew]. January 1, 1960. http://goo.gl/8HWWEJ.

Machlis, Avi. "Firm Building a 'Firewall' against Competitors." *Financial Post*, March 7, 1998.

Martin, Alyson, and Nushin Rashidian. "Martin and Rashidian: Little Green Pill." *National Post* (Canada), April 3, 2014. http://nationalpost.com/opinion/martin-rashidian-little-green-pill.

McCaffrey, Colm, Olivier Chevalerias, Clan O'Mathuna, and Karen Twomey. "Swallowable-Capsule Technology." IEEE *Pervasive Computing* 7, no. 1 (January–March 2008).

Medical Device Daily. "Report from Israel: SpineAssist Is First Miniature Robotic to Receive FDA OK." June 11, 2004.

Merck. "Multiple Sclerosis: Using Hamster Cells to Fight Multiple Sclerosis." January 17, 2015. www.magazine.emerck/darmstadt_germany/innovation/Michel_Revel/multiple_sclerosis.html.

Mishmar. "A Center of Exactness Has Been Established in the Israeli Physics Lab" [in Hebrew]. January 4, 1953. http://goo.gl/jLc83w.

Neiger, David. "Getting to the Point on Security Software." *The Age* (Australia), October 21, 2003.

New Agriculturist. "Hermetic Storage a Viable Option." January 2008. www.new-ag.info/en/developments/devItem.php?a=349.

Newman, Lily Hay. "You Might Be Able to Avoid Colonoscopies Now That the PillCam Is FDA Approved." *Slate*, February 6, 2014. www.slate.com /blogs/future_tense/2014/02/06/fda_approval_for_pillcam_could _mean_swallowing_a_pill_instead_of_having.html.

Ovadia, Avishai. "The Long and Winding Road." *Globes* [in Hebrew], August 7, 2003. www.globes.co.il/news/article.aspx?did=712816.

———. "Taro and Given Imaging Set to Raise a Quarter of a Billion Dollars on the Nasdaq This Week." *Globes* [in Hebrew], September 30, 2001. www .globes.co.il/news/article.aspx?did=524787.

Pagliery, Jose. "Half of American Adults Hacked this Year." *CNN Tech*, May 28, 2014. http://money.cnn.com/2014/05/28/technology/security/hack -data-breach.

Patton, Charlie. "Woman Gets Back Relief with Unique Surgery: Robot Has Key Role to Help Surgeon in Two-Part Procedure." *Florida Times-Union*, February 16, 2014.

Philippidis, Alex. "Top 10 Multiple Sclerosis Drugs." *Genetic Engineering and Biotechnology News*, February 18, 2014. http://www.genengnews.com/the -lists/top-10-multiple-sclerosis-drugs/77900039?page=1.

Pietrangelo, Ann, and Valencia Higuera. "Multiple Sclerosis by the Numbers: Facts, Statistics, and You." *Healthline*, March 24, 2015. www.healthline.com /health/multiple-sclerosis/facts-statistics-infographic.

Pfeffer, Anshel, and Yanir Yagna. "Iron Dome Successfully Intercepts Gaza Rocket for the First Time." *Haaretz*, April 7, 2011. www.haaretz.com /israel-news/iron-dome-successfully-intercepts-gaza-rocket-for-first -time-1.354696.

Press, Viva Sarah. "WHO Ranks IDF Field Hospital as World's Best." Israel21c, November 14, 2016. https://www.israel21c.org/who-ranks-idf-field -hospital-as-worlds-best/.

Rawhani, Anisa. "Pioneering Pot Prof Still Studying at 85." *Kingston Whig-Standard*, June 29, 2015.

Reuters. "Iran 'Rocket Kitten' Cyber Group Hit in European Raids after Targeting Israeli Scientists." November 9, 2015. www.jpost.com/Middle -East/Iran/Iran-Rocket-Kitten-cyber-group-hit-in-European-raids-after -targeting-Israeli-scientists-432485.

———. "Obama Seeks $205 Million for Israel Rocket Shield." May 14, 2010. http://www.reuters.com/article/us-israel-usa-irondome/obama-seeks

-205-million-for-israel-rocket-shield-idUSTRE64C5JO20100513?type=
politicsNews.

Robertson, Bill. "Israel's Iconic Iron Dome: General Danny Gold, Father."
Huffington Post, December 4, 2015. www.huffingtonpost.com/billrobinson
/israels-iron-dome-by-gene_b_8411436.html.

Robinson, Adam. "The History of Robotics in Manufacturing." *Cerasis*, October 6, 2014., http://cerasis.com/2014/10/06/robotics-in-manufacturing/.

Rosenberg, David. "BRM Bets Big on the Internet." *Jerusalem Post*, March 5,
2000.

Rubin, Uzi. "Hezbollah's Rocket Campaign against Northern Israel: A Preliminary Report." *Jerusalem Center for Public Affairs* 6, no. 10 (August 31,
2006). www.jcpa.org/brief/brief006–10.htm.

Sallon, Sarah, Elaine Solowey, Yuval Cohen, Raia Korchinsky, Markus Egli,
Ivan Woodhatch, Orit Simchoni, and Mordechai Kislev. "Supporting
Online Material for Germination, Genetics, and Growth of an Ancient
Date Seed." *Science AAAS*, June 13, 2008. https://www.sciencemag.org
/content/320/5882/1464/suppl/DC1.

San Diego Jewish World. "Behind Israel's Fast Response to Medical Emergencies." April 6, 2014. www.sdjewishworld.com/2014/04/06/behind-israels
-fast-response-medical-emergencies.

Sandberg, Jared. "Even '60 Minutes' Couldn't Turn Computer Crime into
High Drama." Associated Press, February 24, 1995. www.apnewsarchive
.com/1995/Even-60-Minutes-Couldn-t-Turn-Computer-Crime-Into
-High-Drama/id-fd7547b1c7a6cf738de5ad02bfaf4431.

Sandler, Neal. "Israeli Startup Finds Funding Down Under." *Daily Deal*, July
26, 2002.

Sarah, Rachel. "New Israeli Export an Easy Pill for Patients to Swallow." *Jewish
News of Northern California*, November 4, 2005. www.jweekly.com/article
/full/27605/new-israeli-export-an-easy-pill-for-patients-to-swallow/.

Schmeck, Harold, Jr. "Interferon Makes Inroads against Some Infections,
Including Colds." *New York Times*, June 1, 1982.

Schmid, Randolph E. "Tree from 2,000-Year-Old Seed Is Doing Well." June
12, 2008. www.freerepublic.com/focus/f-news/2030302/posts.

Shamah, David. "Bumbling Iran Hackers Target Israelis, Saudis...Badly,
Report Shows." *Times of Israel*, November 10, 2015. www.timesofisrael
.com/bumbling-iran-hackers-target-israelis-saudis-badly-report-shows/

———. "Israel's Drip Irrigation Pioneer Says His Tech Feeds a Billion People." *Times of Israel*, April 21, 2015. www.timesofisrael.com/israels-drip-irrigati on-pioneer-our-tech-feeds-a-billion-people.

———. "Pillcam's Inventor Regrets Sale of 'Biblical' Tech Firm to Foreign Firm." *Times of Israel*, April 23, 2015. www.timesofisrael.com/pillcams-in ventor-regrets-sale-of-biblical-tech-to-foreign-firm/.

———. "ReWalk's Benefits Go beyond Ambulation, Company Says." *Times of Israel*, May 20, 2015. www.timesofisrael.com/ReWalks-benefits-go-beyond-ambulation-company-says.

———. "What Israeli Drips Did for the World." *Jerusalem Post*, August 20, 2013. www.timesofisrael.com/what-israeli-drips-did-for-the-world.

Shauli, Avi. "Another Bonanza? The Innovator behind the Mazor Robot, Worth Today 1.3 Billion Shekels, Tells BizPortal about His Next Innovation." Bizportal [in Hebrew], October 16, 2013. www.bizportal.co.il /capitalmarket/news/article/370886.

Shen-Miller, Jane, Mary Beth Mudgett, J. William Schopf, Steven Clarke, and Rainer Berger. "Exceptional Seed Longevity and Robust Growth: Ancient Sacred Lotus from China." *American Journal of Botany* 82, no. 11 (November 1995): 1367–80. www.botany.org/ajb/82–11–1995–1367.pdf.

Shimoni, Eli. "Mazor's Robot for Back Surgery Raises 10 Million Dollars." *Ynet* [in Hebrew], May 4, 2005. www.ynet.co.il/articles/0,7340,L-3081277 ,00.html.

Shimoni, Mor. "Inspirers: Who Are the Researchers Lighting the Torch This Year?" *Walla* [in Hebrew], March 8, 2015. http://healthy.walla.co.il/item /2836034.

Shipler, David K. "Israel Completes Pullout, Leaving Sinai to Egypt." *New York Times*, April 26, 1982. www.nytimes.com/1982/04/26/world/israeli -completes-pullout-leaving-sinai-to-egypt.html?pagewanted=all.

Shuttleworth, Ken. "Biblical Nazareth Goes High-Tech Thanks to Arab Push." *USA Today*, February 20, 2015. www.usatoday.com/story/tech/2015/02 /18/nazareth-tech-sector/22459503.

Sides, Hampton. "Science Seeks to Unlock Marijuana's Secrets." *National Geographic*, June 2015. http://ngm.nationalgeographic.com/2015/06 /marijuana/sides-text.

Siegel-Itzkovich, Judy. "30 E. J'Lem Arabs Become Hatzalah Emergency Medics." *Jerusalem Post*, October 16, 2009.

———. "Ambucycle Zooms into AIPAC Conference." *Jerusalem Post*, March 3, 2015. www.jpost.com/Diaspora/Ambucycle-zooms-into-AIPAC-conference-392729.

———. "Before the Ambulance Comes." *Jerusalem Post*, September 13, 2009.

———. "Birds on His Brain." *Jerusalem Post*, November 6, 2005. www.jpost.com/Health-and-Sci-Tech/Science-And-Environment/Birds-on-his-brain.

———. "Capital's Light Rail Survives First Simulated Terror Attack." *Jerusalem Post*, July 26, 2012.

———. "Is This Where Charity Ends?" *Jerusalem Post*, October 24, 2004.

———. "Opening Their Eyes." *Jerusalem Post*, December 20, 2015. www.jpost.com/Business-and-Innovation/Health-and-Science/Opening-their-eyes-437828.

———. "Robots Back Breakthrough Surgery." *Jerusalem Post*, March 6, 2011. www.jpost.com/Health-and-Science/Robots-back-breakthrough-surgery.

———. "The World Is Going to Pot." *Jerusalem Post*, May 18, 2014. www.jpost.com/Health-and-Science/The-world-is-going-to-pot-352563.

Sironi, Vittorio A. "Origin and Evolution of Deep Brain Stimulation." *Front Integrated Neuroscience* 5, no. 42 (2011), www.ncbi.nlm.nih.gov/pmc/articles/PMC3157831.

Sobel, Bill. "Segway Inventor Dean Kamen: Science Isn't a Spectator Sport." *CMS Wire*, January 6, 2015. www.cmswire.com/cms/customer-experience/segway-inventor-dean-kamen-science-isnt-a-spectator-sport-027638.php.

Sobelman, Batsheva. "One Country That Won't Be Taking Syrian Refugees: Israel." *Los Angeles Times*, September 6, 2015. www.latimes.com/world/middleeast/la-fg-syrian-refugees-israel-20150906-story.html.

Sokol, Sam. "Fighting Together to Save Lives." *Jerusalem Post*, December 12, 2012.

———. "The Marijuana Maven." *Jerusalem Post*, April 6, 2012.

Solomon, Shoshanna. "Can Cannabis Treat Asthma? Jerusalem Experts to Find Out." *Times of Israel*, October 24, 2017. https://www.timesofisrael.com/jerusalem-cannabis-guru-to-study-effect-of-weed-on-asthma/.

Steinberg, Jessica. "Disease Be Not Proud." *Jerusalem Post*, February 27, 2004.

Steiner, Rupert. "Army Fired an Enthusiasm to Wage War on Hackers." *Sunday Times* (London), July 13, 1997.

Stewart, Lain. "How Can Our Blue Planet Be Running out of Fresh Water." BBC. www.bbc.co.uk/guides/z3qdd2p.

Strange, Adario. "FDA Approved First Robotic Exoskeleton for Paralyzed Users." June 30, 2014. http://mashable.com/2014/06/30/fda-approves -robotic-exoskeleton-paralyzed-ReWalk/#FUfHo81qRgqI.

Struck, Doug. "Birder Sows Goodwill in Mideast." *Washington Post*, April 9, 1998. www.washingtonpost.com/archive/politics/1998/04/09/birder -sows-goodwill-in-mideast/a72fe666–966f–4766–86a2–0827d64cca44/.

Sudilovsky, Judith. "Arabs Make Gains in Joining Israel's High-Growth, High-Tech Industries." Catholic News Service, January 7, 2013.

Tan, Thomas. "Dr. Michel Revel Elected to ISICR Honorary Membership." *International Society for Interferon and Cytokine Research* 10, no. 2 (April 2003): 1–4. http://cytokinesociety.org/wp-content/uploads/2016/11 /Newsletter10.2.pdf.

Tarnopolsky, Noga. "At 82, He's the World's Most Eminent Pot Scientist." *Eureka Times Standard*, August 27, 2013. http://www.times-standard.com /article/ZZ/20130827/NEWS/130828962.

TEDMED. "The Fastest Ambulance? A Motorcycle." April 2013. www.ted.com /talks/eli_beer_the_fastest_ambulance_a_motorcycle?language=en.

Tidhar, David. *Encyclopedia of the Founders and Builders of Israel* [in Hebrew], vol. 7 (1956), 2945. www.tidhar.tourolib.org/tidhar/view/7/2945.

Times of Israel. "Iran Said to Hack Former Israeli Army Chief-of-Staff, Access His Entire Computer." February 9, 2016. www.timesofisrael.com/iran-said -to-hack-former-israeli-army-chief-of-staff-access-his-entire-computer.

———. "Israeli Generals Said among 1,600 Global Targets of Iran Cyber-Attack." January 28, 2016. www.timesofisrael.com/israeli-generals-said-a mong-1600-global-targets-of-iran-cyber-attack.

Tower. "IDF Medical Units Treat Wounded Syrians." August 9, 2016, www .thetower.org/3759-watch-idf-medical-units-treat-wounded-syrians/.

Tzipori, Tali. "Mazor Robotics Worth 7 Times More in a Year; How Did the Company Do It?" *Globes* [in Hebrew], July 4, 2013. www.globes.co.il/news /article.aspx?did=1000859350.

Udasin, Sharon. "A Drip Revolution around the World." *Jerusalem Post*, April 22, 2015. www.jpost.com/Israel-News/A-drip-revolution-around-the -world-398660.

————. "Israel Bird Expert Wins 25,000 Euro German Prize." *Jerusalem Post*, November 14, 2012.

————. "Zvi Tabor, Solar Pioneer, Dies at 98." *Jerusalem Post*, December 17, 2015. http://www.jpost.com/Israel-News/Zvi-Tabor-solar-pioneer-dies-at-98-437563.

Ungerleider, Neal. "How Check Point Became the Fortune 500's Cybersecurity Favorite." *Fast Company*, June 4, 2013. www.fastcompany.com/3012414/the-code-war/how-check-point-became-the-fortune-500s-cybersecurity-favorite.

Uni, Assaf. "Meet the Man Who Discovered Weed's Secret Ingredient." *Vocativ*, December 18, 2014. www.vocativ.com/culture/science/raphael-mechoulam-thc-marijunana/.

Van Heerden, Adam. "Professor Raphael Mechoulam, the Father of Marijuana Research, Talks to NoCamels about His Studies and Breaking the Law in the Name of Science." NoCamels, September 24, 2013. http://nocamels.com/2013/09/professor-raphael-mechoulam-the-father-of-marijuana-research-talks-to-nocamels-about-his-studies-and-breaking-the-law-in-the-name-of-science.

van Vark, Caspar. "No More Rotten Crops: Six Smart Inventions to Prevent Harvest Loss." *Guardian* (UK), October 27, 2014. www.theguardian.com/global-development-professionals-network/2014/oct/27/farming-post-harvest-loss-solutions-developing-world.

Vancouver Sun. "Long-Dead Teenager Tells Tale of Pot-Smoking in Era of 300 AD." May 20, 1993.

Wade, Lizzie. "Researchers Are Finally Studying the Other Chemical in Pot." *Wired*, June 4, 2015.

Waldoks, Ehud Zion. "Bright Ideas." *Jerusalem Post*, October 1, 2008. http://www.jpost.com/Features/Bright-ideas.

Wallis, Jake. "Saving Their Sworn Enemy." *Daily Mail*, December 8, 2015. www.dailymail.co.uk/news/article-3315347/Watch-heart-pounding-moment-Israeli-commandos-save-Islamic-militants-Syrian-warzone-risking-lives-sworn-enemies.html.

Walker, Joseph. "New Ways to Screen for Colon Cancer." *Wall Street Journal*, June 8, 2014. www.wsj.com/articles/new-ways-to-screen-for-colon-cancer-1402063124.

Wantanbe, Lauri. "Independence Technology Discontinues the iBOT." *Mobil-*

ity Management, February 1, 2009. https://mobilitymgmt.com/Articles /2009/02/01/Independence-Technology-Discontinues-the-iBOT.aspx.

Ward, Charles. "Protestant Work Ethic That Took Root in Faith Is Now Ingrained in Our Culture." *Houston Chronicle*, September 1, 2007. www .chron.com/life/houston-belief/article/Protestant-work-ethic-that-took -root-in-faith-is-1834963.php.

Weinreb, Gali. "Out of Zion Shall Go Forth Medicines." *Globes* (Israel), March 1, 2006. www.globes.co.il/en/article-1000067051.

Weise, Elizabeth. " 43% of Companies Had a Data Breach This Past Year." *USA Today*, September 24, 2014. www.usatoday.com/story/tech/2014/09/24 /data-breach-companies-60/16106197.

Whalen, Jeanne. "Tiny Cameras to See in the Intestines." *Wall Street Journal*, February 29, 2016. www.wsj.com/articles/tiny-cameras-to-see-in-the -intestines-1456776145.

Wickham, Chris. "'Bionic Woman' Claire Lomas Is First Woman to Take Robotic Suit Home." *Independent* (UK), September 4, 2012. www .independent.co.uk/news/science/bionic-woman-claire-lomas-is-first -woman-to-take-robotic-suit-home-8104838.html.

Wile, Anthony. "Dr. Raphael Mechoulam: The Promise of Cannabis." *Daily Bell*, October 19, 2014. www.thedailybell.com/exclusive-interviews/35732 /Anthony-Wile-Dr-Raphael-Mechoulam-The-Promise-of-Cannabis.

Winter, Jana. "Suspected Arizona Gunman Reportedly Planned Shooting in Advance." Fox News Channel, January 9, 2011. www.foxnews.com/politics /2011/01/09/fbi-director-robert-mueller-takes-lead-arizona-shooting -investigation.html.

Winter, Rhonda. "Israel's Special Relationship with the Solar Water Heater." Reuters, March 18, 2011. www.reuters.com/article/idUS31161215362011031 8.

Xinhua News Agency. "Israeli Agro Expert Offers Farmers Bug-Free Solutions." November 29, 2011. www.soyatech.com/news_story.php?id=26217.

Ya'akovi, Netta. "Given Imaging Is Planning Another Giant Public Offering – Mostly Selling Shares of Interested Parties." *The Marker* [in Hebrew], January 28, 2001. www.themarker.com/wallstreet/1.95619.

Ynet. "Hi-Tech: Gil Shwed." Ynet [in Hebrew]. www.ynet.co.il/Ext/App/Ency /Items/CdaAppEncyEconomyPerson/0,8925,L-3836,00.html.

———. "A Thriving Green Economy" [in Hebrew]. December 15, 2015. http://www.ynet.co.il/articles/0,7340,L-4739893,00.html.

Zar, Atiya. "Professor Moshe Shoham, Who Heads the Technion Robotics Lab, Believes That Everyone in the Future Will Have a Personal Robot." *Arutz Sheva*, July 15, 2010. www.inn.co.il/Besheva/Article.aspx/9690.

INTERVIEWS

(Titles shown are accurate as of the time of the interview.)

Abu Rashid, General (Ret.) Mansour – Chairman, Amman Center for Peace and Development, Jordan. Phone, December 13, 2016.

Abramowitz, Yosef – Chief Executive Officer, Energiya Global Capital; former President, Arava Power Company, Israel. Washington, DC, March 8, 2017.

Adler, Yoav – Head of Innovation and Cyber-technology, Israel Ministry of Foreign Affairs. Tel Aviv, April 12, 2016; August 5, 2016. Phone, December 19, 2016.

Asli, Muhammad – Head East Jerusalem volunteer, United Hatzalah. Phone, May 25, 2016.

Alexander, Dahlia, MD – daughter of Harry Zvi Tabor; Faculty of Medicine, Tel Aviv University. Jerusalem, July 16, 2015; November 2017; phone, March 28, 2016.

Arnon, Prof. Ruth, PhD – Immunology, Weizmann Institute; laureate, Israel Prize. Rehovot, July 13, 2015.

Bassi, Shaul – Chief Executive Officer, BioBee. Kibbutz Sde Eliyahu, June 29, 2016.

Barak, Naty – Chief Sustainability Officer, Netafim. Kibbutz Hatzerim, July 5, 2015.

Baruch, Yehuda, MD – former Director-General, Abarbanel Mental Health Center, Israel. Phone, December 15, 2016.

Bar-Natan, Bernard – innovator, Emergency Bandage. Givatayim, July 10, 2015; phone, May 24, 2016.

Beer, Eli – Founder and President, United Hatzalah. Washington, DC, March 21, 2016; phone, May 31, 2016.

Ben Dov, Oded – innovator, Sesame Phone. Washington, DC, March 25, 2017.

Ben-Hur, Prof. Tamir, PhD – Head of Neurology Department, Hadassah Medical Center. Phone, December 12, 2016.

Bergman, Prof. Hagai, MD, PhD – Department of Medical Neurobiology, Hebrew University of Jerusalem. Phone, January 1, 2016.

Berry, Orna, PhD – former Chief Scientist, Israel; Vice President, Dell EMC; General Manager, Israel Center of Excellence. Phone, December 22, 2016.

Benabid, Prof. Alim-Louis, MD, PhD – innovator, deep brain stimulation; Member, French Academy of Sciences. Phone, January 12, 2016.

Bloom, Peter – Chairman, DonorsChoose.org; former Managing Director, General Atlantic Partners. Phone, May 23, 2016; New York, December 26 2016.

Brand, David – Chief Forester and Head of Forest Department, Jewish National Fund, Israel. Eshtaol, July 14, 2015.

Brand, Meir – Vice President, Europe, Middle East, Africa Emerging Markets, Google; Israel Chief Executive Officer and Middle East, Russia, and Turkey Regional Director, Alphabet Inc. Tel Aviv, June 24, 2016.

Braun, Prof. Erez, PhD – Faculty of Physics, Technion Israel Institute of Technology. Phone, February 16, 2016.

Bronicki, Dita – Founder and former Chief Executive Officer, Ormat Technologies. Yavneh, July 13, 2015.

Bronicki, Lucien Yehuda, PhD – Founder and former Chief Technology Officer, Ormat Technologies. Yavneh, July 13, 2015.

Carvalho, Prof. Maria Otília, PhD – Chair, Institute of Tropical Scientific Research, University of Lisbon. Phone, January 7, 2016.

Cohan, Peter– Lecturer, Babson College. Phone, September 23, 2016.

Cohen, Mattanya – Director for Planning, MASHAV, Ministry of Foreign Affairs, Israel. Phone, October 25, 2016.

Dagan, Mooky – Chairman, Noah Eshkol Foundation. Holon, June 17, 2015.

de Bruin, Tom – Chief Executive Officer and President, Philippines GrainPro. Phone, January 18, 2016.

Dela Casa, Victor – Digital Marketing and Communications Officer, GrainPro. Phone, December 15, 2015.

Dershowitz, Alan – Professor Emeritus, Harvard Law School; author, *The Case for Israel*. Phone, March 29, 2017.

Dinevich, Leonid, PhD – Faculty of Life Sciences, Department of Zoology, Tel Aviv University. Latrun, August 12, 2016.

Distel, Oded – Director of Israel NewTech and Eco Systems, Ministry of Economy and Industry. Jerusalem, June 16, 2015; June 11, 2017; July 25, 2017.

Drucker, Yossi – Vice President and General Manager, Air Superiority Systems Division, Rafael Advanced Defense Systems. Phone, April 5, 2016.

Eddine, Zaïd Salah, PhD – Technical Director, Marrakech Date Palm Project. Phone, March 28, 2016.

Eden, Shmuel (Mooly) – former General Manager, Intel Israel. Shefayim, July 2, 2015.

Einav, Henry – Patent Counsel, Merck Group, Israel. Phone, July 8, 2016.

El Heid, Ahmed – factory owner, Emergency Bandage. Phone, January 29, 2016; Tuba Zangariyye, August 13, 2016.

Elia, Liron – Founder and Chief Executive Officer, Art Medical. Tel Aviv, July 15, 2015.

Engelhard, Prof. Dan, MD – Head of Pediatric AIDS Center, Hebrew University-Hadassah Medical Center; Professor of Pediatrics, Hebrew University-Hadassah Medical Center. Phone, November 10, 2016.

Erlanger, Steven – London Bureau Chief, *New York Times*; former Jerusalem Bureau Chief, *New York Times*. Phone, December 19, 2016.

Ezra, Aviv – Director for Congressional Affairs, Israel Ministry of Foreign Affairs. Phone, July 5, 2016.

Feinstein, Ari – Founder, World-Check; Founding Principal, Annex Ventures. Phone, September 24, 2015; July 26, 2016.

Fragman-Sapir, Ori, PhD – Scientific Director, Jerusalem Botanical Gardens. Phone, December 2, 2016.

Gerson, Mark – Cofounder, Gerson Lehrman Group. New York, October 27, 2016; December 27, 2016.

Giffords, Gabrielle – former Member of US Congress. Personal correspondence, July 17, 2017.

Goffer, Amit, PhD – Founder, President, and Chief Technology Officer, Rewalk Robotics; innovator, UPnRIDE. Yokneam, June 15, 2015.

Goldberg, Eric, MD – Director of Capsule Endoscopy, University of Maryland School of Medicine. Phone, December 29, 2016.

Goodall, Jane, PhD – Founder, Jane Goodall Institute; UN Messenger of Peace. Personal correspondence, February 5, 2017.

Grinstein, Gidi – Founder and President, Reut Institute. Phone, March 20, 2017.

Gummert, Martin – Senior Scientist, International Rice Research Institute. Phone, November 17, 2015.

Guzman, Prof. Manuel, PhD – Biochemistry and Molecular Biology, Madrid Complutense University. Phone, June 1, 2016.

Halperin, Avner – Chief Executive Officer, EarlySense; co-developer of the contact-free hospital pad. Tel Aviv, July 12, 2015.

Hadomi, Ori – Chief Executive Officer, Mazor Robotics. Hatzuk Beach, July 15, 2015.

Hirschson, Ambassador Paul – Ambassador to West Africa, Israel Ministry of Foreign Affairs. Jerusalem, July 7, 2015.

Howlett, Prof. Allyn, PhD – Physiology and Pharmacology, Wake Forest School of Medicine. Phone, June 2, 2016.

Isaacson, Elie – Cofounder, Agilite. Washington, DC, March 8, 2015.

Jayaraman, Arun, PhD – Director, Rehab Technologies and Outcomes Research, Rehabilitation Institute of Chicago; Associate Professor, Northwestern University. Phone, October 15, 2015.

Kabishi, Areej – Head of Quality Assurance , First Care Products. Phone, February 1, 2016.

Kandel, Eugene, PhD – Chief Executive Officer, Start-Up Nation Central, Israel. Tel Aviv, April 18, 2016; Washington, DC, March 22, 2017.

Katz, Anat – Head of Trade Mission, Israeli Embassy in the United States. Washington, DC, May 21, 2015; May 30, 2017.

Katz, Yaakov – Editor-in-Chief, *Jerusalem Post* ; co-author, *The Weapon Wizards*. Jerusalem, July 6, 2015; June 11, 2017; August 6, 2017.

Kaufmann, Yadin – Cofounder, Sadara Ventures, Middle East Venture Capital Fund. Ra'anana, July 9, 2015.

Kessler, Jonathan – Director of Strategic Initiatives, American Israel Public Affairs Committee (AIPAC). Washington, DC, January 13, 2015; May 11, 2015; May 12, 2016; Tel Aviv, August 2, 2017.

Kirschbaum, Bernhard, PhD – former Executive Vice President of Research and Development, Merck Group. Phone, June 28, 2016.

Kribus, Prof. Abraham, PhD – Faculty of Engineering, Tel Aviv University; former head of Fluid Mechanics and Heat Transfer Department, Tel Aviv University. Phone, June 27, 2016.

Kurzon van Gelder, Shulamit – Director, Planning, Information, and Evaluation, MASHAV, Ministry of Foreign Affairs, Israel. Phone, November 1, 2016.

Kula, Rabbi Irwin – President, National Jewish Center for Learning and Leadership (CLAL). New York, October 12, 2015; phone, January 17, 2017.

Latzer, Doron – Senior Partner, Pearl Cohen Zedek Latzer Baratz. Herzliya Pituach, July 12, 2015.

Leshem, Prof. Yossi, PhD – Founder and Director, International Center for the Study of Bird Migration at Latrun, Israel; Senior Researcher, Department of Zoology in the Faculty of Life Sciences, Tel Aviv University. Phone, July 31, 2016; September 16, 2016. New York, October 28, 2016. Jerusalem, July 13, 2017.

Levine, Chanoch – former Head, Iron Dome Program, Rafael Advanced Defense Systems. Rockville, Maryland, May 20, 2016.

Loebenstein, Prof. Gad, PhD – former Head, ARO-Volcani Center; former Chief Scientist, Israeli Ministry of Agriculture. Phone, December 7, 2016.

Malessa, Orly – filmmaker, Israel. Phone, November 11, 2016.

Madai, Roee – Chief Executive Officer, First Care Products, Israel. Rosh HaAyin, July 14, 2015.

Margolin, Ron, PhD – research fellow, Shalom Hartman Institute, Israel. Phone, July 26, 2016.

Mechoulam, Prof. Raphael, PhD – Medical Chemistry, Hebrew University of Jerusalem; Member, Israel Academy of Sciences and Humanities; past President, International Cannabinoid Research Society. Personal correspondence, May 28, 2016.

Maisel, Dov – Vice President of International Operations, United Hatzalah, Israel. Washington, DC, March 21, 2016. Phone, June 1, 2016. Jerusalem, July 8, 2016; August 6, 2017.

Moran, Dov, PhD – innovator, DiskOnKey (aka flash drive); Managing Partner, Grove Ventures. Nazareth, June 13, 2015; Yarkona, June 26, 2015.

Navarro, Shlomo, PhD – innovator, Grain Cocoon; former Head of ARO-Volcani Center's Department of Stored Products. Rishon LeZion, June 25, 2015; phone, December 16, 2015; December 17, 2017.

Oren, Michael, PhD – Deputy Minister for Diplomacy, Prime Minister's Office, Israel; Former Israeli Ambassador to the United States. Phone, January 8, 2017.

Oron, Yoram – Chairman and Managing Partner, Red Dot Capital, Israel; Founder and Managing Partner, Vertex Venture Capital. Phone, March 6, 2017.

Peres, Nechemia ("Chemi") – Cofounder and Managing General Partner, Pitango Venture Capital. Phone, November 30, 2016.

Plesser, Yeshurun – Latin America Director, BioBee. Kibbutz Sde Eliyahu, June 29, 2016.

Preis, Itai – Adjunct Lecturer, IDC Herzliya. Tel Aviv, June 16, 2015.

Ramati, Yair – former Head, Israel Missile Defense Organization. Phone, March 2, 2016.

Rivkind, Avi, MD – Head of Shock Trauma Unit, Department of General Surgery, Hadassah Medical Center. Phone, December 11, 2016.

Rivlin, Reuven ("Ruvi") – President of Israel. Personal correspondence, January 1, 2017.

Revel, Michel, PhD – innovator, Rebif; Professor Emeritus, Biochemistry and Molecular Genetics, Weizmann Institute of Science; Chief Scientist, Kadimastem Ltd. Ness Ziona, June 20, 2015. Jerusalem, August 14, 2016.

Rosen, Rabbi David – former Chief Rabbi, Ireland; International Director of Interreligious Affairs, American Jewish Committee (AJC). Jerusalem, July 21, 2016; July 18, 2017.

Ross, Ambassador Dennis – Distinguished Fellow, Washington Institute for Near East Policy; former US Special Middle East Coordinator. Washington, DC, January 6, 2017.

Rubinstein, Prof. Menachem, PhD –Professor Emeritus, Department of Molecular Genetics, Weizmann Institute, Israel. Phone, July 4, 2016.

Rymer, William Zev, MD, PhD – Director of Research Planning, Rehabilitation Institute of Chicago; Professor of Physiology and Biomedical Engineering, Northwestern University. Phone, October 14, 2015.

Sallon, Sarah, PhD – co-innovator, Judean Date Palm Resurrection; Director, Natural Medicine Research Center, Hadassah University Hospital. Phone, December 9, 2015. Jerusalem, August 1, 2016.

Sella, Eitan – Managing Director, Hybrid Accelerator, Nazareth, Israel. Washington, DC, March 25, 2017.

Senor, Dan – co-author, *Start-Up Nation*. Washington, DC, March 26, 2017. Phone, August 21, 2017.

Shafrir, Amit– former Executive President and Director of Badoo; former President of AOL Premium Services. Reston, VA, January 4, 2017. Tysons Corner, VA, February 27, 2017; May 18, 2017.

Shamni, Hadas – Israeli school administrator, Israeli Ministry of Education. Reut, July 20, 2016.

Shelhav, Chava, PhD – innovator, Child'Space Method. Tel Aviv, June 28, 2015, July 10, 2015.

Shevach, Regine – Managing Director, Biopharma, Research and Development, Discovery Technologies, Merck Group. Phone, July 8, 2016.

Shoham, Prof. Moshe, PhD – Innovator, Mazor Robot; Founder, Mazor Robotics; Head of Robotics Lab, Technion Israel Institute of Technology; faculty of Mechanical Engineering, Technion Israel Institute of Technology. Phone, May 11, 2016.

Shoshani, Michal – Member, Noah Eshkol Foundation. Holon, June 17, 2015.

Shushan, Shlomit – former Head of Informal Education, Brenner Regional Council, Israel. Matzliach, June 13, 2015; phone, October 30, 2016.

Siegel, Seth M. – author, *Let There Be Water*. Washington, DC, March 21, 2016. New York, October 28, 2017.

Simon, Laurence, PhD – Professor of International Development, Brandeis University; Director of the Center for Global Development and Sustainability, Brandeis University; former Head, American Jewish World Service (AJWS). Phone, December 16, 2015.

Singer, Saul – co-author, *Start-Up Nation*. Jerusalem, June 17, 2015; April 13, 2016.

Singer, Wendy – Executive Director, Start-Up Nation Central, Israel. Jerusalem, June 17, 2015; Tel Aviv, April 18, 2016.

Sivan, Prof. Uri, PhD – Director, Nanotechnology Institute, Technion Israel Institute of Technology; Faculty of Physics, Technion Israel Institute of Technology. Haifa, July 8, 2015.

Solowey, Elaine, PhD – co-innovator, Judean Date Palm Resurrection; Director, Center for Sustainable Agriculture, Arava Institute for Environmental Studies. Jerusalem, June 25, 2015; phone, January 21, 2016.

Spigelman, Guy – Chief Executive Officer, PresenTense Israel. Jerusalem, July 13, 2015. Washington, DC, October 27, 2015; Tel Aviv, July 20, 2016; phone, December 8, 2016.

Spungen, Ann, EdD – Associate Director of the Veterans Affairs Rehabilitation Research and Development National Center of Excellence for the Medical Consequences of Spinal Cord Injury; Associate Professor of Medicine and Rehabilitation Medicine at the Icahn School of Medicine at Mount Sinai. Phone, November 10, 2015.

Steinberg, Shimon, PhD – Chief Scientist, BioBee. Kibbutz Sde Eliyahu, June 29, 2016.

Swidan, Fadi – Cofounder, Hybrid Accelerator, Nazareth, Israel. Washington, DC, March 25, 2017; Nazareth, August 2, 2017.

Tabor, Harry Zvi, PhD – innovator, Tabor Solar Water Collector (*dud shemesh*). Jerusalem, July 16, 2015.

Tabor, Vivienne – wife of Harry Zvi Tabor. Jerusalem, July 16, 2015.

Tzuk, Nir, PhD – Adjunct Professor for Entrepreneurship, Hebrew University of Jerusalem; Strategy and Corporate Development Advisor, Idealist.org. Tel Aviv, July 21, 2015; Washington, DC, July 6, 2016; Jerusalem, August 6, 2016.

van Rijn, Prof. Jaap, PhD – innovator, Zero Discharge Recirculating System for intensive culture of freshwater and marine fish; Faculty of Agriculture, Food and Environment, Hebrew University of Jerusalem. Rechovot, June 22, 2016.

Vardi, Yossi – serial entrepreneur; Israel's unofficial ambassador of technology. Tel Aviv, July 9, 2015; Hamptons, July 3, 2017; Tel Aviv, August 6, 2017.

Volkow, Nora, MD – Director, US National Institute on Drug Abuse. Personal correspondence, May 31, 2016.

Wertheimer, Stef – Founder, ISCAR; former Member of Knesset, Israel. Phone, November 8, 2016.

Yaacovi, Yoram – General Manager, Microsoft Israel. Phone, December 28, 2016; Haifa, August 2, 2017.

Yaron, Avi – Founder, Visionsense. Nazareth, April 16, 2016.

Yonath, Prof. Ada, PhD – Nobel Prize Laureate; Director, Center for Biomolecular Structure, Weizmann Institute of Science. Personal correspondence, July 1, 2016.

Younis, Imad – innovator, GPS for the Brain; Cofounder and President, Alpha Omega, Israel. Nazareth, June 23, 2015, August 3, 2017.

Younis, Reem – innovator, GPS for the Brain; Cofounder, Alpha Omega, Israel. Latrun, July 17, 2017. Washington, DC, September 13, 2016; February 29, 2016; Nazareth, August 3, 2017.

Vidyasagar, Prof. Polana, PhD – Chair, Date Palm Research, King Saud University. Phone, December 21, 2015.

Zehavi, Eli – Chief Operating Officer and Vice President of Research and Development, Mazor Robotics. Phone, May 25, 2016.

Zilka, Yahal – Cofounder of Magma Venture Partners. Phone, March 29, 2017.

Zuaretz, Orit, PhD – former Member of Knesset, Israel. Tel Aviv, July 9, 2015; Washington, DC, May 16, 2016.

Index

251